TECHTV'S SECRETS OF THE DIGITAL STUDIO: INSIDER'S GUIDE TO DESKTOP RECORDING

James Maguire

with Jim Louderback

CONTENTS AT A GLANCE

A Division of Pearson Technology Group, USA
201 W. 103rd Street
Indianapolis, Indiana 46290

TECHTV'S SECRETS OF THE DIGITAL STUDIO: INSIDER'S GUIDE TO DESKTOP RECORDING

International Standard Book Number: 0-7897-2686-6

Library of Congress Catalog Card Number: 2002100457

Printed in the United States of America

First Printing: April 2002

05   04   03   02   4   3   2

Trademarks

Warning and Disclaimer

ASSOCIATE PUBLISHER
Greg Wiegand

ACQUISITIONS EDITOR
Angelina Ward

DEVELOPMENT EDITOR
Sydney Jones

MANAGING EDITOR
Thomas F. Hayes

PROJECT EDITOR
Tonya Simpson

PRODUCTION EDITOR
Benjamin Berg

INDEXER
Mandie Frank

PROOFREADER
Andrea Dugan

TECHNICAL EDITOR
Jordan Tishler

TEAM COORDINATOR
Sharry Gregory

MEDIA DEVELOPER
Michael Hunter

INTERIOR DESIGNER
Anne Jones

COVER DESIGNER
Planet 10

COVER PHOTOGRAPHER
Shawn Roche

PAGE LAYOUT
Cheryl Lynch

TECHTV HEAD OF BUSINESS DEVELOPMENT
Glenn Farrell

TECHTV VICE PRESIDENT/ EDITORIAL DIRECTOR
Jim Louderback

TECHTV MANAGING EDITOR
Andrew Guest

TECHTV LABS DIRECTOR
Andrew Hawn

CONTENTS

CONTENTS

ABOUT THE AUTHOR

James Maguire is a journalist, audio producer, and multimedia sound designer. He has worked extensively as a composer and MIDI programmer and has been very active in developing audio for Web applications. As an engineer/producer, he has been nominated twice for an Emmy award for Excellence in Audio Production. Maguire has an M.A. degree in interactive communications and writes extensively about pop culture and technology, including covering the John Lennon Artificial Intelligence Project for *Wired*, and interviewing artists such as Philip Glass and Suzanne Vega. This is his second book about audio technology. He can be reached at jmaguire@omnibeam.com.

DEDICATIONS

To Joan and Bruce Maguire, for being the greatest, and to Corinne, who keeps the music playing.

ACKNOWLEDGMENTS

Special thanks go to the forward-looking bunch at TechTV, especially Jim Louderback, for their help and support. Additionally, the editorial assistance provided by Sydney Jones, Ben Berg, and Jordan Tishler was the best form of tough love. Thanks also to Angelina Ward, the most helpful acquisitions editor a writer could ever hope for. And thanks also to my agent, Agnes Birnbaum, for her advice and advocacy. Very special thanks to two friends and audio pros, Perry Emge and Steve Higdon, whose assistance made all the difference.

TELL US WHAT YOU THINK!

As the reader of this book, *you* are our most important critic and commentator. We value your opinion and want to know what we're doing right, what we could do better, what areas you'd like to see us publish in, and any other words of wisdom you're willing to pass our way.

As an associate publisher for Que, I welcome your comments. You can fax, e-mail, or write me directly to let me know what you did or didn't like about this book—as well as what we can do to make our books stronger.

Please note that I cannot help you with technical problems related to the topic of this book, and that due to the high volume of mail I receive, I might not be able to reply to every message.

When you write, please be sure to include this book's title and author as well as your name and phone or fax number. I will carefully review your comments and share them with the author and editors who worked on the book.

Fax: 317-581-4666

E-mail: feedback@quepublishing.com

Mail: Greg Wiegand
           Que Corporation
           201 West 103rd Street
           Indianapolis, IN 46290 USA

INTRODUCTION

Around the year 1450, Johannes Gutenberg invented the movable type printing press. That first press was an ungainly affair, slow (it took him two years to print the first Bible), and of course hand operated. But it caused a sea change in the production of books and other printed matter. Before Gutenberg's invention, printing was done chiefly by hand-engraved wood blocks, or even worse, by scribes who copied by hand. This meant it was far too expensive for anyone but a tiny elite to produce written material.

Over the course of years (quite a few years, actually—things moved slowly back then), the printing press made producing printed matter widely accessible. Any rabble rouser or wild-eyed revolutionary could print up a pamphlet and distribute it on street corners. What was once only for the elite became available to the commoner, creating an enormous surge in literacy.

In our own time we're seeing a similar change. In the last few years, audio recording technology—really good audio recording technology—has become accessible to home users. Like the changes created by Gutenberg's original printing press, the production equipment once available only to an elite is now accessible to most anyone with a song in their head.

It used to be that to produce a high-fidelity recording, you had to buy time in a recording studio. These were (and still are) expensive places. They are typically used only by the lucky few who have 1) a substantial savings account and a willingness to spend it, or 2) a recording contract, which means appeasing the deities at record labels. Or, perhaps a band could pool its meager gig proceeds and get in the mood to produce the definitive recording between 11 a.m. and 4:30 p.m.

Studio equipment is operated by the equivalent of those monks who used to print books by hand: audio engineers, a mysteriously trained cadre who control rows of gleaming buttons in a manner generally beyond the comprehension of the mere musicians who pay them.

But things have changed. Year by year through the '90s, audio recording technology kept getting ever more affordable—and better.

The PC became a self-contained recording studio, able to inexpensively host a full-fledged audio workstation. Audio hardware was increasingly replaced with software, and the software became ever more sophisticated, enabling home-based users to shape and bend audio in ways that would have been impossible at any price several years earlier.

Now, in the early twenty-first century, more audio tools fit in a laptop than even existed in the mid '80s. More importantly, a radical deflation has occurred—what once cost six figures can now be had for about $999 (or much less). The difference between a "home" studio and "pro" studio has gotten mighty blurry.

There's definitely a buzz about this new technology. The Internet has been part of this. With its abundance of music and audio software to download, it has helped create the idea of the PC as music studio. Musicians and sound enthusiasts of all stripes are aware that the humble box on their desktop can, with little but a Net connection, be a surprisingly powerful audio production tool.

But there's a question—in fact there are a lot of questions. Sure, the equipment is amazingly cheap for the capability, but—what about the knowledge necessary to use it? How do you mix a song? What does it mean to mix a song? What does an audio compressor do, and how do you use one? What software do you use? How do you get started?

That's where this book comes in. It's a navigational tool. It helps you figure out the maze of software and hardware options, learn basic audio theory, and discover the techniques and tools to make your music sound professional and polished. Armed with this book (and plenty of tinkering time), you'll learn how to turn your PC into a raging music machine, and to use that music machine to make your audio projects sound their sweetest.

The good news is that, while building and learning how to use a desktop audio studio requires serious time and effort—quite a bit, actually—it tends to be interesting and fun work. The creative abilities offered by modern audio equipment are vast. If you can hear it in your mind, it's likely that today's technology enables you to create it, right there on your desktop. That's cool.

And these capabilities will influence the future of music. How could music not be affected by an entire generation with the ability to create, mix, and master high-quality projects using affordable home equipment? It makes you wish all those earlier generations of musicians had desktop studios—those early blues musicians we never heard, those talented rock 'n' rollers who deserved a recording contract but never got one. Fortunately for us, we live in a time when anyone with a PC and little know-how can create a faithful document of his or her musical creativity.

As for music and creativity, a small note to bear in mind. Please don't let the gee whiz nature of today's audio technology make you lose sight of what really counts. The new audio tools have a lot of buttons and knobs and squiggly lines representing sound waves. If you find yourself thinking about all of this rather than getting into the music itself, please turn off the PC, go outside, and sing loudly until the neighbors tell you to stop.

Then, of course, boot up the software again and keep right on going. There are beautiful sounds to be made, and the tools to make them are right there in your hands.

James Maguire

January 2002

PART I

AUDIO STUFF II REALLY HELPS TO KNOW

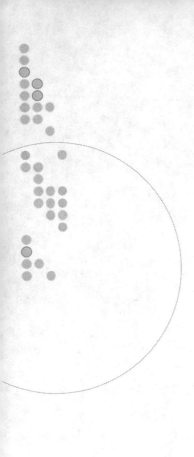

CHAPTER 1

OUR ANALOG ANCESTORS AND THE BASICS OF SOUND

In This Chapter

- Find out the basis for all sound
- Learn the fundamental audio principles of frequency and amplitude
- Find out how sound was recorded prior to the digital era, which continues to influence modern recording
- Be a fly on the wall in a vintage recording session

FREQUENCY, AMPLITUDE, AND ELVIS

The year is 1961 and Bill Porter, Elvis's audio engineer, is recording the king of rock 'n' roll. It's a big session, and the challenges facing Porter are considerable. He's recording the most blazingly famous musician of his time, not to mention a roomful of hotshot studio players. Everyone is at the top of his game, and Porter better be, too. This recording might get used in an album—a vinyl record album, on shiny black plastic—that will be heard on little transistor radios from Long Island to Los Angeles.

But on top of all that is still another challenge for the young audio engineer. Porter has to record the king of rock 'n' roll using *analog recording equipment*.

And that's a headache. Because long before there were CDs or home computers, decades before you could turn up the volume by clicking Increase Gain, sound was recorded with analog equipment. And that means Porter's job was a tough one.

Let's be a fly on the wall in RCA's Studio B in Nashville, one of the recording studios in which Elvis recorded his hip-shaking rock 'n' roll hits. We'll look at how audio was recorded before the digital era, and along the way we'll examine the basics of sound itself. Although recording has come a long way since its analog roots, many of the basic concepts remain the same. These concepts are as essential to the desktop recordist as they were to the young Bill Porter.

Hot Link: Sun Studio (`http://www.sunstudio.com/`)

If there's a recording studio that can claim to be the birthplace of rock 'n' roll, it's Sun Studio (see Figure 1.1). The young Elvis first recorded there, and this Memphis studio also recorded such greats as Jerry Lee Lewis, Carl Perkins, and Johnny Cash. The studio's Web site lets you take a virtual tour.

All right, audio trivia buffs, who made the very first sound recording? The answer: Thomas Edison, who invented the phonograph in 1877 (he also invented electric light, as well as scads of other things—and did it all without using computers). Said Edison, "Of all my inventions, I liked the phonograph the best…Life's most soothing things are sweet music and a child's goodnight." On the Edison Historic Site (`www.nps.gov/edis/sounds.htm`), you can hear excerpts of hit songs from 1901, such as "Who Threw the Overalls in Mrs. Murphy's Chowder?" and "Which Switch is the Switch, Miss, for Ipswich?"

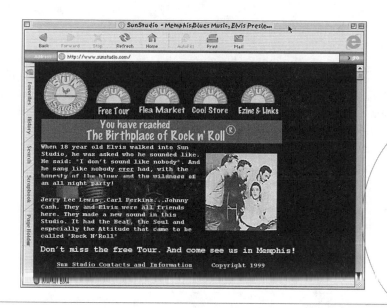

Figure 1.1

Sun Studio is where Elvis first recorded his signature vocals.

Tape Is Rolling: Take One

Let's take it from the top. As Elvis opens his great pouty lips, out comes *sound*–vibrations transmitted through the air in waves. These waves are the basis of all audio and music. If you zoom in to that sound wave it looks like Figure 1.2.

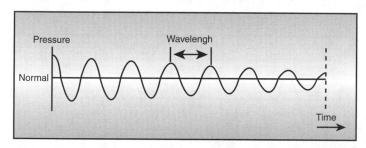

Figure 1.2

Notice this sound wave's peaks and valleys.

We know what this wave sounds like by measuring its peaks and valleys. This measurement determines the sound's *amplitude* and *frequency*.

9

Amplitude

The distance from the wave's peak to its valley is its amplitude. The greater the distance between these points, the greater the amplitude. The greater the amplitude, the louder the wave sounds (see Figure 1.3). When Elvis was at the climax of "Don't Be Cruel," his sound waves had a big span between peak and valley. But when he sang softly and intimately into the microphone, as he did toward the end of "In the Ghetto," his sound waves had just a tiny amplitude. This low amplitude singing caused a swooning feeling in his female teenage fans.

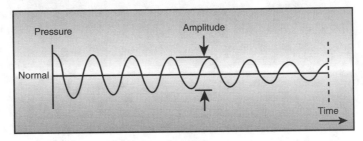

Figure 1.3

Amplitude is a measurement of the distance between each wave's peak and valley.

Frequency

When a wave travels from peak to valley and back to peak, that's referred to as a *cycle* (see Figure 1.4). Frequency is measured in *cycles per second*, referred to as *Hertz*. Elvis's voice, being male and hence rather low, was primarily in the 500 to 700 Hertz range.

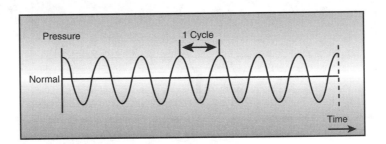

Figure 1.4

Frequency is a measurement of how many times a wave completes a cycle in one second.

JARGON

Heinrich's Legacy

The concept of cycles per second, or Hertz, is named after the 19th century German physicist Heinrich Hertz. The abbreviation *kHz* stands for kilohertz, which refers to a thousand Hertz.

Elvis's soul-tinged sound waves travel to the microphone (a Telefunkun U-47). A thin diaphragm inside the microphone vibrates in response to the frequency and amplitude of Elvis's sound waves. These vibrations turn the sound waves' acoustic energy into mechanical energy, and then into electrical energy. This electrical energy, carrying information about the sound wave's frequency and amplitude, travels to the reel-to-reel tape machine (guided by Porter's skillful movements at the recording console).

NOTE

As sound travels from one place of equipment to another in a recording studio it changes from one form of energy to another—even if the studio is as small as a desktop PC. The process of changing from, for example, acoustic energy (generated by a singer's voice) to electric energy (which is how it travels through the microphone cable) is called *transducing*.

This analog tape machine spools a reel of tape a quarter of an inch wide over its record heads. When the electrical energy carrying Elvis's voice arrives at the tape machine's record heads, a little magic happens.

This thin piece of reel-to-reel tape is coated with magnetic particles in a polymer base. Think back to those science experiments you did in school, in which you dumped some iron shavings on a piece of paper and moved them around with a magnet. That's similar to what's going on at the tape machine's record head.

As the electrical energy reaches the record heads, it imprints an electromagnetic design in the magnetic particles on the surface of the recording tape. The peaks and valleys represented by this electromagnetic design are analogous to the peaks and valleys of Elvis's sound waves—hence the term analog.

Hot Link: Abbey Road Studios (`http://www.abbeyroad.co.uk/`)

This London recording studio (see Figure 1.5) was the home of the Beatles, who recorded their worldwide hits with an analog tape machine. Abbey Road continues to be a top studio, and in recent years has worked with bands like Radiohead, the Eurythmics, and Echo and the Bunnymen.

THE BASICS OF SOUND

1

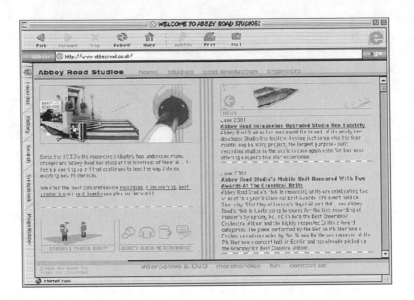

Figure 1.5

Abbey Road Studios was where the Beatles recorded their legendary hits.

When the King leaves the studio, this tape can be played back, and even in the great rock 'n' roller's absence, the listener hears his voice. It's a minor miracle—a singer's voice stored on the surface of a thin piece of tape (and Elvis's, no less). The technological advance from analog to digital is minor compared to the original feat of storing a sound's frequency and amplitude using mechanical and electrical devices.

This analog technology, by the way, is still used by the cassette machine that's gathering dust in your closet. You might want to get the thing out and dust it in honor of this major audio advance.

Pity The Audio Engineer

But back to the challenges facing Bill Porter. What were the difficulties inherent in analog audio recording?

Analog recording adds a layer of hiss over music. However, if Porter records a strong enough signal to tape, the music masks this hiss. If he records too strong a level, the recording is distorted—he has to tell Elvis that his once-in-a-lifetime performance is unusable. In addition, each piece of tape can store only one performance at a given point in the tape. This is in contrast to a digital system, which can theoretically record an unlimited number of takes and place them anywhere within the editing interface. And since analog multitrack recording offers a limited number of tracks, there were instances when an artist would have had to *record over* a previous take hoping for a better performance—which means *erasing* the previous performance; it's lost forever.

Hot Link: VintageAudio.com (http://www.vintageaudio.com/)

As recording technology has progressed, there has been a movement to preserve the virtues of earlier recording equipment and techniques. Many top audio engineers use up-to-the-minute digital gear, but keep handy, say, a vintage tube microphone from 1965. The VintageAudio site (shown in Figure 1.6) specializes in upgrading and modifying work on audio gear from previous eras.

Figure 1.6

Vintage Audio specializes in upgrading audio gear from earlier eras.

Analog tape is linear (it lacks digital's nonlinear capability), so if the musicians wanted to go to another point in the song, Porter would have to hit rewind and wait. We hope he can do this quickly, because he has a roomful of famous musicians waiting for him.

And, when it comes time to edit the master, the engineer had to get out a razor blade and *physically cut the tape*. What if he cut in the wrong place? What if he dropped a piece to the studio floor, losing part of a performance that would have been a nationwide Top 40 hit?

You might suggest making a safety copy of the master before editing it, but that adds yet another layer of hiss to the music. So it's best to use the razor blade on the irreplaceable master. Yes, Porter's achievement is an impressive one.

JUST ONE MORE GLANCE BACK BEFORE PLUNGING MADLY AHEAD

The reel-to-reel tape machine that Bill Porter used to record Elvis now sits silently. Whatever its virtues, analog is a thing of the past.

But some people, believe it or not, prefer analog audio, the recordings made in an earlier age. They say analog is warmer, it feels more "present." Digital audio, they feel, is cold and impersonal—something is missing. Maybe they like the fuzzier, soft focus that analog recording's layer of hiss gives a sound. In fact, some audio engineers (fewer and fewer) still record to analog tape and then store their recordings in a digital format.

Hot Link: Audio Recording: History and Development (http://www.digitalcentury.com/encyclo/update/audiohd.html)

This Digital Century site is a well-done history of audio from Edison up to the present day (see Figure 1.7). There's a particularly interesting discussion of radio vs. records in the early 1930s. With the advent of radio, experts asked, "Who's going to buy music when they can hear it for free?"—a debate that echoes our 21st Century debate about Napster-style file swapping vs. buying music.

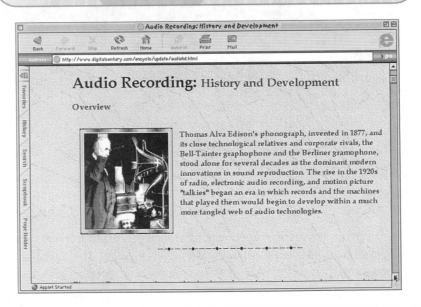

Figure 1.7

The Digital Century site offers an extensive history of audio technology.

Some of the nostalgia for analog recording is about the music itself. In earlier decades recording tended to be looser and more spontaneous. Listen to a recording of the '60s rock band The Mamas and the Papas, and notice how the band claps along in rhythm. If you listen closely, you'll hear that not everyone is exactly on the beat, but the feeling is great.

In a big-budget pop recording circa 21st Century, it's likely that this would be completely controlled. The record producer might decide to go for a looser feel—so he'd hire professional percussionists who could clap around the beat. In today's more highly professional—and more highly processed—sound recordings, spontaneity is still possible, and some groups achieve it, but it is easy to lose.

And remember, the great treasures of Western music are all recorded in analog. You name it...Louis Armstrong to Benny Goodman, Bruce Springsteen to Led Zeppelin, the Berlin Philharmonic to the Beatles' White Album—all recorded in analog, and some of the most profound sound ever committed to recording media.

So you can do great things with an analog recording deck. But you can do even greater things with a digital recorder. Besides, you've got one right on your desktop. Kind of inspiring, isn't it?

Bill Porter is still engineering. He teaches audio engineering at Webster University in St. Louis. Elvis, sadly, is no longer with us. He created his last sound wave in 1977.

CHAPTER **2**

FAST FORWARD: DIGITAL AUDIO AND THE NONLINEAR NOW

In This Chapter

- Discover the basics of digital audio
- Learn about sample rates
- Find out about the role audio frequencies play in sound
- Learn about the Nyquist Frequency

SO WHAT IS DIGITAL AUDIO?

Digital audio has what I call a "shiny surface." It has a kind of high-tech chic—a compact disc gleams, the buttons and knobs on a software mixer look really cool, audio software invites you to manipulate complex music mixes with a single mouse click (see Figure 2.1). Even on the surface, digital audio has a serious gee whiz factor.

Figure 2.1

Today's digital studio is a high-tech place.

But let's go beneath the surface, inside the digital world, to uncover its secrets. You didn't know those WAV files on your PC had an inner life, did you? Today's audio technology is even more fascinating inside than it is on its high-tech surface. And besides, a basic knowledge of how it works really improves your sound design capabilities.

Digital audio does something that might seem unlikely. A digital sound file stores all the wildness of sound—tuba shrieks, cranking guitar solos, and sexy whispers—as a series of numbers. That's right, those WAVs and MP3s on your PC reduce the infinite variations of sound and music to a series of ones and zeros.

A digital audio file stores its zillions of ones and zeros as *sample rate* and *bit depth*. These two numbers measure how accurately that sound file can reproduce its music or sound.

In this chapter we'll look at sample rate; in the next we'll explore bit depth.

Hot Link: TSC Audio Forum (http://www.trinitysoundcompany.com/bbs/)

Got a question about audio? Post it at the TSC Audio forum—there's a multitude of audio enthusiasts who visit and respond (see Figure 2.2).

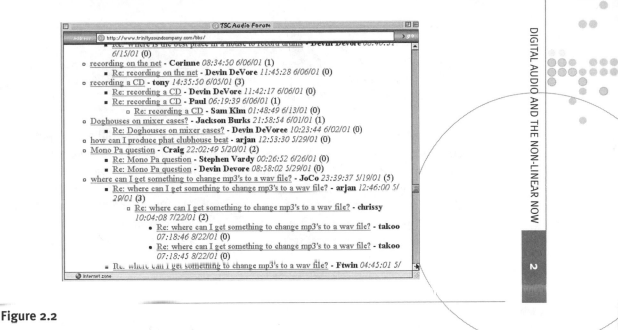

Figure 2.2

You can post your audio questions at the TSC Audio forum.

SAMPLE RATE

The squiggly lines in Figure 2.3 represent digital sound. It's a WAV file of me saying "Mary had a little lamb." That's what Thomas Edison said when he invented the phonograph in 1877. (Needless to say, that first recording was very analog.)

Figure 2.3

This WAV file's sample rate is 44.1kHz and its bit depth is 16 bit. (Already you can see the numbers creeping in.)

A *sample* is a measurement of a sound wave's amplitude at a brief moment in time. As a sound wave cycles through its peaks and valleys, your digital recorder takes a snapshot of how far each peak and valley travels from the mid point. The further the distance from the mid point, the greater the amplitude.

Hot Link: AES (`http://www.aes.org/`)

The Audio Engineering Society offers a wealth of information about audio sample rates and other sound-related topics. Take a look at the Audio Education and Resources link.

Your recorder must take thousands of samples—think of them as little snapshots—to accurately capture that wave's shape (see Figure 2.4). *Sample rate* is a measurement of how many samples a digital recorder captures per second. The higher the number of samples, the more faithfully that sound file can reproduce its audio content. The sample rate of my WAV file is 44.1 kHz, which means the file contains 44,100 samples every second. So your computer, proving it is indeed a wondrous machine, can measure a sound's amplitude 44,100 times (or more) in one second.

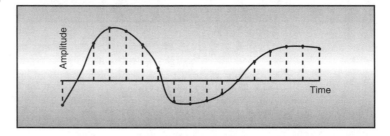

Figure 2.4

When a wave form is sampled, its amplitude is measured.

Here's a digital audio phenomenon I've always found interesting. Sound is essentially made up of frequency (how high or low its pitch is) and amplitude (how soft or loud its volume is). So you'd think that a digital recorder must record both frequency and amplitude, right?

Well, actually, a digital recorder captures a sound's frequency by measuring its amplitude across time. As your recorder takes snapshots of a wave's peaks and valleys (measuring amplitude), it also records the number of these cycles the wave completes in a second (which measures frequency—remember, cycles per second equals Hertz, which is a measurement of frequency). Cool, huh?

A Sample of Confusion

The term *sample* gets used in a couple of different ways, which creates confusion. A *sample*, as we've just seen, is a snapshot of a sound wave's amplitude. But the word *sample* is also a slang term for a bite-sized digital audio file; for example, a short recording of a drumbeat or a saxophone riff. Electronic musicians often talk about searching for samples to add to their techno-mixes. A *sampler* is a synthesizer-like device that enables you to record audio and manipulate it, maybe stretching it out or raising its pitch. So, to see how confusing this could be, you could talk about the sample rate of your sampler, and say you're searching the Web for samples to download—but you only want high-sample-rate samples. Make sense?

Hot Link: SampleNet (http://www.samplenet.co.uk/)

To find out about samples (the small music recordings) check out SampleNet (see Figure 2.5). This U.K.-based page is home base for many sample-obsessed electronic musicians. You'll find samples of everything from orchestra hits to drums to horns.

Figure 2.5

SampleNet is a great place to find samples to download.

You might ask, "Does it really take 44,100 samples in one second to accurately reproduce a sound?" It's a tribute to the human ear that the answer is yes, the ear is that subtle a sound receptor. If that seems a bit extreme, try listening to a sound file that's at 22kHz instead of 44.1kHz. If you listen closely, especially if you have good speakers, you'll hear a dramatic difference between sound sampled 22,000 times a second and sound sampled at 44,100 times a second.

Hot Link: MTSU Department of Recording Industry (`http://www.mtsu.edu/~record/`)

If you're thinking about getting serious about audio on a professional level, take a look at the well-respected program at Middle Tennessee State University.

If you want a really dramatic example, listen to a sound at 11kHz. Now remember, this is a sound file that takes 11,000 samples of a sound in one second. And yet, if you listen to an 11kHz sound file, your ear knows the difference. The music has much less brightness or "sparkle"—you might wonder if your speakers are malfunctioning.

The Ear Versus the Eye

Compare audio with film. Like digital audio, film uses a series of rapidly changing snap-shots—still images—to create the illusion of movement. But film uses a wimpy 24 frames a second. That's right, digital audio uses 44,100 snapshots a second, and film uses a grand total of 24. So the ear really is one of the most amazing bodily organs. Not, perhaps, the most beautiful one, but I suppose that's a matter of opinion.

Hot Link: Full Sail (`http://www.fullsail.com`)

Many audio engineers got their start in the program at Full Sail. Located in Florida, this school is dedicated to training students in a wide array of digital/multimedia technology, and is particularly known as an audio training facility.

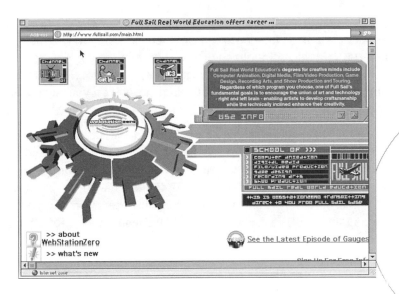

Figure 2.6

Many audio engineers have trained at Full Sail.

 NOTE

Frequency Ranges

Looking at the chart in Figure 2.7, we can see the approximate frequencies of many commonly heard sounds.

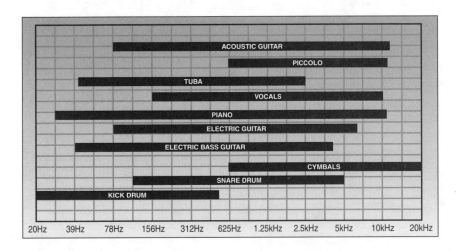

Figure 2.7

Chart representing sounds at various frequencies.

In a perfect world, the range of human hearing goes from 20Hz all the way up to 20,000Hz, or 20kHz. If the truth be told, down there at 20Hz sound is more felt than heard. And up at 20KHz? Well, not too many people can hear all the way up there. One of the culprits of this inability to hear higher frequencies is loud music. Sustained exposure to high volume (for example, Motley Crue at volume level 9 on your stereo all evening long) creates hearing loss.

Some audio engineers—both pro and casual—lose a significant portion of their hearing because they monitor their mixes at high volumes for long periods. And those folks who mix sound at live concerts? We pity their ears. This is a very important point: Protect your ears! Hearing loss is irreversible. Many sound designers keep ear plugs with them at all times (they fit on your key chain) and when they find themselves in a high volume situation, they pop them in. The couple of bucks you spend on ear protection is money very well spent.

Hot Link: Music and Audio Connection (`http://www.musicandaudio.com/`)

The Music and Audio Connection site has a good selection of audio links, including educational resources and audio schools, as well as a tasty collection of software to download (see Figure 2.8) .

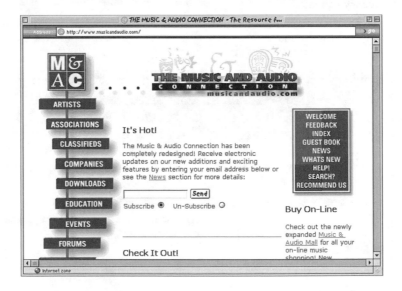

Figure 2.8

The Music and Audio Connection site offers software to download and links to educational resources.

IMPORTANT DIGITAL AUDIO TERMS, OR, HOW TO USE JARGON TO IMPRESS YOUR FRIENDS

Imagine this. You're working with a friend at your desktop recording studio, perhaps building a hard, driving techno-electro piece. You find a Web site full of samples and you download one; its sample rate is 22kHz. You notice that it lacks the clarity of your 44.1kHz samples. It's "fuzzy" sounding, and there's an extra layer of noise in the sound.

You say to your friend, in a scholarly voice, "Yup, it's a good example of the Nyquist Theorem—this sample just doesn't capture the full frequency spectrum."

Whoa. At that point you are a cool dude or dudette, dazzling your companion with some technical jargon. Impressive. You've just discovered the second reason it helps to have a fuller understanding of digital audio technology. It enables you to dazzle your friends with obscure terminology. This can increase your sense of self worth without all those pesky therapy sessions.

But the first reason to delve deeper into digital audio technology is to improve your ability to create artistic sound design. Let's leave your friend where we last saw him—gaping in awe—and take a look at an advanced digital audio concept.

Hot Link: The Physics of Music (`http://online.anu.edu.au/ITA/ACAT/drw/PPofM/INDEX.html`)
Yes, this is a long URL, but there's a lot of information here. It's a scholarly overview of sound put together by a professor at the University of Australia.

Nyquist Frequency

Why, you might ask, does sound recorded at high sample rates, like 44.1kHz, sound so much better than those recorded at low sample rates, like 11kHz?

When you record sound digitally, you must use a sample rate that's at least double the audio frequency of the sound wave you're recording. Otherwise your recording suffers. The frequency that a given sample rate can reproduce is called its *Nyquist frequency*.

A WAV audio file recorded with an 11kHz sample rate has a Nyquist frequency of 5500Hz. (Remember, 1,000 Hertz equals 1 kilohertz, or kHz, so 11kHz is twice as big as 5,500Hz.) This 11kHz audio file cannot reproduce frequencies above 5500Hz. Pretty limited, huh? Because we can hear (theoretically) up to 20kHz, this 11kHz sample rate captures only a small portion of what we can hear. To capture the entire range of human hearing, we have to use a 44.1kHz sample rate. This can reproduce frequencies up to 22.05kHz—the full range of human hearing and then some.

Audio engineer Harry Nyquist first published an article describing this concept in 1928. (At that time he was researching factors affecting telegraph speed. He proved that the minimum bandwidth for effective transmission is equivalent to half the number of code elements a second.) So this central audio concept is named after him—see, Harry understood about impressing his friends with terminology.

Hot Link: The Music Lab at California Institute of Technology (`http://www.its.caltech.edu/~musiclab/`)

Take a look at these photos of the music lab at CalTech—these folks are into some wild stuff (see Figure 2.9). Also, peruse the article "There's Life Above 20khz."

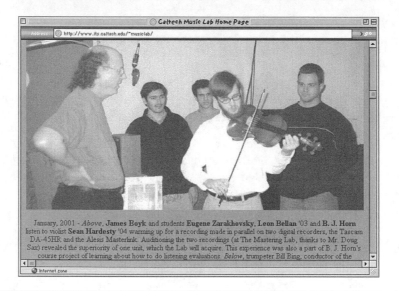

Figure 2.9

Some wild audio happens at CalTech's music lab.

It's helpful to understand the Nyquist frequency when preparing audio for limited bandwidth situations, like uploading to the Web. Audio files with a 44.1kHz sample rate require twice the download time of those with 22kHz sample rates. But if you're putting speech-only files online, it's okay to use 22kHz files. The Nyquist frequency of a 22kHz WAV file is 11,000 Hertz, which is a wide enough bandwidth to reasonably reproduce the spoken word. To find out more about preparing audio for the Web, see Chapter 22, "Preparing Your Sounds to Be Uploaded."

Why is Nyquist's theorem true? Look at sound waves, and compare the movement of low-frequency sound waves with those of higher frequency waves (see Figure 2.10). A low-frequency sound, like the lowest note on a bass guitar, takes much longer to complete a single cycle. So it doesn't take very many samples—instantaneous measurements of amplitude—to capture that slowly cycling sound wave. But high frequency sounds, like a soprano's top note, have thousands of cycles per second. If you don't sample that sound wave rapidly enough (like 44,100 times a second) you won't record all of that wave's rapid movement as its amplitude cycles from peak to valley.

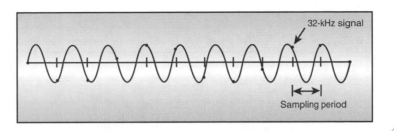

Figure 2.10

If you attempt to record a 32kHz signal with a 44.1kHz sample rate, you will encounter problems with aliasing.

To accurately record a sound you need to capture at least two points in every cycle in a sound wave. This means you need at least two samples per cycle (remember, cycles per second is Hertz). For example, a sound wave with a frequency of 13kHz—like the upper wail of a saxophone—contains 13,000 cycles per second. So to capture two points in that wave's cycle you need to sample it at least 26,000 times a second. Your 44.1 digital recorder does a good job of this.

Aliasing: A Bad Thing

But what if you throw caution to the wind and try to record a symphony orchestra with a 22 kHz sample rate? Does your computer blow up? Are you an uncool dude or dudette? Well, no, but you do encounter something called *aliasing*. Aliasing occurs when the recorder's sample rate is too low to accurately record the music's higher frequency sound waves.

Remember, when you record at 22kHz (which you would never do, we know) your Nyquist frequency is 11,000kHz. So not only does your recording lack all the frequencies above 11kHz (all the gorgeous high tones), but several erroneous signals appear in the audio recording.

Hot Link: The Virtual Acoustics Project (`http://www.isvr.soton.ac.uk/FDAG/vap/`)

Freaky is a good word to describe what goes on at the Institute of Sound and Vibration Research. Sponsored by the University of Southhampton in England, this is pioneering research into the nature of sound. Take a look at "the analytical simulation of the sound field scattered by a rigid sphere." The Web graphics alone make it worth a visit (see Figure 2.11).

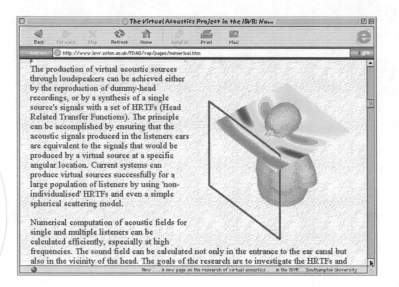

The production of virtual acoustic sources through loudspeakers can be achieved either by the reproduction of dummy-head recordings, or by a synthesis of a single source's signals with a set of HRTFs (Head Related Transfer Functions). The principle can be accomplished by ensuring that the acoustic signals produced in the listeners ears are equivalent to the signals that would be produced by a virtual source at a specific angular location. Current systems can produce virtual sources successfully for a large population of listeners by using 'non-individualised' HRTFs and even a simple spherical scattering model.

Numerical computation of acoustic fields for single and multiple listeners can be calculated efficiently, especially at high frequencies. The sound field can be calculated not only in the entrance to the ear canal but also in the vicinity of the head. The goals of the research are to investigate the HRTFs and

Figure 2.11

Check out the wild and wonderful graphic representations of sound at the Institute of Sound and Vibration Research.

At this low sample rate your recorder encounters a kind of sampling confusion. It's not taking enough samples per second to record both the peak and the valley of the upper-frequency sound waves. Your recorder, having sampled these upper frequencies inaccurately, folds these errant frequencies back into the audio bandwidth. This is why aliasing is also known as *foldover*.

But don't lose too much sleep worrying about aliasing. This is the kind of phenomenon that designers of audio gear think about all the time, so they've come up with a solution. Digital recorders *bandlimit* the recorder's audio input with a *low pass filter* to *attenuate* frequencies above the Nyquist frequency.

Whoa, did we just start speaking another language? Let's look at those terms:

- **Bandlimit.** To bandlimit audio means to block certain frequencies while allowing others to pass. Audio engineers sometimes take a full-fidelity recording and give it a telephone quality by bandlimiting it to allow only the mid-range frequencies to pass. Since a telephone is very "mid-rangey," this bandlimiting technique mimics the sound of the telephone. In the case of an anti-aliasing bandlimiter for a 44.1kHz digital recorder, the analog to digital converter's bandlimiter would eliminate all frequencies above the Nyquist frequency, or 22.05.

- **Low Pass Filter.** A low pass filter lets low frequencies pass through but blocks frequencies above a user-determined cutoff point. In the case of a low pass filter to prevent aliasing, it would block all frequencies above the Nyquist frequency. For a 44.1kHz digital recorder, that means blocking all frequencies above 22.05kHz.

- **Attenuate.** This is a fancy way of saying "to turn down the volume." Or, to put it in audio-ese, to decrease the amplitude.

You'll see many audio devices boasting of 96kHz sample rate capability. Using the Nyquist theory, we know that this device can reproduce frequencies to 48kHz—yet human hearing stops around 20kHz. So why would anyone build an audio device with 96kHz capability?

Remember the aliasing filter we mentioned a couple of paragraphs back? This is a "brick wall filter" that allows no frequencies above a certain frequency to be recorded as you record digital audio. For a device that can record at 44.1kHz, this brick wall aliasing filter must be at 22.05kHz. This prevents a 44.1kHz recorder from recording frequencies above 22.05kHz, which would get folded in with the lower frequencies and cause a degraded recording. However, and this is really a fine point, some sounds have harmonics (high frequencies that are overtones of fundamental frequencies) that exist above 22.05kHz. In addition, some people claim they can hear at or above this range. So to fully accommodate these higher frequency demands, a recorder must have an aliasing filter that allows these frequencies to pass. Hence the audio recorder that can record at 96kHz sample rate, with an aliasing filter that allows everything up to 48kHz to pass through.

Some designers of audio gear say that the brick wall filter in a 44.1kHz recorder harms the upper range of audible frequencies, and that 96kHz systems have cleaner and clearer highs. Ultimately, you can let your ears be the judge.

CHAPTER 3

DIGITAL AUDIO, CONTINUED

In This Chapter

- Learn more about the basics of digital audio
- Find out about quantization and bit depth
- Understand the concept of a 16-bit word
- Learn about dither

QUANTIZATION: ONE STEP AT A TIME

Say you got an assignment from a photo editor: There's a new statue of Abraham Lincoln in the park, and she wants you to go photograph it. In fact, says your editor, we're doing a complete photo essay on this new statue, and we need you to photograph it from every possible angle.

This process of taking thousands of snapshots is like sampling. When you assemble all the photos (or samples) together, you'll know exactly what that statue of Abe (or your sound wave) looks like. That is, *if* the snapshots are high quality.

That's the question: How good is each snapshot? Did you shoot them with a cheap disposable camera, or with a high-end Nikon 35 millimeter? If each photo (or each sample) is low quality, it doesn't matter how many you have. You still won't get a faithful reproduction.

> **Hot Link: Webmonkey (`http://hotwired.lycos.com/webmonkey/multimedia/audio_mp3/`)**
>
> This audio tutorial offered by the tech-savvy folks at Hotwired is one of my favorites (see Figure 3.1). It's geared for desktop musicians, and it's clear and to the point.

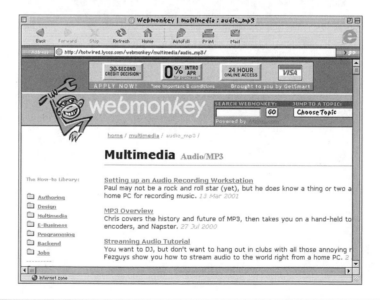

Figure 3.1

The Webmonkey site is full of good audio tutorials.

The quality of each sample, its *bit depth*, determines how many volume variations it can reproduce. The bit depth of audio files is typically 16-bit, 20-bit, or 24-bit. (Occasionally you'll come across an 8-bit audio file—avoid them.) The greater a sound file's bit depth, also referred to as its *resolution*, the more accurately it reproduces a sound's changes in volume.

Sample Rate and Bit Depth: Related Terms

Sample rate is how many samples you take; *bit depth* is how good each sample is.

Let's look at bit depth. Sound can occur at a virtually limitless number of volume levels. From an autumn leaf falling, to a baby laughing in the next room, to a band practicing next door, not only are a vast variety of volumes possible, but most sounds are constantly and subtly changing volume—that's what makes them interesting and beautiful.

The process of digitally recording a sound's volume changes is called *quantization*. If you want your quantization to be faithful to the original sound, you'll need sufficient bit depth.

Hot Link: Audio Forums
(http://www.audioforums.com/forums_frame.html)

We can't think of a topic related to desktop audio that's not discussed—at length—at Audio Forums (see Figure 3.2). Mac OS, Windows OS, audio hard drives, music software...the list seems never ending. It's also an online gathering spot for musicians, engineers, and producers.

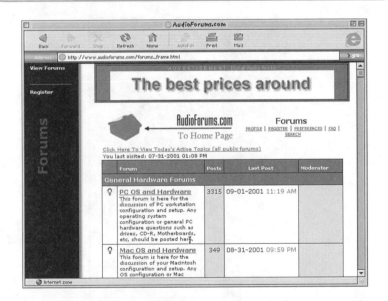

Figure 3.2

The Audio Forums site is a great place to learn about music technology.

NOTE

The *decibel* is named after Alexander Graham Bell, who invented the telephone in 1876. (What did people do before that?) While the decibel, or dB, is most commonly used as a measurement of sound pressure level (loudness), it's actually a ratio between two values. As a measurement of sound pressure level, its base reference is 0 dB, the lowest level at which the human ear can perceive sound. Sound is said to double in perceived volume with every 10 dB increase. Sound pressure level ranges from the threshold of hearing at 0 dB to the ear-splitting loudness of 130 dB, as you can see from the chart in Figure 3.3. But there are other types of decibels: dBv and dBm, for example. In dBv, based on voltage, the base reference is 1 volt, so 0 dBv = 1 volt. In dBm, which describes a signal's wattage, the base reference is 1 milliwatt, so 0 dBm = 1 milliwatt.

A related concept to sound pressure level is the Fletcher Munson equal-loudness curve. This is very important to understand if you want to create mixes that sound good at various volume levels. Fletcher and Munson were researchers at the Bell Labs who examined the human ear's perception of volume at different frequencies. They found that the mid-range frequencies sound the loudest to the ear, in particular the 2 to 5kHz range. To make low and high frequencies sound equally loud requires them to be played at higher dB (the lower frequencies need the most boost). What this means in practical terms is that when you mix at high volumes you'll hear those rich lows and bright highs, but when a listener plays it back at a lower volume the mid range is the most predominant. In short, it's always good to listen to your audio project at lower volumes before deciding you're finished.

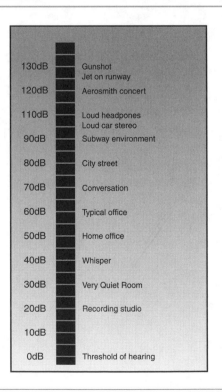

Figure 3.3

Here are some examples of the sound pressure levels of various common sounds.

> **Hot Link: The Recording Web Site**
> (`http://www.recordingwebsite.com/`)
> This site is a good resource for the home recording enthusiast, with a
> library of product reviews and tips on recording (see Figure 3.4).

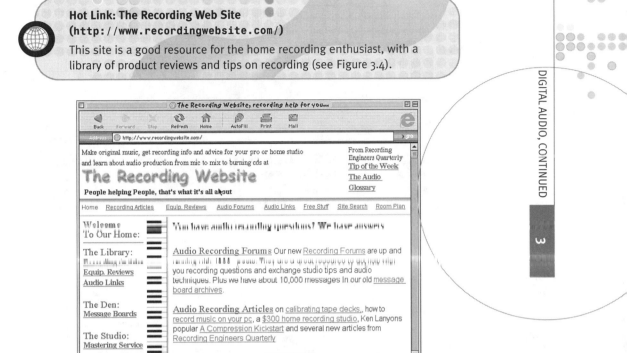

Figure 3.4

Check out all the home recording resources at the Recording Web Site.

But What's a Bit?

You may think your computer is devious (it seems mine knows just when to crash), but at
root it's pretty simple. In a computer's world, everything is either a 1 or a 0. This two-digit
system is called the binary number system, and binary digits are referred to as bits (Binary
digITs).

A one-bit piece of data, a 1 or a 0, can only store two values: on or off. However, a two-
bit piece of data, such as 01, can store four possible combinations: 00, 01, 10, 11.

A four-bit piece of data can represent 16 possible values, and an 8-bit piece of data can
store 256 values.

Keep adding numbers and you'll arrive at a 16-bit piece of data, otherwise known as a 16-
bit word. Here's an example of a 16-bit word:

1010101111100001

It's not the kind of word you'd use in a conversation, is it? But it's a useful word, especially
for audio. A 16-bit word can represent 65,536 volume variations.

> **Hot Link: Home Recording (http://www.homerecording.com/)**
>
> The Home Recording site is a well-known site, dedicated to audio education (see Figure 3.5). It's also part of a Webring, so it includes links to many similar sites.

Figure 3.5

You can learn about many aspects of do-it-yourself audio at Home Recording.

The 16-Bit Word and Quantization

Let's look at how this 16-bit word helps us record. In the diagram in Figure 3.6, each of the stair steps represents one of the 65,536 volume levels a 16-bit recorder assigns to a sound wave. (Our illustrator didn't want to draw all 65,536 stair steps, but you get the idea.)

As sound is recorded digitally, a sample and hold circuit inside the analog-to-digital converter measures that wave's amplitude thousands of times a second (this is the sampling process). The A-D converter then assigns that amplitude a binary number (in the case of a 16-bit recording, it could be any one of 65,536 values).

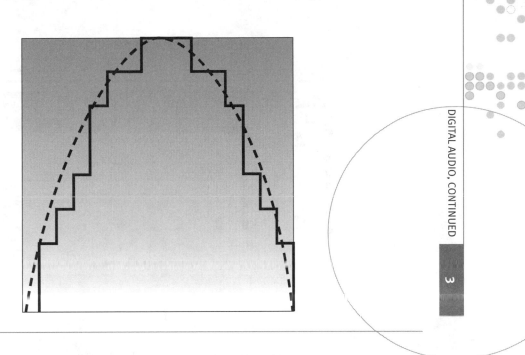

Figure 3.6

Notice how the rounded contours of a sound wave are represented by many small stair steps. This is the process of quantization.

The quantization process assigns a sound wave's volume level to one of these 65,536 stair steps. In the case of 16-bit recording, the resulting sound files can reproduce 65,536 different volume levels, from silence to rock-band loud.

Think about it. If a digital recorder is set to record at 44.1kHz, 16-bit, it's taking 44,100 samples a second, and each one of these samples is assigned to one of 65,536 possible quantization values. Whew. That's a lot of work for one second of audio.

Hot Link: ModernRecording (http://www.modernrecording.com)

The ModernRecording site is a labor of love by four experienced engineers/producers (see Figure 3.7). It covers the gamut of techniques and audio gear, and has an interesting Question and Answer page.

Figure 3.7

The ModernRecording site covers all manner of audio technology issues.

THE EAR PROVES (ONCE AGAIN) IT HAS A LOT TO OFFER

It's at this point that we encounter one of the great tricks of digital recording. Take another look at Figure 3.6. Notice that the sound wave is smooth, but the quantization stair steps form a jagged pattern.

How, you might ask, can we record a smoothly changing volume with something that uses stair steps?

A digital recorder, like a great dancer who can move up stair steps with an effortless smoothness, replicates a subtly changing volume level by assigning each small change to a given stair step.

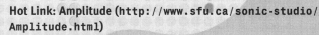

Hot Link: Amplitude (`http://www.sfu.ca/sonic-studio/`
`Amplitude.html`)

Amplitude, shown in Figure 3.8, lays out a lot of information about audio theory with very little words. We especially like the example in which they offer downloads of different-shaped sound waves (click the Waveform link).

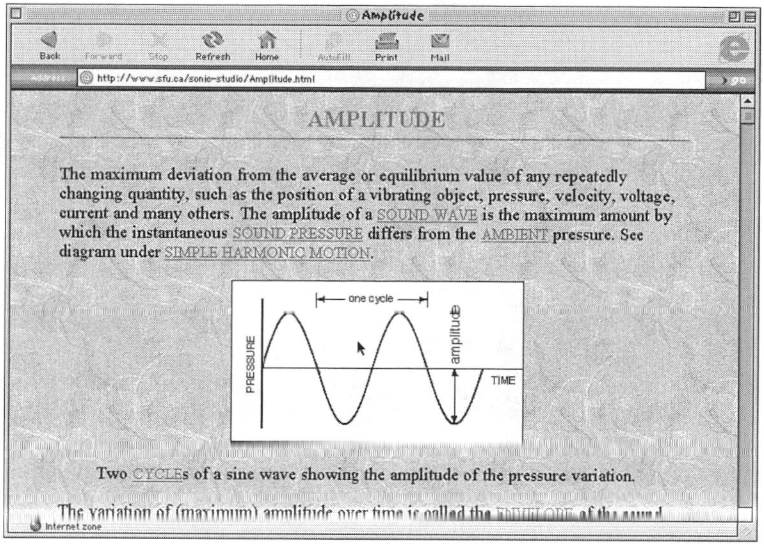

Figure 3.8

Amplitude offers downloads of various types of sound waves.

The key factor that gives a digital recorder the ability to accurately capture subtly changing volumes is *how many* steps it uses. In the case of an 8-bit audio file the number of volume gradations is 256. So an 8-bit recording quantizes all the volumes we hear, from whispery soft to jet engine loud, to 256 possible stair steps.

That seems like a lot, right? You'd think so, but once again the ear—that amazing organ—demonstrates what a superlative sound receptor it is. Because 8-bit sound does not fool the ear. Oh, it's adequate. You can distinguish a dog bark from a car engine. But to create audio that satisfies the ear as high fidelity, you need the 65,536 stair steps of 16-bit audio (16-bit audio is used in CDs, among other many other uses).

So this is digital recording's sneaky trick. It reproduces gradually changing volumes by using stair steps. But each step is so tiny that it fools the ear into thinking it's a smooth unbroken line. Pretty tricky, huh?

While 16-bit is a popular standard, as sound technology moves forward more applications offer 20-bit and 24-bit sound. Audio at 24-bit depth has a mind-boggling 16,777,216 volume gradations. That's probably enough.

Hot Link: Electronic Musician (`http://www.electronicmusician.com`)
Back before the desktop studio was the phenomenon it is today, this mag was doing a good job of covering it, and it still provides a lot of well-written commentary and advice (see Figure 3.9).

Figure 3.9

Electronic Musician does a great job of covering desktop recording.

Dynamic Range

The term *dynamic range* refers to the difference between the softest possible signal and the loudest possible signal a system can reproduce. The better the bit depth of an audio file, the more dynamic range it can reproduce. Here are the dynamic ranges of various bit depths:

- 16-bit audio has 96dB of dynamic range.
- 18-bit audio has 108dB of dynamic range.
- 20-bit audio has 120dB of dynamic range.
- 24-bit audio has 144dB of dynamic range.

These figures are theoretical. In the real world, factors like speaker quality influence the dynamic range of an audio playback system.

DITHER: COMPENSATING FOR A DIGITAL PROBLEM

But what about volume levels that fall in between two steps? Too bad—the analog to digital converter can't accept "in between" values. It must round off a volume level to one step or another. (This problem doesn't exist in analog recording; analog equipment records subtly changing electric voltages without assigning them to quantization stair steps.) The difference between the wave's actual voltage versus the stair step it must be rounded off to is called *quantization error*. This quantization error can lead to audible noise, which is more noticeable with low amplitude (low volume) recordings. That's why it's a good idea to record at the maximum level of input that your system can handle.

Hot Link: EQ Magazine (http://www.eqmag.com/)

The good thing about this magazine is that even though it's information-packed, it's still accessible to the beginner (see Figure 3.10).

Figure 3.10

EQ magazine has a lot of articles for the desktop audio designer.

Low amplitude waves cause problems for digital recorders. The difficulties arise when the analog to digital converter rounds off the sound wave's voltage to the closest stair step. That's not a problem with high amplitude sound waves, which use the full quantization range, or most of the 65,536 values. But since low amplitude signals use only the bottom few steps, the recorder doesn't have many stair steps to round off to. This leads to inaccuracies in the digitization process that can cause quantization distortion.

But this is no reason to dump your PC and go back to analog recording, because a good digital recording system compensates for low signal quantization distortion using *dither*. (Finally, a technical term that has a fun name. Just say it to yourself a few times...*dither*...it's a lot more pleasant than quantization value, huh?)

Hot Link: Mix Magazine (http://www.mixonline.com)

You've got to be a serious dude or dudette to read *Mix* magazine (see Figure 3.11). It's the recording industry trade magazine, and it's aimed at professionals. Still, even if you're not mixing big-budget film sound in L.A., it's got a ton of good information. If you want to know how the pros do it, take a look at *Mix*.

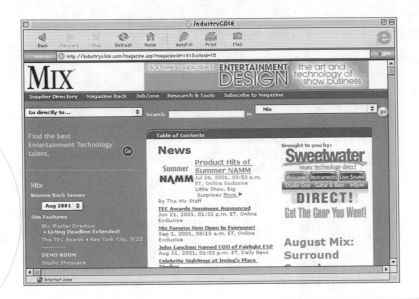

Figure 3.11

Mix magazine is geared for the audio professional.

Dither is a small amount of white noise—yes, that's right, a digital recorder actually adds noise to the sound wave. (This allows the analog aficionados to say, *see, analog is better.* But not so fast.) This noise is added to the sound wave before it is digitized. This aids the quantization process by allowing samples with insufficient bit depth to be properly quantized. This added noise gives a necessary boost to the low amplitude sound waves, allowing them to retain their original shape. It helps the input signal to come closer to the quantization stair steps much more often. Moral of the story: A little added noise (in the form of dither) is a good thing.

CHAPTER 4

MIDI: THE VIRTUAL ORCHESTRA

In This Chapter

- Learn the basics of MIDI, the computer music language that has profoundly changed desktop music making
- Find out how musicians use MIDI
- Learn about MIDI software
- Take a look at some seriously cool MIDI hardware

IS IT LIVE...OR IS IT MIDI?

Since the time when MIDI first became commonly used in the mid '80s, it's been an important part of music production. It's become standard practice to combine recordings of live musicians with tracks programmed with MIDI sequencers. Often, the MIDI tracks are amazingly life like—mixed in with live players in the right way, you might not be able to tell the difference.

In fact, in MIDI's early years, some people thought: Someday, this is going to put live musicians out of business. You'll be able to program a musical part on your computer, say, the perfect funk drum part, and that will be the end of live drummers.

But as the '90s rolled on, it became clear that those early fears that the live musician could be replaced were unjustified. Yes, you could program some pretty impressive parts with a MIDI sequencer. If you had the right bank of synthesizers, you could create an entire movie score with your PC. But still, put that side by side with live symphony, and the difference is clear. Humans bring a feel that is, well, human.

That said, some ear-blowing things can be done with MIDI. Few things expand the capability of the musician the way that MIDI sequencers do. Used musically, avoiding the more robotic MIDI techniques, some amazingly musical things can be created.

In fact, is that recording a live player...or is that MIDI...?

A BUNCH OF JARGON

Before we go any further, let's pause for some terminology. MIDI definitely has its own language.

NOTE

You'll often hear MIDI music musicians talk enthusiastically about *patches*, as in, "Whoa, I created this really cool electric guitar patch." This is not a piece of fabric to repair a guitar. Rather, it's a sound. The term patch is synonymous with sound, but it's usually more than just a plain electric guitar sound. Many synthesizers enable you to layer and filter individual sounds to create sounds that are all your own. Some MIDI players spend hours doing this.

In the early days of MIDI, each musical part—the strings, the drums—required its own keyboard. Fortunately this limitation is distant history. Now, most keyboards or sound modules will play several parts at once—they are *multitimbral*. Send your synthesizer the drum part on channel 10, and the piano part on channel 1, and it will play both simultaneously. This is a good thing, but realize that every synthesizer can only play so many parts at a time. And your synth has another limitation as to what it can play at the same time. If your keyboard has 32-voice *polyphony*, it will only play 32 notes at the same time, no matter what. You might have a string part that plays 8 notes simultaneously, and a piano part that plays 5 notes simultaneously—that's 13 notes. So the keyboard can only play 19 more notes (32 minus 13 equal 19).

MIDI Spotlight: The Roland XV 5080

A serious sound generator, the 5080 boasts 1,024 patches—right out of the box (see Figure 4.1). And since this synthesizer is also a sampler, it allows you to create and manipulate still more sounds. It offers 128-voice polyphony and is 32-part multitimbral. It also comes with 8 expansion slots in case you want to add on to its sound generating capabilities.

Figure 4.1

The Roland XV5080 is a serious sound generator.

Photo courtesy of Roland.

What Is MIDI?

MIDI arose out an unusual situation. In the early '80s the synthesizer industry was still in its infancy, but it understood the value of creating a common language so keyboards made by different manufacturers could work together.

Before 1983, a Yamaha synthesizer was a wonderful music-making piece of gear, as was a Roland or Korg synth. But there was no use hooking them up together, because they weren't going to speak to each other.

MIDI changed that, hence its name—Musical Instrument Digital Interface. It allows sound gear made by different companies to work together, which means that one PC, running one piece of software, could turn a bank of synths made by different companies into a cohesive orchestra (or rock band, or jazz ensemble, or just about anything). Using a MIDI sequencer—a program that allows you to record and edit MIDI data—you can compose music with a speed and flexibility that dwarfs older composing methods. And you can save these tunes as files in a format that allows easy collaboration.

 MIDI Spotlight: Korg Triton

This is one of Korg's top of the line synthesizer/samplers (see Figure 4.2). In addition to a massive amount of sounds—from drums to guitars to things your ears have not yet heard—it enables extensive real-time control of your sound.

Figure 4.2

The Korg Triton is a top of the line synthesizer.

Photo courtesy of Korg.

MIDI's capabilities caused an explosion in electronic music making. By the late '80s, MIDI was everywhere—in a multitude of albums, in big concerts and small club dates, and in studios of every stripe. Even music that sounds completely acoustic often includes at least some small use of MIDI (and sometimes much more).

(This compatibility between manufacturers is a minor miracle. Imagine if the manufacturers of other equipment tried to make their equipment work together, MIDI-style. It would be as if Apple and Microsoft decided to create computers that could be used interchangeably. Fat chance. Now you see how radical the MIDI agreement is.)

MIDI Spotlight: Alesis A6 Andromeda Waveform Synthesizer

Whoa, check out the knobs on this baby (see Figure 4.3). The Andromeda is what's known as an analog synthesizer. So you don't use this 16-voice polyphony, 16-part multitimbral unit to simulate real instruments. When you play this unit, everyone knows it's a synthesizer—but that's part of its charm. All those knobs on the unit (72 of 'em, not to mention 144 buttons) enable you to tune and filter the keyboard's very electronic-sounding output. A cool unit if you're going for that vintage sound.

Figure 4.3

The Alesis A6 does a good job of creating vintage sounds.

Photo courtesy of Alesis.

MIDI has become the ubiquitous language of the recording studio. The MIDI communication protocol has come a long way from its original use—one keyboard sending a signal to another. MIDI is now used to control much more than keyboards—it's used as a communication protocol for a wide array of studio gear, including signal processors (such as reverb boxes) and mixing consoles. And, it's also handy for sending patch data (information about that patch's sound, like amount of high end) from keyboards to storage devices, and for MIDI sync (more on that later).

MIDI is similar to digital audio itself in that it reduces the various elements of a musical performance to number-generated commands. Using numbers, the basic MIDI language tells a synthesizer or other tone generator the following information:

* What note to play: the *note number*
* When to start and stop that note: *note on* and *note off*
* How loud to play that note: this is called *key velocity*
* What the parameters are for: pitch bends, modulations, wheel moves, and sustain pedal use
* What patches to play, and when, and whether or not the patch changes (you might start with a wicked electric guitar patch, then send a MIDI message to change the synthesizer's voice to a gentle acoustic patch)

 MIDI Spotlight: Kurzweil K2600R Rackmount

The K2600R is packed with realistic, natural-sounding patches (see Figure 4.4). But, this high-end synthesizer/sampler has enough on-board effects processors to manipulate this bank of sound to become as unnatural as you like—mix and match to your heart's content. It features 48-voice polyphony and is 16-part multitimbral. This unit is a top seller.

Figure 4.4

This Kurzweil synthesizer has enough sounds for most any use.

Photo courtesy of Kurzweil.

Can I Turn a MIDI File into a WAV File?

A MIDI file contains no audio—it just stores information. It contains all the information needed to tell a keyboard how to play a piece of music. It tells the keyboard to, for example, start at a medium fast tempo with a funky eighth note pattern. The actual sound for the song is in your keyboard (or your PC or your sample), not in the MIDI file.

So if you want to turn a MIDI file into WAV file (and remember, WAV files contain actual audio), you need to record the audio output of the keyboard that's playing the MIDI file. You might say, "I play MIDI files on my PC and I hear them even without a keyboard." That's true—that's because the sound is coming from your PC's sound card (and in fact might not be too good because of this).

So yes, you can turn a MIDI into a WAV, but you'll need to do some recording to do so, and save the resulting file as a WAV (or AIF, or QuickTime, or some other high-quality format).

This "no audio, just information" format makes MIDI files really small. Compare the file size of a WAV file of a song to that of a MIDI file and you'll probably gasp—the MIDI is tiny. But, as in many things, small is beautiful when it comes to computer files. MIDI files' small size makes them easy to e-mail or upload to the Web. Have you ever received an e-card, and a little piece of corny music started to play with it? That's a MIDI file. The card makers embedded a MIDI file with the text and graphics—they know it's small enough to download quickly, and your PC's sound card is sufficient to play the music.

MIDI Spotlight: EMU Mo' Phatt

This unit's mission in life is to create grooves (see Figure 4.5). Its 32MB Urban Sound ROM gives you the sound source to make hard-thumpin', head-bobbin' grooves. The unit's effects processor lets you filter and redesign the sounds to keep your grooves fresh.

Figure 4.5

The Mo' Phatt is a groove machine.

Photo courtesy of E-Mu/Ensoniq.

Realize that when you send people a MIDI file, you don't know how it will sound to them. If you're used to listening to that MIDI arrangement with a $40,000 dollar rack of synths and they have nothing but that $69 discount sound card, they might wonder why you were so moved by this music. But that's life in MIDI city.

MIDI Spotlight: Midiman Midisport 1x1

If you're looking for an affordable low-tech way to get MIDI in and out of your PC, a MIDI interface unit like this will do the trick. The Midisport plugs into your USB port. These bare-bones units usually retail somewhere around $50; that's about as cheap as you can go for a new MIDI interface (but shop for a used one if you want to go still lower; these units hold up well). Notice that it only provides you with one MIDI in and one MIDI out, hence the name 1x1. You say you have more than one keyboard? That's okay: Using daisy chaining (hooking one keyboard into another, into another, into another), you can hook up several keyboards with a 1x1 unit.

THE BRAINS OF A MIDI SYSTEM: SOFTWARE

For many musicians, the first time they sit down with a MIDI keyboard/sequencer combination is a major thrill. It's amazing to realize that you can click Record, hold forth in any style you want, and when you're done, there it is: The software has notated all your meanderings, in a medium that lets you edit with meticulous detail.

For composers used to notating with paper and pencil, this is especially liberating. Most of the tedious, time consuming notation work is done for you, allowing you more time to create. Beautiful.

MIDI sequencing software is indeed a musician's liberation. You can edit each note individually (or entire verses and choruses) until you get the effect you like. You can transpose your performance to a higher pitch with a few clicks of a mouse, and you can speed up or slow down the tempo without changing the pitch—that's impossible with tape recording (because speeding up the tape would increase the frequency, thus raising the pitch), and only partially possible with digital audio recording.

MIDI Spotlight: MOTU MIDI Express XT USB

When you have a full-blown MIDI studio, you need a unit like this MIDI interface by Mark of the Unicorn (see Figure 4.6). This unit provides you with eight independent MIDI inputs and outputs; it will handle 128 MIDI channels—enough for most uses, wouldn't you say? The MIDI Express also enables SMPTE read/write, which is crucial if you're synchronizing your MIDI rig with a tape machine or a video deck.

Figure 4.6

MOTU's MIDI Express XT will handle all your studio's MIDI interface tasks.

Photo courtesy of Mark of the Unicorn.

If you want to move your notes closer to the beat—or farther away—you can select those notes and decide how rhythmically accurate you want them be. And if you played your part on a keyboard assigned to a flute sound, you can then assign that part to a saxophone, or bass, or drums, or something really weird like a Space Invader sound. Cutting and pasting a performance from one song section to another is as easy as it would be with a word processor.

All this new freedom and creative flexibility is achieved with the help of your MIDI software—the command center of many electronic musicians' studios. Let's look at a typical program, Mark of the Unicorn's Digital Performer, shown in Figure 4.7, which is one of the leading MIDI programs. Over the years it has grown into a full-fledged audio editor, allowing multitrack recording with its MIDI sequencing. If you're looking for a program to be your main audio/MIDI workhorse, this would be a good choice.

The transport panel   MIDI Machine Control

Your MIDI score

Digital audio tracks

MIDI mixing console

The Fade tool

Video Playback

Software effects devices

Music notation

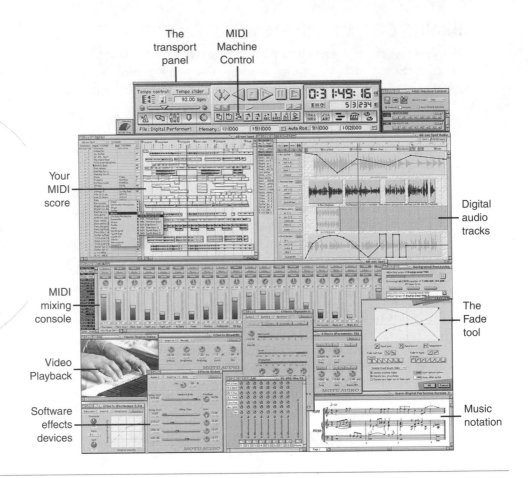

Figure 4.7

Today's leading MIDI software is complex but highly capable.

Graphic courtesy of Mark of the Unicorn.

Looking at this screenshot, my first impression is: Holy Moly, it looks complicated, doesn't it? All those buttons and knobs—even though we know what they mean, we still think it looks pretty Star Trek. Beam us up, Scotty; how do we land this thing?

Fortunately, if you understand half a dozen or so concepts, you'll know what all these software buttons and knobs do. The following list gives information about each:

- **The transport panel.** This panel enables you to record and play back your music. Notice the number in the top right: 0:31:49:16. This is real time—31 minutes, 49 seconds, 16 frames (there's 30 frames in every second). Underneath this is another number, 5/3/234. This helps you find your place in the song—5th measure, 3rd beat, 234 clicks (various software divides a beat into various amounts of clicks; some have 480). Typing a new number in either box enables you to go directly to that point. Notice also the Tempo Slider and the bpm (beats per minute) box. Use these to adjust the speed of your song—even while the song is playing.

- **MIDI Machine Control.** This is where you control external sync. This enables you to synchronize the PC with your MIDI software using another machine, such as a digital tape machine you use to record live musicians.

- **Your MIDI score**. On the left is the list of musical instruments; on the right the little squiggly pictures represent groups of notes each instrument is playing. Each instrument has its own track. You can click any one of the notes and edit any of its values: pitch, length, volume, and so on. You can also select groups of notes, like an entire verse, and repeat, delete, transpose, or otherwise edit it. Notice the vertical line; this represents the playback head.

- **Digital audio tracks.** These are not MIDI tracks. Not all MIDI sequencers enable you to record audio as Digital Performer does. These audio tracks play in sync with the MIDI tracks. The curvy and square lines represent volume changes the user has decided to draw in to mix audio with MIDI in a musically pleasing way.

- **A MIDI mixing console.** This enables you to route tracks from one location to another; for example, to send a track to a reverb chamber to make it sound more "spacious." The mixing desk also indicates the volume level of each track.

- **Software effects devices**. These help you color and enhance the music using tools like reverb and equalization (more about that in Chapter 17, "Mixing.")

- **Video Playback.** This feature enables you to synchronize your MIDI composition with a video deck. This is something only high-end sequencers enable you to do, although more and more MIDI software enables you to do this. This picture is the video the composer is creating music for. But by watching the video while composing, you can see how the musical punctuation points—the "hits"—are matching the video.

- **The Fade tool**. Using this tool you can subtly shape the way one section blends into another.

- **Music notation**. Perhaps the only thing on the screen that an 18th Century composer would recognize, this is good old-fashioned music notation. We wonder what this would have done for Beethoven's output—he may have written a half dozen more symphonies. The software notates the music as you play it, which is exponentially faster than paper and pencil.

How Musicians Use MIDI

MIDI as a musical element is much like a tasty spice. You probably don't want your entire song to be played by MIDI instruments, but it's a great way to enhance your arrangement. Many songs are recorded with a combination of live musicians and MIDI instruments. Preferably, the MIDI drum part is played or programmed by a skilled drummer; the MIDI keyboards are tickled by someone who really plays the piano. Or, perhaps you record one real horn player, and you mix the real horn part in with a MIDI horn section to make the whole section feel more musical.

MIDI is a songwriter's best friend. It enables a songwriter to play a demo version of a new song without hiring musicians. With a MIDI keyboard, software, a microphone and a recorder, a tunesmith can turn a musical idea into a fully realized song.

MIDI Spotlight: Parker MIDI Fly

A MIDI guitar—cool! For years, MIDI composers would try to play a MIDI keyboard and make it sound like a guitar. Okay, so you have a guitar patch on your keyboard, but the two instruments are played so differently that a keyboard can never quite sound like a guitar. Since the Parker has MIDI output, you can add a completely authentic guitar track to your MIDI mix (see Figure 4.8).

Figure 4.8

The Parker MIDI Fly lets guitarists lay down MIDI tracks with their instrument of choice.

Photo courtesy of Parker Guitars.

One of MIDI software's great strengths is that it enables someone who doesn't play a particular instrument (or any instrument) to compose. You can pick the notes out slowly, or simply type in the notes at any speed you want. A MIDI software function called *quantize* enables you to shift the sloppy notes you just played as close to the beat as you want. The MIDI function called *humanize* (not all programs have this, and some of them call it something different) enables you to shift the notes away from the beat if they are too rigidly correct.

General MIDI and Standard MIDI Files

When you're done with a MIDI song arrangement, you may want to save it in a format that can be read by any MIDI program. Say you use Digital Performer but you have a friend who uses Cubase. They're both good MIDI sequencing programs, but Cubase can't open a Digital Performer file, and vice versa. Each sequencer program saves files in its own proprietary format.

One solution is to save your work as a Standard MIDI File (SMF). Any sequencer that supports this format (and most do) will save your file in a manner that's readable by any SMF-compatible sequencer. This is good news because it enables you to e-mail or upload your MIDI arrangement without worrying whether it will play in someone else's setup. It also enables you to collaborate with MIDI composers anywhere without fear of file incompatibility.

MIDI Spotlight: Digitech Studio Quad 4

This digital reverb unit is an example of the many uses of MIDI (see Figure 4.9). This unit allows MIDI control of program changes and effects parameters, among other mix elements. So you can send it a MIDI signal in the middle of a song to change from, for example, a short delay to a long delay, enabling you to get more use from a single effects box. The Quad 4 allows four independent audio inputs and outputs, so with the added flexibility enabled by MIDI, this box gives you an extensive sound palette.

Figure 4.9

The Digitech Studio Quad 4 allows MIDI control of program changes.

Photo courtesy of Digitech.

However, there are some compromises to be made for this cross-platform compatibility. The Digital Performer sequence you created might call for a specific clarinet sound, but you might lose this information when you save your work as a SMF. Yes, it will be a melodic instrument of some kind, but it might not be that cool layered clarinet patch you've created.

The good news for MIDI composers who spend a lot of time picking out patches is an improvement to the SMF file format called General MIDI (GM). Any sound module that conforms to this format will play a GM file with the (mostly) correct sounds.

To be GM compatible, a synthesizer must have the standard set of 128 instrumental patches, and it must be able to play 16 channels simultaneously with 24-part polyphony. The assignment of instruments is always the same; patch 1 is always the piano, patch 80 is always the Ocarina (hey, wait a second, is the Ocarina such a popular instrument that it gets a place on the GM map? C'mon, when was the last time you composed for Ocarina?). Channel 10 is always the drum channel. The GM standardized specifications also include specifications as to how a synthesizer responds to commands like velocity, pitch bend, and tuning.

Many manufacturers now use GM as their standard. And many of today's sound cards and synths include the GM standard and then some—a good synth will be able to respond to more than 16 channels of information, and play more than 24-note polyphony (64-voice or more is not unusual) .

NOTE

MIDI Spotlight: Digitech Whammy!

Yes, this is a whammy pedal that's MIDI controllable (see Figure 4.10). In case you're not a guitarist, a whammy pedal gives you all kinds of cool and wild guitar effects, such as the classic dive-bomb slide. It's one more example of how virtually every aspect of modern music making somehow involves MIDI.

Figure 4.10

Have you always wanted to do the "dive-bomb" slide? The Digitech Whammy will let you realize your dreams.

Photo courtesy of Digitech.

A couple manufacturers, notably Roland and Yamaha, have created extensions to the GM standard. (While manufacturers worked together to create MIDI compatibility, that doesn't stop them from trying to go one better than each other.) Roland's GS extension adds extra sounds to the 128 GM standard, as well as a special sound effect set. Yamaha's XG format requires 32-voice polyphony, three independently controllable effects processors, and several sound effects banks (those extra sound effects make the gamers happy).

In the real world, even a simple GM file like a percussion-saxophone duet will sound significantly different on different synths; volume might be set differently, or modulation wheel messages (which are used to shift pitch) might be interpreted differently, not to mention the inherent differences in synth sound quality. Remember, MIDI is just information. The sound itself always comes from the sound card or rack module.

What is a SysEx?

System Exclusive Message (SysEx) enables a MIDI module to transmit and receive information that relates only to a particular MIDI device. A SysEx message contains a manufacturer ID that allows it to distinguish a specific MIDI module from the other MIDI devices in the chain. Composers typically use SysEx messages to send custom patch information to a sequencer or patch librarian, which enables them to store those patches they've spent so many hours creating.

Hardware Ins and Outs

Take a look at the back of a MIDI keyboard, and you'll see three MIDI connection points: In, Out, and Thru. As you might guess, you plug a MIDI cable into a keyboard's In jack to send it information—this keyboard is then the slave. You plug a cable into a keyboard's Out jack to send information from it—this keyboard is the master. So perhaps your master keyboard doesn't have a good electric guitar sound. No problem. Just hook up a cable from its Out jack to the In jack of your synthesizer that has a good crunchy guitar, and use your master keyboard to play notes on the slave synth.

But what about the MIDI Thru jack? Any information the keyboard receives in its In jack is routed back to its Thru jack. This enables you to *daisy chain* several MIDI sound modules together. So you can hook up half a dozen or so MIDI synths to one master synth, as shown in Figure 4.11, press a note on the master, and all the slave synths will play the same note.

(By the way, the phrase Slave Synths is a good name for an '80s retro band. You're welcome to use it if you like; we just want free backstage passes.)

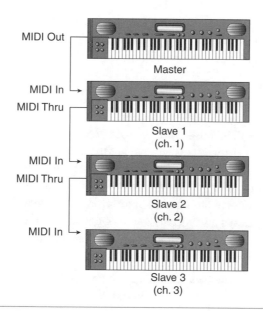

Figure 4.11

The MIDI daisy chain: with one master synth, you can control many slave synths.

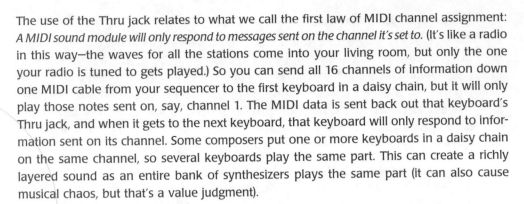

The use of the Thru jack relates to what we call the first law of MIDI channel assignment: *A MIDI sound module will only respond to messages sent on the channel it's set to.* (It's like a radio in this way—the waves for all the stations come into your living room, but only the one your radio is tuned to gets played.) So you can send all 16 channels of information down one MIDI cable from your sequencer to the first keyboard in a daisy chain, but it will only play those notes sent on, say, channel 1. The MIDI data is sent back out that keyboard's Thru jack, and when it gets to the next keyboard, that keyboard will only respond to information sent on its channel. Some composers put one or more keyboards in a daisy chain on the same channel, so several keyboards play the same part. This can create a richly layered sound as an entire bank of synthesizers plays the same part (it can also cause musical chaos, but that's a value judgment).

Figure 4.11 shows a master keyboard controlling several slave synthesizers, but in today's typical home studio, all of your synthesizers are controlled by the MIDI software running on your PC. To enable your computer to communicate with your keyboards, you'll need a piece of hardware called a *MIDI interface.* You plug this device into a port on the back of your computer. MIDI interfaces come in all sizes and capabilities, depending on budget. A good one includes multiple MIDI Ins and Outs; remember, each MIDI Out can handle 16 channels. So a MIDI interface with four MIDI Outs will give you 64 channels—enough for most applications, but you never know. (At some point you'll probably want 128.) A pro-level MIDI interface also includes synchronization capability (more on that in Chapter 15, "Audio Synchronization.")

There's one more thing you'll need to make your MIDI setup sing: some kind of MIDI operating system to enable your sequencer software to communicate to with your MIDI interface. Mac musicians will probably use Opcode's OMS (Open MIDI system) or FreeMidi by Mark of the Unicorn. Windows musicians will install MIDI drivers that are typically included on the MIDI software's master disks/CD. These aren't programs you typically spend a lot of time with; you install them and they do their work. They enable your computer to know which MIDI devices are connected to your MIDI interface (say, the Korg M1, or the Roland Sound Canvas). These programs also recognize the patch names in your various synths, as well as perform real-time processing such as delay and pitch shifting.

I'm Sending a Signal to a Synthesizer, but It's Not Responding. Why?

So, your synthesizers are all hooked up, you send them MIDI data, but you near nothing. What might be wrong?

- Many times the problem is channel assignment. Remember, a MIDI module will only respond to messages sent on the channel it's set to. If your Yamaha MIDI module is set to channel 7, and you're sending it messages on 2, you'll hear only the sound of silence. Peaceful, but frustrating.
- Are both keyboards turned on?
- Is the MIDI cable faulty? Try switching it with a cable you know for sure works.

- Is the channel muted or made nonplayable by some button you've clicked? This is an example of operator error, and though we don't like to admit it, operator error is the most common problem.

- Try turning the keyboard off and back on again. This process of *power cycling* can help many pieces of studio gear, which seem as susceptible to bad moods as we humans are.

- Is the analog output of the synth plugged into a speaker system—and is that speaker system actually turned on?

ADDITIONAL MIDI LINKS

The Internet is one of the desktop musician's best resources. Here are some sites to help you expand your MIDI knowledge and download some free MIDI files. Enjoy!

- **MIDI on About.com** (http://midimusic.about.com). Hosted by MIDI guru Steve Allen, this site is a sprawling online encyclopedia. Find everything from software to files to How To advice.

- **Cubase** (http://www.cubase.com). To many MIDI composers, Cubase is where it's at. It's clearly one of the best sequencer programs.

- **Cakewalk Software** (http://www.cakewalk.com). Clearly one of the most popular MIDI sequencers, Cakewalk is worth checking out. And while you're there, take a look at Sonar, a complete MIDI and audio editor.

- **Emagic** (http://www.emagic.de). This company makes the highly popular Logic Audio sequencer—especially big in Europe.

- **Coda Music Technology** (http://www.codamusic.com). This company makes Finale, a leading notation program, and SmartMusic, a tutorial program.

- **Opcode** (http://www.opcode.com). Are you a Mac MIDI user? Take a look at Opcode's Studio Vision program, as well as some of its other Mac-related audio applications.

- **PG Music** (http://www.pgmusic.com). If you're a MIDI composer, this site is a must visit. It makes the popular Band-In-A-Box program, which gives you fully orchestrated MIDI files in all the popular music styles. You can open them up and customize them to your own liking.

- **Voyetra Turtle Beach** (http://www.voyetra.com). One of the most popular music software companies, it offers a full range of sequencing and notation applications.

- **FindMIDIs.com** (http://www.findmidis.com). Download scads of MIDI files by radio-driven pop acts: Eminem, Destiny's Child, all your favorite boy and girl bands.

- **MIDI Network** (http://www.midi-network.com). Hundreds of rock and pop MIDI files by well-known acts. Download them and customize them to create your own music.

- **Punk and Metal Midi Archives** (http://www.geocities.com/SiliconValley/4063). Yes, it is what it sounds like: the music of many of your favorite head bangers, misanthropes, and anarchists, all saved as MIDI files. Enjoy!

- **Country Guitar** (http://midistudio.com/midi/DA_AF.htm). The MIDI Studio itself is worth a look around, and in particular, take a listen to the MIDI stylings of Dick Anderson, who records these files with his Fender Strat.

- **MIDIWorld.com** (http://midiworld.com). The list of MIDI files for download just keeps going and going[el]

- **A Passion for Jazz** (http://www.apassion4jazz.net/juke.html). This site is a good one for an overall jazz information; the MIDI download section contains a good selection of classic tunes.

- **Broadway MIDI** (http://www.broadwaymidi.com). Someone spent some serious time putting this site together: It offers thousands of MIDIs from hundred of musicals, not to mention opera, Christmas, TV, and other music. Start downloading.

- **Chuckie's Movie Midi Files** (http://movies.musicpage.com). Chuckie has posted a vast collection of movie soundtracks; this site has been a big one since the mid '90s.

PART **II**

LET'S START BUILDING

THE DESKTOP PHILOSOPHY: VIRTUALLY EVERYTHING SHOULD BE VIRTUAL, OR, HOW CAN WE DO THIS CHEAPER AND BETTER?

In This Chapter:

- Get ready to design your desktop studio
- Discover ways to build your studio more cheaply
- Learn about the all-in-the-box philosophy
- Find out many good places to shop for gear

THE ETERNAL RULES OF DESKTOP AUDIO

So you have a PC or a Mac, a little machine that purrs quietly and has tons of potential. They don't look like much, do they? But they are definitely cool tools, able to think a lot faster than we are, to store a library of information, to connect with the Internet. They can't think creatively, but that's where you come in. You and your computer could make some beautiful music together.

But how, exactly? Okay, your machine has made some bleeps and blips, maybe helped you download an MP3 or two, but you want to do more. You know this box could really sing. It's time to start building.

Setting up a desktop studio can be a lot of fun, and it can also be incredibly confusing. The fun part is knowing how much you can do with your home setup--an entire audio universe can be contained in your humble PC. That boring-looking little box is chock full of sound possibilities: techno tracks, sound effects, sample manipulation, music composition, burning CDs...the list goes on.

But as you consider your options for how to assemble your studio, it can get confusing. Quickly, the vocabulary created by the manufacturers starts to blur together with the actual audio vocabulary: VST and VAST, SCSI and PCI, DSP and IO, FireWire and mLAN. It's easy to get bogged down in jargon overload. That's understandable. It's one of the great truths of keyboards and audio gear that they rarely have simple, nontechnical names. So you hook up your VSR9000 to the MOTU Interface, which in turn is routed to the Yamaha 02R, and then into the Digi 001. If all that makes you scratch your head, don't feel alone.

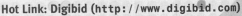

Hot Link: Digibid (http://www.digibid.com)
Digibid is an all-inclusive online music and sound gear auction (see Figure 5.1). You'll find everything from amps to speakers to guitars to keyboards. Even if you don't want to buy there, it's a good idea to browse the site and get a sense of prices before making your final purchase. The selection of used gear is so extensive that it's likely you'll find a price on whatever you're looking for.

It All Comes Down to You

Step One in the great task of fearlessly building a desktop studio is to figure out your goals. You could build a wildly elaborate studio, with every audio whirly-gig known to man, but you don't need to if you just want to layer techno tracks from samples you download from the Web. A simple (but versatile) setup will do you just fine, and we'll talk about that.

Figure 5.1

Digibid is an online music and sound gear auction.

Or perhaps you're a songwriter and you want to create polished demos. That's a common use for desktop studios (and if you create one, expect your musician friends to call more often). But the demo songwriter doesn't need some of the extra gear that's needed by, for example, a recordist who's in business recording bands. Those groups will want all the bells and whistles, and when you tell them you haven't bought the XLR95XB (whatever that is), and so you can't re-resonate the de-emphasis (whatever that means), they'll be disappointed. A relatively simple setup enables the songwriter to turn out polished demo-quality mixes.

For many of today's audio production tasks, you don't need anything more than a fast PC, a big hard drive, some software, an audio card, and a CD burner (good speakers and a sweet mic or two also help). So before you bring your credit card into one of those electronic music shops filled with incredibly seductive gear--careful, sailor--give some thought to what you really want to do.

The point is: Figure out your goals first. When you know exactly what you want to accomplish, it will help you wade through the blizzard of VSTs, I/Os, and SCSIs.

Hot Link: eBay (http://www.ebay.com)

Of course the selection at eBay, shown in Figure 5.2, is massive, but the problem is what keyword to use to search for PC music gear? We've had good results with "midi," which yielded 21 pages of MIDI gear for sale (although it's worth searching with other keywords--you'll find just about any type of audio gear on eBay). The prices are often far below retail: It pays to shop around.

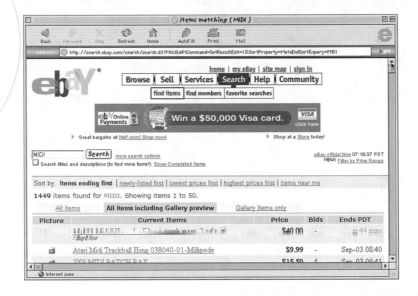

Figure 5.2

You'll find a large selection of music gear on eBay.

Some Rules That Will Save You Money

Of course your goals may change with time, but no matter; remember Eternal Rule 1 about buying audio gear:

It's much better to start simply and add on. You don't want to be making a credit card payment for that cool piece of gear that's gathering dust. Make sure you find yourself saying "Wow, I really wish I had the 'what's-a-majigger'" at least several times before you let a salesperson tell you that you need it.

And when you try to sell a piece of used gear you don't need, you'll encounter Eternal Rule 2 (and this is the important one):

There's a huge market for used audio gear. We mean massive. You can find everything you see in all the catalogs in the classifieds and online under "used instruments." All that bright and shiny gear is about 30 percent cheaper or more (or should be--if it's not, make them an offer. There are so many other people trying to sell gear they'll probably have to come down).

This mondo-sized market exists for used gear because--and we don't want to be too discouraging, but you may as well know this--the world is full of enthusiasts who get seduced by the awesome possibilities of the equipment. It can bend, shift, shape, layer, and morph to your heart's content. It can make people who have never touched an instrument sound like musicians.

Hot Link: Full Compass (http://www.fullcompass.com/)
A complete audio gear retailer, Full Compass has it all (see Figure 5.3). The photo displays at the site enable you to get a good look at the equipment.

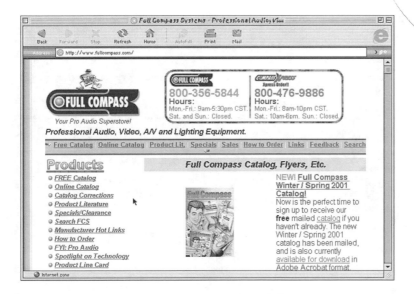

Figure 5.3

Full Compass carries a complete selection of audio gear.

But here's the part that people forget. (Goodness, we're coming to the discouraging part; please proceed with caution.) At the end of the day, making music, creating vital audio sound design, can be a really hard, tedious process. The gear is full of whiz-bang buttons and knobs, but there are plenty of moments where it's no more fun than sitting at an old fashioned piano and practicing scales.

This is what helps create the used market for audio gear--dreams that hit a brick wall. The equipment looks sexy--and it is sexy--but the work gets long. There are few things as creatively inspiring as a fully equipped audio studio, but realize as you build that it's going to be work. That knowledge will help you when you bring home that new piece of gear and discover the manual has been translated from Japanese.

VIRTUALLY EVERYTHING SHOULD BE VIRTUAL

Before we begin to look at the nuts and bolts of a desktop studio, let's look at an approach to audio production that's becoming increasingly popular. This is the approach we recommend you take in turning your PC into a sound studio. It can be summed up with the phrase "everything in the box." Simply put, it's an approach that emphasizes the PC as the center of the audio studio. All recording, editing, and mixing is done with software, and many of the auxiliary audio tools also reside within the PC.

Hot Link: Markertec (http://www.markertec.com/)

"Home of the Unique and Hard To Find" is the Markertec motto, and this site lives up to it. Acoustic foam? They've got it. Audio test equipment? You bet. If it's audio or video gear, you'll probably find it at Markertec (see Figure 5.4).

Figure 5.4

You'll find much of the gear needed for a home audio studio at Markertec.

To put this trend in context, we state what we think of as the three eras of audio recording. We have to oversimplify a bit to fit things into three neat eras, but bear with us and you'll see where we're heading.

Era 1: Traditional Analog

Time period: 1940s to 1985.

Everything was analog. Recording studios had big clunky gear, and all the equipment was separate. The mixing console routed audio signals, the tape deck recorded, and if you wanted to add a special effect (like reverb) you routed your audio to still another piece of equipment. The big change in this era occurred in the 1960s when multitrack recording became common, enabling much greater control over the sound of individual instruments. Prior to that the entire band had to be recorded to one stereo master (or mono master), so if one member made a mistake in an otherwise timeless performance, the whole group had to do it again.

Hot Link: B&H: The Pro Audio Section (http://www.bhphotovideo.com)
This online retailer offers both new and used audio equipment, although we weren't too impressed with the used selection. It does offer a full array of pro audio gear though (see Figure 5.5).

Figure 5.5

The audio section of B&H offers both new and used audio equipment.

Era 2: Digital Traditional

Time period: 1985 to the mid- to late-'90s.

Over the course of this period, the various pieces of studio gear became digital. This caused a great increase in sound quality. In addition, advances in multitrack recording gave precise control over the sound of each instrument; individual musicians could do endless takes until they created perfect performance (with the help of editing). The digital audio workstation (DAW) was developed, giving audio engineers the benefit of a software interface for hard disk recording. But these DAWs were very expensive. And equipment remained separate entities, so a professional studio would have a digital mixing console and a digital tape deck; if an engineer wanted to add an effect like delay or chorus, he would route it to a separate digital effects box. A recording studio--an inordinately expensive thing to own--was a room full of hardware.

> **Hot Link: Digital Pro Audio (http://www.digitalproaudio.com/)**
>
> This site specializes in outfitting home and project studios, but there's enough pro-level gear to satisfy a full-fledged studio (see Figure 5.6). This site, like all online retailers, only charges sales tax to the residents of the state it's located in (in this case, New York). So buying online is a good way to avoid those pesky state sales taxes.

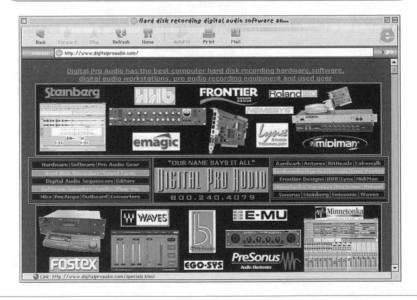

Figure 5.6

Digital Pro Audio carries gear for both the home and professional studio (is there a difference anymore?)

Era 3: All Digital

Time period: 2000 onward.

Each of the various pieces of gear has migrated into the PC, replaced by software. The price of a DAW has fallen to affordability, or you can download freeware from the Web and run it on your home PC. The multitrack tape machine is nearing extinction, replaced by hard disk recording. Your mixing desk, where you set relative sound levels (among other tasks), is now visible on your computer screen. The effects boxes that add reverb and delay are now software plug-ins that you control onscreen with the click of a mouse. Even the synthesizers are software. Most everything is all in the box. The modern studio can be an incredibly compact place--the recording artist Moby has one in his laptop.

This all-in-the-box era is a boon for the desktop recordist for the following reasons:

- A PC full of software is a heck of a lot cheaper than a studio full of hardware, and in some cases more capable.
- You can download much of what you need to get started--for free. (But of course to really get some cookin' software you will need to part with some cash.)

EXCEPTIONS TO ALL-IN-THE-BOX

However, not everyone uses the all-in-the-box approach. There are still people who use, for example, the ADAT machine. The Alesis Digital Audio Tape (ADAT) is a reasonably priced digital multitrack recorder that became popular in the early '90s. Before the ADAT, owning a digital multitrack was out of the question for all but the most high-end studios. When Alesis put out the ADAT it was immediately popular. And as the price of ADATs fell they became wildly popular; it was one of the key factors that dramatically increased home studio usage. You'll still find a multitude of home studios equipped with these digital multitrack recorders.

Hot Link: Gearsearch (http://www.gearsearch.com)
This site, shown in Figure 5.7, is a kind of search engine for music gear. It redirects you to other places to find gear online, so it's a good place to locate online music equipment retailers. The desktop musician's motto: I will pay the lowest price. (Repeat daily).

Figure 5.7

Gearsearch helps you find online gear retailers.

But ADATs don't go along with the all-in-the-box philosophy. The ADAT is an external tape machine--it's essentially the same type of tape machine that's been used for decades, except it's digital. And my prediction (and it's a pretty safe one) is that the ADAT and machines like it are rapidly becoming dinosaurs.

In the new era of all-in-the-box, the ADAT is replaced by the audio hard drive. Instead of recording to a tape machine (even a digital one), today's recordists are using software-based recording systems that store all sound files on a hard drive.

The ADAT can't begin to compete with hard drive–based recording. When you record, edit, and mix with a hard drive, you're using a random access system--there's never any rewinding or fast forwarding, and if you want to cut and paste that verse and chorus, it just takes a couple of mouse clicks. Then burn a CD or upload a file with a few more mouse clicks. That's audio in the 21st Century.

Hot Link: Mars Music (http://www.marsmusic.com/)

Mars Music sells music gear from A to Z, including a vintage section for those looking for sounds from the pre-digital era, and a "scratch n' dent" section that offers refurbished gear (see Figure 5.8) .

Figure 5.8

You'll find most any type of audio gear at Mars Music.

There are plenty of other pieces of audio hardware that are being replaced by software-based recording. Instead of having a rack filled with compressors or effects units (more on them in Chapter 13, "The Recordist's Tools,"), today's recordist can accomplish these tasks with computer hardware and software. So "all in the box" means your studio is compact and versatile. And it's a lot easier (and cheaper) to download a software upgrade than to go out and buy a new effects box.

Still, though, when you go shopping to set up your desktop studio, you'll see plenty of offers for this external gear. Walk into a well-stocked music gear store and you'll see all sorts of units, apparently still selling well, that are quickly on their way to the dust heap. You'll see compressors, effects units, and digital tape machines--all hardware. Yes, they are an option, but in most cases one you don't need to consider. Think hard drive and think software. And those friends of yours who have ADAT machines? Please break the news to them gently.

Hot Link: J and R: Audio (`http://www.jandr.com/audio`)

J and R sells the full range of consumer electronics. You'll find plenty of home theater stuff here (see Figure 5.9). It's more of a place to buy your peripherals (speakers, cable) than the core of your system.

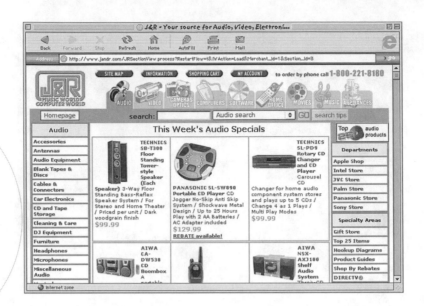

Figure 5.9

J and R offers a full range of consumer electronics.

But those users who are not all-in-the-box devotees might say, "Hey, I don't want to weigh down my PC that much. And my ADAT machine works great." And they have a point. There's nothing wrong with this approach. Some great tunes have been recorded with an ADAT and plenty of external processing hardware.

Hot Link: zZounds.com (http://www.zzounds.com/)

A well-stocked online music retailer with an interesting sales technique. The site allows you to download MP3 samples from dozens of its sound modules, with the theory that this will help you decide if you like that particular synthesizer (see Figure 5.10). Many of the units have several accompanying samples for download. Someone did a lot of work.

Figure 5.10

Zzsounds allows you to download MP3 samples from many of its sound modules.

Many highly capable home project studios have been cobbled together through the years using external hardware. Perhaps you know people who started in, say, 1991, who are still turning out great mixes. They don't want to completely reconfigure their studios, and they probably don't need to. But it's not the best approach if you're starting out now.

Another school of thought says that software-based effects processors are inferior to hardware-based processors. If you're working on big-time audio projects, software alone won't cut it, says this camp. They'll tell you that you're not going to record the reigning king or queen of Top 40 with a PC-only setup. You'll need a full rack of exotic and wonderful (probably handmade) hardware to doctor and enhance the sound. They'll explain that you will spend a fortune accumulating this hardware, and it will need to be replaced or upgraded next year. Then again, Ricky Martin's smash hit *Livin' la Vida Loca* was recorded and mixed exclusively in the Pro Tools system. The producers of this big-budget pop hit had all the studio gear imaginable at their disposable, but they chose an all-in-the-box approach.

Hot Link: Sweetwater (http://www.sweetwater.com)

A well-respected music store with a great selection. You can call it and get advice, too (see Figure 5.11).

Figure 5.11

Sweetwater has a tremendous selection of audio gear, and the salespeople are always willing to help.

Of course software alone can't replace some things. Microphones and microphone pre-amps are still very much real-world physical items. And depending on your goals, a basic mixer comes in handy--although those 64-channel monsters are even going out of style in pro studios. And some engineers have a fondness for vintage compressors or reverb units (again, more on this gear later). So all-in-the-box is a guiding philosophy, not a written-in-stone rule.

But here's the point: If you're just starting out, building your audio facility from scratch, the most efficient and powerful (and cheapest) approach is to base your studio as much as possible in your PC.

And the center of that PC-based studio? Software, of course. Which brings us to our next chapter....

CHAPTER **6**

SOFTWARE: THE BASICS

In This Chapter

- Learn about how software has revolutionized music production
- Discover the importance of software in your desktop setup
- Look at some leading recording/editing programs
- Find many Web sites that offer audio shareware

THE JOY OF SOFTWARE

Audio software is the tool that turns your humble PC into a righteous music-making machine.

Boot up, say, Pro Tools—one of the best audio programs—and it's as if you're an aural painter, with sound as your palette. Brighten this, lift the volume on that, stretch this, layer all these, cut and paste, filter and flange, dream and create—the only limitation is your imagination.

Click a sound file and, in a few seconds, make it much shorter or longer—without changing the pitch. Or change the pitch, correcting the singer's tuning, but keep the length the same. And that guitar riff, the one that was played thirty seconds into the song? What would it sound like if it came in a few seconds later? No problem, just click it, assign it a new time, and it now plays later.

Hot Link: Shareware Music Machine (`http://www.hitsquad.com/smm/`)

There aren't too many online sources of software that top Shareware Music Machine, shown in Figure 6.1. From recorder/editors to CD burning utilities to audio file converters, this site offers it all.

Figure 6.1

Shareware Music Machine is the motherlode of downloadable software.

Whoops—there's a tiny click in the flute part. Who knows where it came from, but it ruins an otherwise flawless (and probably unrepeatable) performance. Don't sweat it. Simply zoom down to the sample level, find the click, and remove it, re-drawing the waveform to minimize any loss.

And what about that singer? He's really inconsistent; he sang an inspired version of the chorus exactly once, and all his other takes were flat. But you'll make him sound good. Select his rare moment of inspiration and paste it into all of the song's choruses, making slight volume and effect changes to provide the necessary variety.

And now that you've heard the song, your intuition tells you to replace the last solo and chorus with two verses—a strange idea but you think it might work. Use your software to shift chunks of music until your song sings as you imagine it. Hmmm…now that you hear it, you like the old version better—that's okay; reverting to the original requires just a few mouse clicks. Anything else you'd like to try?

Hot Link: AnalogX (http://www.analogx.com/contents/download.htm)

AnalogX (shown in Figure 6.2) offers a good collection of Windows audio software to download, including speech synthesis programs and a program that helps you scratch like a DJ.

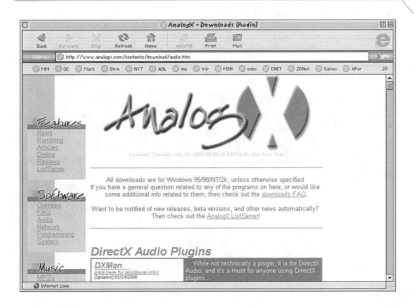

Figure 6.2

AnalogX offers a Windows software for download.

As audio software has grown in power and flexibility, it has caused a revolution in music recording. In the analog era, all the bending, twisting, and shaping that's common in the digital era was only dreamed of. The audio recordist, while important, was ultimately a skilled accompanist, the facilitator of something greater.

Now, with the ocean of possibilities created by software (and the hardware to run it), what the musicians do is just part of the creative process. The recordist is no longer just a nerdy fellow who's good with a screwdriver. Now he or she is a sound designer, a co-creator, someone who's expected to have vision and imagination. The individuals with their hands on the software are now central players. It's only a slight exaggeration, and perhaps not one at all, to say the sound designer is more important to the finished product than the musicians themselves. In fact, with the capabilities offered by today's PC-based recording, the job of musician and recordist is merging.

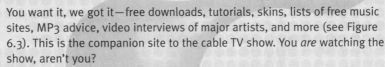

Hot Link: TechTV AudioFile Web Site (`http://www.techtv.com/audiofile/`)

You want it, we got it—free downloads, tutorials, skins, lists of free music sites, MP3 advice, video interviews of major artists, and more (see Figure 6.3). This is the companion site to the cable TV show. You *are* watching the show, aren't you?

Figure 6.3

The AudioFile section of TechTV is loaded with sound and music resources.

Peace, Love, and Nondestructiveness

Audio software enables you to do something that's quite nearly magical: nondestructive editing. That is, you can edit a recording of a flute solo into a hundred pieces, realize that all your edits were mistakes, and instantly call up the original—just as it was before you edited it.

You see, the software provides a *user interface* that accesses that sound file from your hard drive. It enables you to manipulate that file beyond recognition but keeps the original safe on your hard drive. You can combine it with 40 other tracks, pitch shift it, make it 10 percent shorter, and still the original file sits untouched on your hard drive.

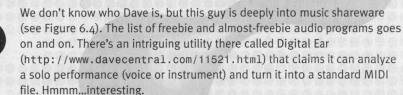

Hot Link: DaveCentral (http://www.davecentral.com/audio.html)

We don't know who Dave is, but this guy is deeply into music shareware (see Figure 6.4). The list of freebie and almost-freebie audio programs goes on and on. There's an intriguing utility there called Digital Ear (http://www.davecentral.com/11521.html) that claims it can analyze a solo performance (voice or instrument) and turn it into a standard MIDI file. Hmmm...interesting.

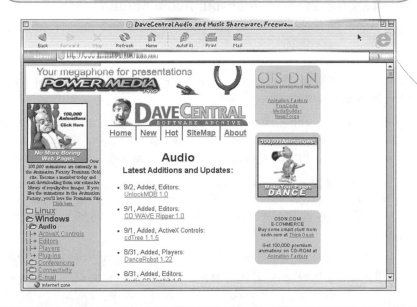

Figure 6.4

DaveCentral has a list of free and almost free audio programs to download.

This software also means you can create a six-hour piece of music from a sound file that's only six minutes long. Simply loop that file and it will play as long as you like. There's no actual six-hour file on your hard drive, but the software creates the illusion that there is. Whether this is good music is a matter of opinion, or more accurately, how creatively it's looped and layered. But the capabilities of audio software technology have given birth to an entirely new style of music—techno—that is loop heaven. Everything is looped (again and again and again) and it's audio software that makes this possible. It's safe to say that without MIDI and nonlinear digital audio techniques, the style called techno would hardly exist.

The Joy of User Definability

The other really magical thing about audio software is its user definability. To put it in technical-ese, it allows dynamic allocation of resources. That is, data flow and overall configuration of your software-based studio is up to you. You can add more tracks with a few mouse clicks—try doing that with a hardware-based recorder. And if your computer's audio card allows for a certain amount of audio processing, you can decide to allocate these processing resources any way you want. Do you want to spend your card's processing power by booting up 37 software reverb units? Okay then, you now have 37 reverbs. Wild. It's as if some audio deity suddenly decided to endow you with great sonic riches. This flexibility is another way that software greatly enhances audio creativity.

Your Software Is the Center of Your Audio Studio

The most important choice you'll make in creating your home studio is which software you choose. In many cases it will be your mixing board, your effects processor, your compressor, expander, and more. Your software determines which plug-ins you can use to expand your studio. You want to choose a program that enables you the greatest imagination and flexibility in your sound design creativity.

Along with your main program you'll probably have a suite of helper software: CD burning software, MP3 encoders, perhaps a separate MIDI program (although this is often part of the main program), maybe an application that's specially designed to convert files.

But it's your central program that determines how good your desktop studio is. Yes, you need a powerful hardware base—a fast processor, plenty or RAM, hard drive storage, and good audio card/interface—but if your main software workhorse is limited, your choices are limited.

Hot Link: CNET Music Center (http://music.cnet.com/)

This site rivals ZDNet as one of the Web's best audio meccas (see Figure 6.5). There are scads of links to software to download, as well as a lot of clearly written tutorials on basic and not-so-basic audio techniques. CNET offers its own list of most frequently downloaded software—an interesting glimpse on what's going on in desktop audio.

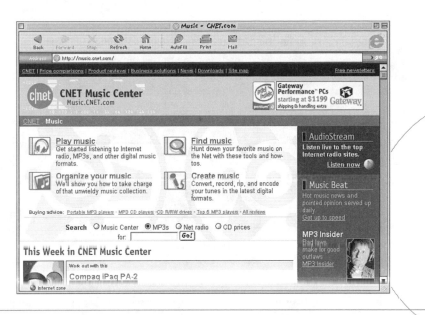

Figure 6.5

CNET Music is a leading music technology Web site.

In fact, it's often a good idea to make your hardware choices based on what software you want to use. Decide what kind of computer port or external hard drive you need based on accommodating your audio workhorse. If program x, for example, will only work properly with a FireWire drive, make sure you get a FireWire. In short, design your studio around this central software program. If you have to spend more than budgeted to afford the audio editor/recorder of your dreams, then scrimp on another area, like buying a cheaper synthesizer or not getting that second tone module.

IT'S A DIGI, DIGI, DIGI WORLD

So, given that your audio recorder/editor is so important, which one should you choose?

My personal opinion is Pro Tools, made by Digidesign.

> **Hot Link: Pro Tools Free (http://www.digidesign.com/ptfree)**
> You can download a bare-bones version of this monster recorder/editor (see Figure 6.6). And yup, it's free!

Figure 6.6

The Digidesign site offers a free version of Pro Tools.

We've watched the development of audio software since back when Early Audio Man was still using razor blades to cut tape. Although many programs are as capable as Pro Tools, none is more clearly designed and more intuitive to use. The program makes sense and it's solidly built. It's not glitchy or cranky, and it's not prone to crashes. And the ease of use, flexibility, and power it offers enable you to take sound design as far as you can envision.

Let's look at the development of this leading audio editor. Pro Tools, through much of the '90s, was in a crowded field of audio software programs. As analog production died in the late '80s, many manufacturers of digital audio workstations (DAW) rushed to fill the demand for nonlinear audio technology. Some of the names that grabbed early market share are no longer with us. Synclavier's Post Pro, for example, was a formerly promising contender that has seen better days.

Hot Link: SynthZone Software Archives (http://www.synthzone.com/ softarch.htm)

A lot of this is MIDI stuff mixed in with links to general audio software. It's not a flashy page but it offers some resource-rich links (see Figure 6.7).

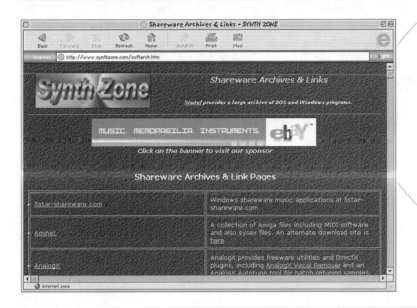

Figure 6.7

Download both MIDI and audio recording software at SynthZone.

Pro Tools, through this highly competitive period, was found in many home studios built on the cheap, but it was also found in some professional recording studios. It acquired a substantial user base of both home and high-end users. In 1995, the company that makes Pro Tools, Digidesign, was bought by Avid, the leader in nonlinear digital video editing. So this versatile audio program is fully compatible with an industry leading video-editing program. In the last few years, Pro Tools has moved into position as a leader in high-end audio production. Hollywood blockbusters like *Gladiator* and *Pearl Harbor* were mixed on Pro Tools systems.

Pro Tools continues to be scalable—you can scale it up to do most anything, or scale it down for casual use. You can spend tens of thousands of dollars and get an audio tool capable of mixing a symphony orchestra for a major film release. Or you can spend less than a thousand and get a happenin' home setup that turns your desktop into a semi-pro project studio.

Or, you can spend absolutely nothing, and download the free demo version that is as capable as most mid-level audio software. It will do multitrack editing and mixing, and includes basic effects software. It's highly unusual that one program would meet the needs of such a wide spectrum of users. In one day, this same software is being used to mix a Hollywood mega-release, and across town, an MP3 enthusiast is using it to string together a bunch of free downloaded songs. (Granted, the Hollywood mixers have a much more expensive version of the software, with all sorts of big-bucks hardware to beef it up.)

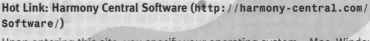

Hot Link: Harmony Central Software (http://harmony-central.com/Software/)

Upon entering this site, you specify your operating system—Mac, Windows, of whatever—and then go to a page full of audio applications for your system (see Figure 6.8).

Figure 6.8

Harmony Central has got a lot for everyone—it even has DOS software.

Pro Tools' large user base gives its users an important advantage. There are so many studios that use it, both home and professional, that collaborating with other musicians in another town—or country—is easy. If you lay down some basic tracks in your home studio in Dubuque Iowa, but you want your friend in New Jersey to lay some sax riffs over your song, you can burn a CD-R of your session and send it off (or e-mail your files). The New Jersey sax player can riff wildly, and then send the session on to a percussionist in San Francisco, who opens the session and adds some blistering tracks before sending it back to Dubuque.

Hot Link: AudioTools (http://www.audiotools.co.uk/)

Hail to the Brits—they're the one group that seems as Internet-obsessed as the U.S.; Web-based audio in particular seems huge in England. This U.K.-based site (see Figure 6.9) offers a full complement of audio programs.

Figure 6.9

Check out the downloadable software at AudioTools.

This compatibility feature taps into a powerful trend in music and sound production. The world's a small place these days. With the Internet and next-day mail delivery, artists' collaborations are no longer limited by geography. To take advantage of this larger network, it helps to use the software that everyone's using. Sure, you could just send them WAV or AIF files and they could open the files in whatever they're using. But that's several important steps behind opening up a session and having all the tracks, sends, and effects all laid out and ready to go.

As a last note: While Pro Tools is a great tool, there are many great tools available. Cubase, Sound Forge, Logic—the list is long, and each has its (well deserved) passionate fans. The bottom line is: Does it do everything you need it to do, and does it allow you to be your creative best? So talk with a lot of users to get first-hand feedback, and realize that there is no "best" piece of audio software. It's truly a matter of opinion.

Hot Link: Partners In Rhyme (http://www.partnersinrhyme.com/)

This isn't the largest collection of shareware, but it includes some good stuff—its offering of file converters (to change an AIF to MP3, for example) seems particularly extensive (see Figure 6.10). There's a also a heapin' helpin' of royalty-free sound effects and samples.

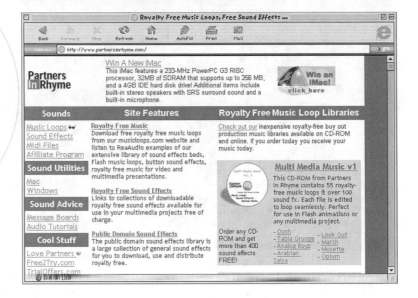

Figure 6.10

You'll find plenty of audio file converters as well as sound effects and samples at Partners In Rhyme.

Audio software comes in a lot of flavors: file conversion (WAV to MP3, for example), MIDI, CD burning, effects plug-ins. You'll find overviews of each of these software types in various chapters in this book, but for the following section, We've assembled some programs that could function as your main workhorse. There are of course many more choices than those listed here, but the following are used happily by many desktop musicians.

Cool Edit Pro

Cool Edit Pro (http://www.syntrillium.com) is one of the most popular desktop editing programs (see Figure 6.11). This view shows a multitrack session, with the various tracks on top of each other (notice the list of instruments on the left: snare, toms, keys, and so on).

One of the great aids of computer-based audio editing software is the amount of detailed information you get from the visual display. The recordist no longer has to rely on ears alone. This visual display enables you to know, for example, exactly how the tracks line up with each other: Does that timbale rhythm line up with the piano the way it should? It's easy to use the visual display to find a certain sound, and then modify it with one of the software's functions.

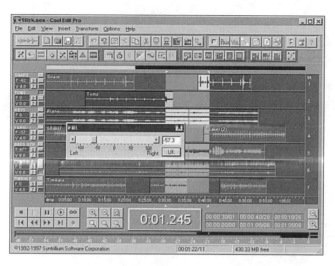

Figure 6.11

Find Cool Edit at Syntrillium.com.

In this view the Pan function is being used. Moving the center tab to the left places that track on the left side of the stereo image ("panning it left"). This Pan decision (and all mix parameters) can be stored with the session, so if the musicians come back in six months and want to change just one guitar solo, everything is saved just as you left it.

Look at the boxes containing numbers in the lower right. Those are SMPTE address points. We go into more detail on those in Chapter 15, "Audio Synchronization," but they enable the recordist to click a sound file and move it to any point in time. Simply enter a new time, press Return and the vocal line goes right there.

> **Hot Link: Reviews of PC Audio Software** (http://
> www.webdevelopersjournal.com/studio/soft.html)
>
> We can't vouch for the accuracy of these reviews—everyone has his or her
> opinion (see Figure 6.12). But if you're out browsing various programs, this
> is a good place to find alternative viewpoints.

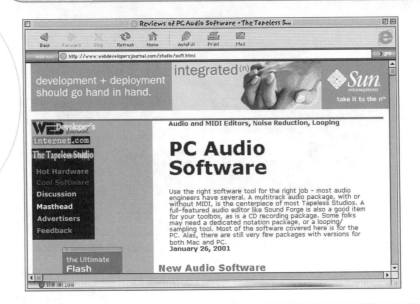

Figure 6.12

Surf to Web Developer's Journal for reviews of audio software.

And notice the little magnifying glasses in the lower left. Those enable you to zoom all the
way down to the sample level, enabling you to remove a small imperfection in the sound.
Or, you can use the zoom tool to zoom all the way out, viewing your mixing in its entirety.
This is helpful if, for example, you want to cut and paste entire verses or choruses into new
locations.

Cool Edit Pro enables 64 tracks of simultaneous recording. For much less money you can
get Cool Edit, which is not as feature rich but is still a powerful desktop tool.

Acid

Acid is great for looping a small musical phrase, often a drum and bass pattern, adding
layer on top of layer until you have a hard drivin' musical groove. The top-of-the-line version comes with a library of 400 snippets to loop—enough for most uses (see Figure 6.13).
And of course a lot of Acid users create their own loops.

Hot Link: Acid (`http://www.sonicfoundry.com`)

Acid is made by Sonic Foundry, which makes Sound Forge, another popular audio editor.

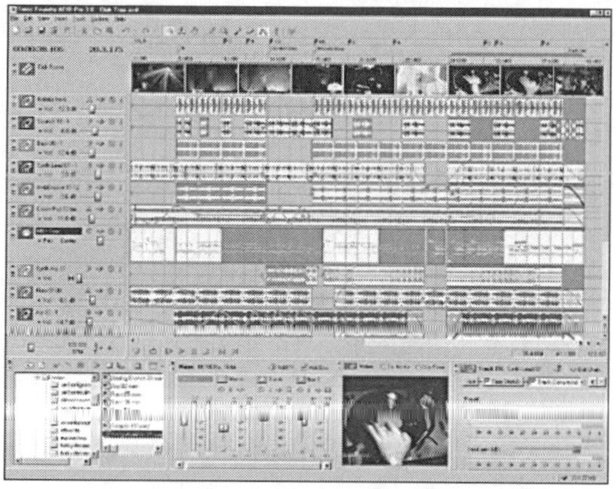

Figure 6.13

Acid is great for looping audio.

Hot Link: Musicware (`http://www.musicware.dial.pipex.com/`)

The best part of this site, which offers audio freeware and shareware, is the Links Directory, which catalogs several types of Web audio resources.

Working with Acid is so intuitive it's like painting with fingerpaints. If you want a funky hip-hop loop to happen earlier in the song, just drag it there. If you want to combine two loops so that one flows into the other, Acid will do the work of matching the rhythms so they segue seamlessly. It enables you to draw in volume and pan and add effects like reverb and chorus. The software will stretch out a phrase, making it faster or slower, and it will also lower or raise pitch. Acid makes it easy; in fact it does a lot of the work for you.

And Acid will run in sync with your MIDI programs, which enables you to layer music from your MIDI program over Acid's prerecorded loops. Acid is available in many popular flavors, including Hip Hop, Latin, Rock, DJ, and Techno.

Sound Forge

Ask a roomful of desktop musicians what their favorite program is, and plenty of them will say Sound Forge. In addition to the full range of basic editing functions, this two-track recorder/editor is chock full of audio effects: from chorus and delay to flange and noise pitch. It's quite easy to use—just drag and drop—and it enables you to export just about any file format you're likely to encounter, from MP3 to WMA. It also supports CD burning.

And, like many leading editors, Sound Forge can handle DirectX plug-ins (more on them in Chapter 7, "Software: The Extras"). So you can add still more wild and wonderful audio processors to this already highly capable application.

Hot Link: Sound Forge (`http://www.sonicfoundry.com`)
Made by Sonic Foundry, Sound Forge is a highly popular audio program.

GoldWave Multiquence

Figure 6.14 shows the main edit screen for Multiquence, a mid-level audio editor made by GoldWave. As you can see from the movie in the top panel, the audio editor enables you to edit and mix audio in sync with video. Somewhere, there's undoubtedly an independent filmmaker who is using this program to add audio to her indie masterpiece. The only cheaper way to do this is if your uncle owns a sound studio.

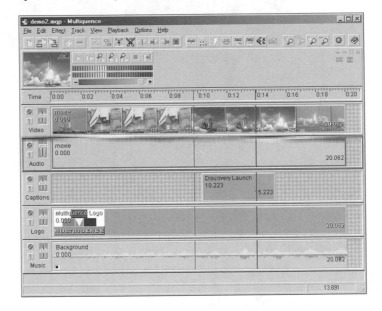

Figure 6.14

The GoldWave Multiquence program.

Hot Link: GoldWave Related Software (`http://www.goldwave.com/utils.html`)
The good folks at GoldWave were nice enough to put together a page full of links to audio software. It's a good collection, including some MP3 encoders and some CD burning software—start your downloader.

The SonicSpot (http://www.sonicspot.com/)

The listings in this software-for-download site run the gamut from MP3 encoders to audio mixing to CD burning. Good collection.

Sometime a few years from now, this advance—a really inexpensive audio program that includes video support—will seem like no big deal. But as of this writing...wow, this really points out the extent to which the revolution in desktop capability provides creative tools without requiring a big budget.

In addition to its video feature, GoldWave Multiquence has many of the features that are now standard in desktop audio editors. It includes a toolbox of audio helpers like flange, an equalizer, drag-and-drop editing, MIDI capability, and an unlimited number of virtual tracks.

Hot Link: The TechZone Music Software Virtual Studio (http:// thetechnozone.com/audiobuyersguide/software/midi/ midi-software.html)

We've rarely seen such a far reaching yet compactly organized list of links about audio software. You'll find plenty of reviews and opinions, as well as a good overview of what's available in plug-ins and sound cards.

Cubase

Cubase is one of the best desktop audio programs available. We wouldn't normally quote a company's product brochure—it's usually too superlative-packed to be worth much—but in Cubase's case it sums it up nicely. "Cubase VST is not just an audio recorder; it's a complete audio studio." That's true, and the legions of users, both professional and casual, will attest to it.

HotLink: The Cubase Download Page (http://service.steinberg.net/ webdoc.nsf/show/download_e)

This site offers a hot collection of audio goodies, all available as free demo versions. Stop by and stock up on helper programs that will round out your studio's functionality.

Hot Link: The Cubase Webring (http://www.dbrown.force9.co.uk/ webring.html)

This is a network of sites—dozens of them—devoted to this popular MIDI/audio software. If you become a Cubase believer (and there are many) you might want to add your own site.

Cubase VST (`http://www.steinberg.net`)

Cubase is made by Steinberg, a German software company that makes a whole shelf full of useful audio editing/manipulation programs (see Figure 6.15). Also by Steinberg is DeClicker, DeNoiser, FreeFilter, and the LoudnessMaximizer.

Figure 6.15

Cubase is a leading audio production tool.

Cubase combines audio and MIDI capabilities into one seamless environment. This comes in handy in a lot of ways; you don't have to worry about synchronizing your MIDI and audio programs, and all your songwriting elements are grouped together.

Open up the window that enables you to mix your audio tracks and you'll find a highly capable array of sound design tools. Each of the 72 channels is equipped with level fader, pan control, solo and mute switches, effects, equalization controls, and a five-stage dynamics section.

In addition, each channel can use up to eight auxiliary sends (which enable you to access Cubase's famed VST plug-in effects rack) and four insert points for internal plug-in effects. Any of the channels can be routed to one of the eight stereo groups, enabling you to submix tracks of your song, say, the drums or vocal harmonies. (For a discussion of auxiliary sends and submixing, see Chapter 17, "Mixing, Part One.")

Cubase's Arrange window enables you to view the various chunks of your songs as they play back; the big red chunk is your verse, the purple chunk is your chorus, and so on. This clear method of "visual song spotting" keeps the emphasis on the music rather than bogging you down in audio technology.

Hot Link: ZDNet Downloads: Audio (http://www.zdnet.com/downloads/mp3.html)

As you might expect from an offering by such a big publisher, the ZDNet audio download site is jam-packed with audio goodies (see Figure 6.16). Start the downloader!

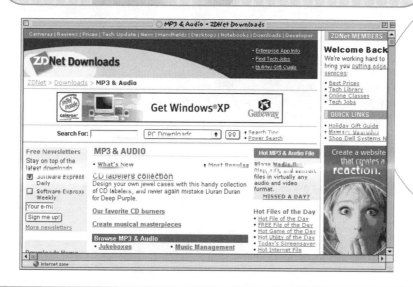

Figure 6.16

This site publishes a list of that week's Top Ten Audio Downloads. It's a good way to track what's hot and what's not.

Some desktop musicians use Cubase primarily as a MIDI sequencer. The program allows you to view and edit your MIDI music using a traditional score, or in the events mode that many MIDI composers favor. In a nice touch, you can edit MIDI even while listening. A related program, Cubase VST Score, enables you to print a professional-level music score.

Understanding that collaboration now happens globally, Cubase includes the Inwire feature, which enables musicians to compose—or just jam—with musicians using the Internet. This is a really cool feature. Your changes are streamed to your partner, who can make additions and stream them back. You can work back and forth for days or hours, as if you were sitting right next to each other. Need to discuss something? No problem. The built-in Internet chat feature enables you to talk in real-time.

CHAPTER **7**

SOFTWARE: THE EXTRAS

In This Chapter

- Find out about plug-ins: DirectX, VST, and others
- Learn about software synthesizers
- Discover programs that convert audio files
- Look at the necessary player utilities

THE EVER-EXPANDING UNIVERSE OF AUDIO PLUG-INS

Your desktop studio probably will revolve around one central piece of software—a big dog that can record, edit, mix, and perhaps even boil an egg. This is the audio workhorse you boot up every time you sit down to work and create. It could be Cool Edit Pro, Sonar, Pro Tools, or one of several other good choices.

But no matter how hot your main program is, at some point you'll want it to do something it can't do. You'll have, for example, a guitar track to which you'll want to give a vintage sound, and Pro Tools by itself can't do this. Or maybe you'll want to add an exotic reverb, and Cool Edit doesn't have this capability built in.

It's a fact of plug-in life that some plug-ins process audio faster than others do. With a fast plug-in, not long after you click Process, your clip is done. And when you're in the thick of it, producing creatively, delays are inspiration dampeners. This is the kind of thing that's hard to find information about ahead of time. You find out by word of mouth or actual experience; we've never seen any specs listed. But it's a good thing to ask, if you're getting the plug-in from a friend.

It's at this point you'll want one of the sound designer's main helpers: the plug-in. No audio studio is complete without a full range of these useful software tools.

Plug-ins add audio capability to your main software. You download one or several (some are free, but the best cost some cash), and install them in a folder recognized by your main program. Suddenly that audio workhorse has more functionality than it did right out of the box. For many of today's most popular programs, from Cool Edit Pro to Cubase, plug-ins add new color to your audio palette: unusual sound manipulation, retro audio mixes, a wider array of reverb and delay, as well as things you've probably never thought of. There are plug-ins that do just about everything, and it seems there are new ones created every day.

The first commercially successful plug-ins were developed for Pro Tools because the hardware that's part of the Pro Tools setup provided the processor boost necessary for the intense calculations that plug-ins do.

As computers became faster and had more RAM, developers started writing plug-ins for software that didn't need proprietary hardware. Some of the leading formats for plug-ins are DirectX and VST, but there are many others. Some manufacturers of audio hardware—such as Drawmer, Focusrite, and Lexicon—have released plug-in versions of their effects gear. Conversely, we've seen some hardware versions of successful software plug-ins, like Line 6's Amp Farm and Antares's Auto Tune.

The last two examples aside, plug-ins are yet another example of how software is replacing hardware. It's a heck of lot cheaper to get a plug-in version of the reverb unit than a hardware version. And, if the plug-in is suddenly upgraded, it's a lot easier to download the new version than go to the music store and get new hardware.

That said, there are plenty of hardware effects boxes that won't be replaced for the foreseeable future. The Lexicon 960L reverb unit comes to mind. Then again, it costs a cool $15,000, so most of us are just going to look at pictures of it anyway.

Real-Time Versus Offline

Many plug-ins are real-time, meaning you can hear their effect as soon as you send audio through them. These software applications don't actually affect the audio itself; they merely change the sound of the audio that returns from that plug-in.

In other cases, you can audition a plug-in, try various settings, and then actually rerecord the audio back into the mix with that effect on it. The advantage of doing this is that you don't have to use your system's processing power for that real-time effect. This technique comes in handy if you have a dozen or so tracks, each with effects, and your PC CPU starts to get cranky and upset.

A Plug-In for Every Occasion

For example, let's look at the plug-ins that are available at The Sonic Spot site. Surf on over to http://www.sonicspot.com/daplugins.html.

There, you'll find shareware and freeware downloads of plug-ins for almost every occasion:

- **The Arboretum Realizer.** This Winamp plug-in enhances MP3 music playback quality in real-time.
- **ClickFix.** This plug-in for Cool Edit Pro helps you fix clicks and pops in your mixes.
- **Maxim VST Plug-ins, Pack 2.** This suite of plug-ins enables you to add compressors, limiters, and gates to your mix (more on these concepts in Chapter 17, "Mixing, Part 1") and also do pitch shift for drum loops.
- **Noise Reduction.** A plug-in designed to restore and repair your audio recordings by taking out unwanted noise.
- **Rhythm'n'Chords.** This is a good example of how plug-ins do more than manipulate existing audio: some even help you create music. Rhythm'n'Chords, designed for Cakewalk Pro, helps you create MIDI rhythm guitar parts.
- **WaveSurround DX.** A cool little addition, this plug-in simulates surround sound output.

And our personal favorite from this page's menu:

- **BJ LoFi.** This strange little plug-in simulates 8-bit sound card noise. Yes, it's actually designed to make you music sound *worse*.

Why, you might ask, do we like this kind of thing? Because so much audio gear is designed to create higher quality sound, to the point that audio hardware and software is spiraling upward toward ever more pristine quality. We like plug-ins like BJ LoFi that add a grungier, more retro sound—it can add character to music if used properly.

We also think the BJ LoFi is kind of funny. Typical retro plug-ins add, say, the sound of the 1959 Fender Amp. This is a beautifully classic retro sound that many rhythm and blues aficionados would appreciate and enjoy. But who really misses the sound of an 8-bit sound card? Well, believe it or not, there's a burgeoning underground 8-bit scene, in which musicians use self-consciously grungy material from sources like—gasp—the Commodore 64 to create music. Moral of the story: Different ears like different things.

The DirectX Files

When you talk about plug-ins, the conversation turns quickly to DirectX. This standard for plug-ins has greatly aided the quantity and quality of plug-ins, for audio as well as many other types of software. With the possible exception of VST, more audio plug-ins are written for DirectX than any other format.

In short, DirectX is a cool thing that can add wildly interesting sound colors to your mix—it can turn a good piece of software into a great piece of software.

DirectX creates a HAL—hardware abstraction layer—that uses software drivers to communicate between your PC and your audio software. This means that developers can create plug-ins without worrying about hardware/software compatibility issues, which get as tangled as a plate of spaghetti really quickly. So, if you run a Windows box, you can (hopefully) rest assured that a DirectX plug-in will work on your system, no matter what specific type of PC you have. There are no Mac DirectX plug-ins, but some companies that make plug-ins in this format also make a Mac version.

Hot Link: Microsoft's DirectX Page
(`http://www.microsoft.com/directx/`)

From this page, you can download the latest version of DirectX and read the FAQ written by the developers themselves. But don't stop here. Webopedia (`http://www.webopedia.com/TERM/D/DirectX.html`) does a good job of making things clear. This page on DirectX also includes a lot of links to find out more. Also check out the DirectX Files Plug In Menu site (`http://www.thedirectxfiles.com/plugins.htm`). This resource-rich site has a lengthy list of plug-ins to download and covers just about any audio need. You'll find plug-ins for Sonic Foundry, Opcode, Steinberg, TC Works, and many more. Some are free and some are pay-to-download.

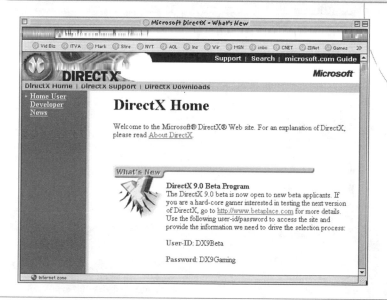

Figure 7.1

This is the first place to visit when you're ready to explore DirectX. Download the latest version and read the FAQ written by the developers themselves.

VST and Plug-Ins

Another dominant technology in plug-ins is VST (Virtual Studio Instruments). If you spend much time with audio software, you'll see the term VST quite a bit. VST is open software technology that's used by many developers to write audio programs. Originally developed by Steinberg for Cubase, it has become a standard format for digital audio production.

VST plug-ins, like DirectX, are available for an almost limitless array of audio functions, from compressors to sweep flanges to old fashioned sounding tremolo effects (useful for creating the classic Hammond B3 organ effect). One of the coolest uses of VST is for software synthesizers–a must have for any serious desktop audio artist.

Hot Link: db-Audioware (http://www.db-audioware.com/vstfree.htm)

When you're ready to add some plug-ins to your software repertoire, db-Audioware, shown in Figure 7.2, is good site to visit.

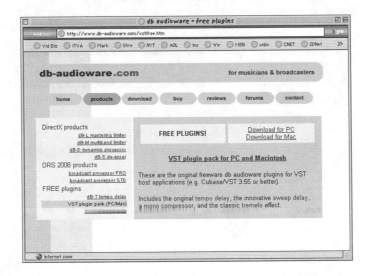

Figure 7.2

This site has an extensive list of software plug-ins, including some free VST plug-ins.

Hot Link: Steinberg (http://www.steinberg.net/infocenter)
The epicenter of VST activity is Steinberg. The site offers a page of freeware plug-ins for download.

SOFTWARE SYNTHESIZERS: EASY TO CARRY

Buying a synthesizer used to require trooping down to the music store, plunking down your credit card, and carting home a plastic and metal thing with keys. These store-bought synths resemble the family piano except they're lighter, have more sounds in them, and nobody has ever has been asked "did you practice your synthesizer today?"

But now VST and other software technologies are used to create synthesizers that are software only. So you can download them and play them onscreen in a manner similar to that of a real-world synthesizer. Software synthesizers come with a library of built-in audio along with a synthesizer-like user interface. So you can layer and alter its sounds in any number of ways, limited only by that virtual keyboard's software.

These virtual synthesizers receive input through MIDI (it would be tough to play the synth itself because it's viewable only through your computer screen). Once a virtual synth receives a MIDI note, it triggers playback from its bank of audio. The more extensive the library of audio, and the more options it allows for filtering, the more versatile that virtual synth. To play a software synthesizer you either need a real synthesizer, so you can send MIDI notes to your software synthesizer, or a MIDI file on your computer.

Steinberg offers a full range of software synths built in the VST format, but many companies have developed virtual keyboards with their own technology.

Hot Link: FXPansion (http://www.fxpansion.com/)
There's software you can get to make VST plug-ins work with DirectX programs. Made by FXPansion, it's available in three different levels of capability.

Hot Link: AudioMidi.com (http://www.audiomidi.com/software/programs/synths.html)
The folks at AudioMidi have really done their homework in this compilation of software synthesizers. A great collection.

Hot Link: A12B3C.com (http://www.a1b2c3.com/free/av01.htm)
Yes, this site has a strange name, but it has a lot of audio freeware and shareware (as well as other non-audio software).

Hot Link: Freebytes (http://www.freebyte.com/music/#synthesizers)
Tons of good links to aid your exploration of software synths.

Propellerhead Software (`http://www.propellerheads.se/index.php3`)

Within this one piece of software is a synthesizer, sequencer, drum machine, and sampler. (See Figure 7.3.) It's not as versatile as some programs in terms of MIDI and audio editing, but offers a lot a capability in a program that's considered easy to learn.

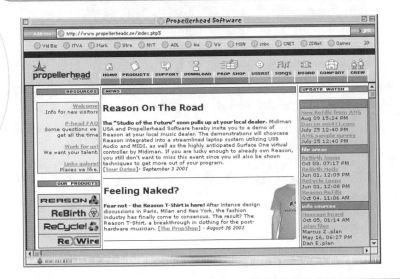

Figure 7.3

Propellerhead makes Reason, an all-in-one music creation program.

SOFTWARE SYNTHESIZERS

Yamaha offers a 90-day free trial of its YXG50 virtual synthesizer. (See Figure 7.4). If you still like it after making music with it for three months, you've got to pay for it. This synthesizer offers 128-voice polyphony and 670 voices, all of which are programmable. In case you get tired of your existing drum sounds, it also includes 21 drum kits, as well as a raft of effects to filter and doctor your sound. It really helps to have a lot of RAM to operate the YXG50, since all of its sounds are loaded into RAM.

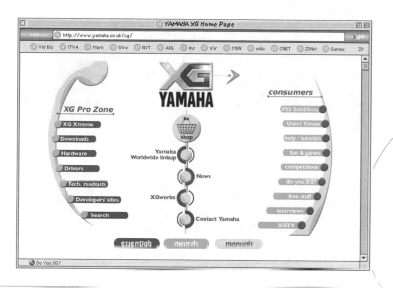

Figure 7.4

You can download a 90-day free trial version of the YXG50 SoftSynth from the Yamaha site (http://www.yamaha.co.uk/xg/).

Hot Link: Roland Virtual Sound Canvas (http://www.edirol.com/index.ddp)

This virtual synthesizer boasts a staggering 902 different sounds—is that enough? If not, it also includes 26 drums sets, in addition to a full complement of effects like reverb, chorus, and delay. This virtual synthesizer, like all the synthesizers, is a convenient way to turn a MIDI file into an audio file. Simply play back the MIDI file using this synthesizer's sounds. The MIDI notes trigger actual audio, which you can record and save as a WAV or MP3. In a nice touch, it's available for both Mac and Windows.

Hot Link: Koblo 9000 (`http://www.digidesign.com/`) (Search Using Keyword "koblo")

Notice in the picture of the control panel that this sampler enables you to design a sound with everything from a Detune function to a Resonance filter (see Figure 7.5). This kind of capability in a hardware sampler would cost much, much more than the Koblo. Download the free demo and give it a spin. You might create some sounds you've never heard before.

Figure 7.5

The Koblo is more than a software synthesizer—it's a sampler, enabling you to import and modify sounds with a mind-boggling array of choices.

CONVERSION SOFTWARE: TURN LEAD INTO GOLD

One of the strange things about the world of desktop audio is the multitude of formats. The proliferation of audio formats is a enough to make even a casual PC sound user ask "what the #&!?"

The formats are too numerous to fully list. There are the biggies like WAV, MP3, WMA, and RealAudio; the reasonably popular ones like QuickTime or MIDI, and—just to add complexity—a large crowd of other formats: SND, Paris, a-law, and Advanced Streaming Format.

And then there are the *really* obscure ones, like the Covox V8, or Gravis Patch. Our personal favorite among ultra-obscure formats: the Lernout & Houspie SBC 8 kpps. Someone, somewhere, has an entire project stored in the Lernout & Houspie format. That's a sad thing.

Okay, say you have an audio file in one format and you want to convert it to another. What do you do? You need software. If you have one of the big programs, like Cool Edit Pro or Sound Forge, it can handle many of these formats. But if you don't, you can get software specifically created for audio conversion. Simply open the file in one of these programs, and save it in a new format. (By they way, if you want to find out about converting files for the Web, see Chapter 22, "Preparing Your Sounds to Be Uploaded.") Some of the following conversion programs can come in handy:

- **Windows converters**:

  - **Audio Magic Ring** (`http://www.hitsquad.com/smm/programs/AudioMagicRing/`). Does a good job of converting any number of audio files between different formats or sample rates (see Figure 7.6).

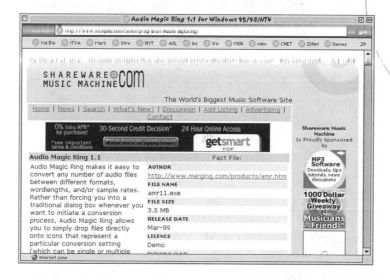

Figure 7.6

With Audio Magic Ring you convert sound files by simply dropping them onto desktop icons.

  - **Media Wizard** (`http://www.filecenter.com/filecenter/details/1079.asp`). A conversion tool that handles all the common formats and a few that are not so common. It has a playlist feature that lets you "create your own concert," enabling you to play back hours of sound files.

- **Macintosh converters:**

  - **Sound App** (`http://www-cs-students.stanford.edu/~franke/SoundApp/`). This one helped us solve a thorny file conversion program. Highly recommended.

  - **S/Link** (`http://www.airworks.com`). Enables drag and drop file conversion and batch processing for a wide variety of file formats.

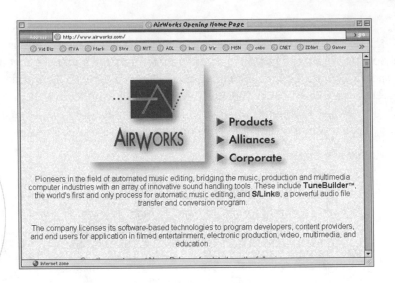

Figure 7.7
S/Link is a bare bones program, but the list of files it handles is impressive. It's inexpensive, too.

- **BarbaBatch** (http://www.audioease.com). A top choice, and a very versatile and powerful batch conversion tool. It can translate just about any format into any other format, and it has a "U Name It" feature that adds any file extension you like, from .wav to .aiff, to each file it converts.

UTILITIES YOU NEED: THE BACKUP PLAYERS

Yes, you have your star software, the one or two pieces that enable you to do most of your work. These are your star players, your Michael Jordans and Sammy Sosas. But your suite of software, to be fully equipped, should also include some unsung heroes—software that cannot claim to be exotic and will not earn you extra points with your friends, but that will come in handy in a lot of occasions. We're talking about RealOne and Windows Media Player.

If you're even "kind of-sort of" interested in audio on the PC, the following applications require no introduction. In case you don't have them, you ought to grab them. They're free, and are an essential (if unglamorous) part of the desktop musician's studio tools:

- **RealOne** (http://www.real.com). The newest multimedia player from Real enables you to play all the major audio and video formats with one player. It also allows you to bookmark hyperlinks to audio and video streams. Look for this player to become standard operating equipment for any desktop musician.

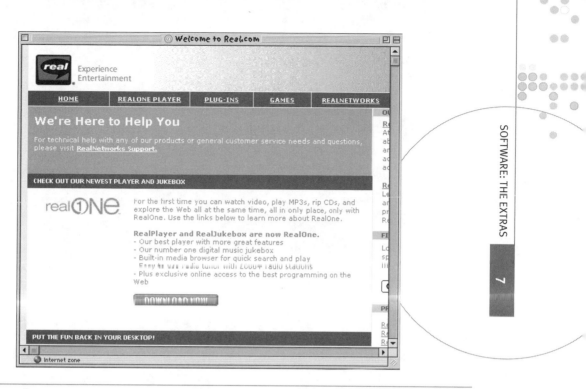

Figure 7.8

Real is still the dominant player in the field of streaming media.

- **Windows Media Player** (http://windowsmedia.com/download/download.asp). RealOne's chief competitor for streaming audio/video player is Windows Media Player, made by a promising software start-up called Microsoft. It's in the number two position behind the Real multimedia player in terms of users, but there's nothing second best about its usability; it's a solid player and a handy tool for any PC sound enthusiast.

CHAPTER 8

HARDWARE: HAVE PC, WILL TRAVEL

In This Chapter

- Discover the many hardware options for the desktop musician
- Learn how to build your own digital audio workstation
- Take a look at audio interfaces
- Learn key concepts you'll need to understand audio hardware

ENOUGH OPTIONS TO MAKE YOUR HEAD SPIN

Choices, choices, and more choices. That's what confronts you when you prepare to set up the hardware aspect of your desktop studio. Audio gear manufacturers, taking advantage of affordable digital technology, have developed a blizzard of options, with each option customizable to a given budget. This has helped build interest in home recording, which has in turn created a still larger market. Manufacturers have seen the market grow and responded by offering ever more configurations of gear. There's a spiraling sprawl of new gear.

Open up any music equipment catalog and you'll see dozens of possible audio hardware configurations. Most of them have wonderfully snazzy—but inscrutable—high-tech names, like the RK783-1Z, which is available with the 24-24 I/O or the 8/16 I/O option. Unless you get the Audio System 96X1, which includes S/PDIF but requires a FireWire port.

Whew! Is your head starting to spin? What's an audio dude or dudette to do?

Well, depending on your goals, maybe you can avoid the subject of extra hardware altogether. You might be able to look at the computer you already have and say, "It's all I need." The audio gear makers don't want you to know this, but in some cases it's true. If you bought your computer sometime in the late '90s or later, it can do a whole lot of audio work without special add-ons.

Take, for example, the audio software Acid. This popular application enables you to layer and loop audio tracks until the cows come home. You can download samples from the Web, perhaps using a prebuilt rhythm bed as a foundation, and build some rich-sounding tracks.

Hot Link: Nuendo (http://www.nuendo.com)
Made by Steinberg, Nuendo is a complete workstation requiring nothing more than software, PC, and a sound card.

The hardware you need to do this? Any PC with a processor speed of around 300MHz and a built-in sound card. In other words, most of the computers that are still in use are suitable. (If you find one that isn't up to this level, you might want to donate it to the Museum of Dinosaur Computers.)

Figure 8.1

Nuendo gives you recording, editing, processing, and mixing in mono, stereo, and eight channels of surround sound in a number of formats.

Many applications, such as Acid, enable you to do all kinds of basic (and not so basic) sound work and require no more hardware than the computer you already have. Armed with, say, Cool Edit, MusicMatch Jukebox, some software synthesizers, and MIDI software, all of which you can download for next to nothing, you would have an entire mini-studio. You could download and convert files, edit and layer, and create your own mix discs. Little extra hardware would be required, and you'd never have to ask the question: "Does the 96-48X12 require an external hard drive?"

It's this low cost of entry that has swelled the ranks of desktop enthusiasts into a huge army of home recordists. And a creative army it is. Have computer, will travel, and fancy gear makers be damned.

But Let's Face the Music: We Want Hardware

As capable as we are with just our home computers, we still want more. Much more. We want our desktop computers to be complete mini-studios, allowing us the full range of sound design options. We want our PCs to be so well equipped it makes major studio owners nervous. So let's give in to our urge to turn our computers into fully souped-up audio machines.

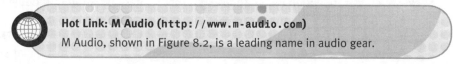

Hot Link: M Audio (http://www.m-audio.com)
M Audio, shown in Figure 8.2, is a leading name in audio gear.

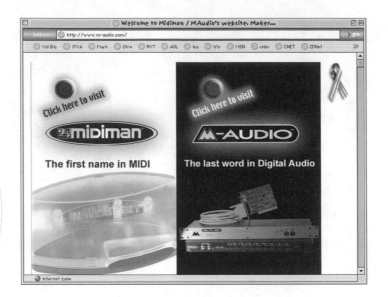

Figure 8.2

If you spend any time looking at audio gear, you'll quickly come across M Audio. They make all manner of audio cards, pre amps, and A/D converters.

But wait. This PC-based approach is not the only affordable desktop audio solution. In fact, this all-in-the-box PC-centered studio is not the only popular solution. Yes, it is our preference, but, believe it or not, there are people who don't agree with us. So before you spend time and money bulking up your PC, realize that you have several other setup options that don't put much weight (or none at all) on your PC. You could, for example, use

- **Portable digital studio.** These are standalone digital recorders, about the size of a bulky laptop. Affordable PDSs are made by Korg, Tascam, Fostex, and other audio gear makers. The predecessor to these units (back in the '80s) was a cassette-based system—not great for sound quality, but they were inexpensive multitrack recorders. Now these units have grown up and gone all digital. Some of them have 24 tracks (or more), XLR inputs, substantial hard drive space, and plenty of on-board effects. Major drawback: the screen that allows you to view your tracks is usually pretty small. But you could do all your recording and editing on one of these, and let your computer gather dust. Plus, they are great for field recording, because they are much more portable than your desktop.

- **MDM (modular digital multitrack).** These units are linear digital multitrack recorders. An example is the ADAT by Alesis. They are referred to as "modular" because you can buy a unit with 8 tracks and then later add another module for an additional 8 tracks—some people build 48-track digital recorders this way. The big plus for the MDM is that they offer digital sound for an affordable price. The big negative is that it's linear tape, which limits editing and sound manipulation capabilities compared to a software-based random access system.

8

NOTE

Random Access Versus Linear

Many modern digital recording systems offer nonlinear editing. But don't be confused. Not all digital recording is nonlinear. If a system is nonlinear, it enables you to access any moment in time without rewinding or fast-forwarding. Tape is linear; disk-based recorders are nonlinear. Nonlinear audio systems are a quantum leap past linear audio systems.

- **Hard disk recorder.** These units are hard drives with software that allows multi-track recording and editing. Some hard disk recorders can interface with your PC using an Ethernet connection. An example is the Tascam MX-2424. This unit allows 24 tracks of 24-bit recording simultaneously. The software runs on your PC, giving you a full screen view for editing. The hard disk recorder has come a long way, enabling sophisticated editing and mix automation. These hard disk systems are close competitors to the PC-based approach. Actually these units *are* PCs; they're simply dedicated to one thing, audio, in contrast to using your main PC, which you probably use for a lot of other things.

These various hardware options give you a lot of recording capability without using your main PC. And any of these options could be quite suitable: Many good project studios use each of them. Some of these users say they can get more audio work done with this hardware than with a PC.

Hot Link: Fostex (http://www.fostex.com)
Fostex is a popular brand of home audio gear. (See Figure 8.3.)

Figure 8.3

Fostex gear is found in home studios everywhere. The company realized there's a market for less expensive versions of high-end digital gear.

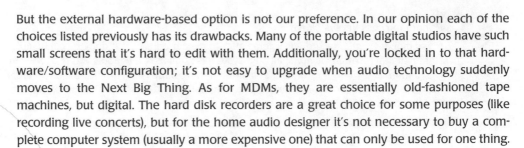

But the external hardware-based option is not our preference. In our opinion each of the choices listed previously has its drawbacks. Many of the portable digital studios have such small screens that it's hard to edit with them. Additionally, you're locked in to that hardware/software configuration; it's not easy to upgrade when audio technology suddenly moves to the Next Big Thing. As for MDMs, they are essentially old-fashioned tape machines, but digital. The hard disk recorders are a great choice for some purposes (like recording live concerts), but for the home audio designer it's not necessary to buy a complete computer system (usually a more expensive one) that can only be used for one thing.

Of course, your choice depends on your goals. There is no one-size-fits-all solution. But our preference is to veer away from these non–PC-based hardware options. A well-equipped, fast PC (and when we say PC we mean Mac or PC) with an audio card/interface and some hot software is your best option for a few key reasons.

- In most cases, a PC gives you the most bang for your buck. This is especially true if the computer you already have is sufficient (or wouldn't cost that much to upgrade). You say you don't have a computer, or the one you have is too old to upgrade? The cost of a computer with software is often less than one of the external audio hardware options listed previously.

- Software is easier, cheaper, and faster to upgrade than hardware. If you buy a standalone hardware recorder, such as an MDM, you're stuck with its capabilities. If some new and unforeseen audio advance comes out (which happens on a regular basis) you may have to get an entirely new unit to take advantage of it. (On the other hand, even using a PC and software may require a new audio card/interface or other auxiliary hardware to keep up with advances. Nothing's easy, is it?)

- Basing your audio work in your main computer means the rest of your software programs are right at hand. What if you want to make a list of all your songs, using a word processing program? Or, maybe the musicians you're recording have gone out for a smoke (again) and you want to play a quick game of computer Risk. You'll have it right at hand. (Heck, if they're boring musicians you can keep playing while working with them.)

- The Internet is conveniently accessed from your PC. Say a friend sends you an audio file. You can download it, add it to your mix, and e-mail back your finished song, seamlessly. That's what the future of audio is all about.

Hot Link: Tascam (`http://www.tascam.com`)

If you visit the Tascam site—and you'll see every kind of digital hardware there—take a look at the CD-302. It's a dual CD player designed to allow DJs to do real-time scratching. Cool. (See Figure 8.4.)

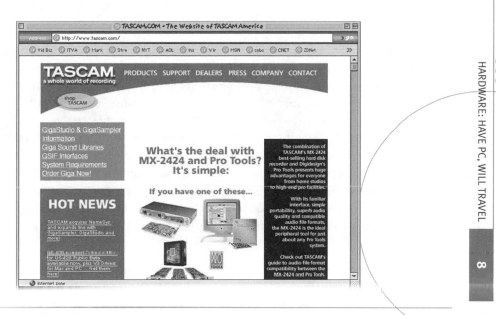

Figure 8.4

Visit the Tascam site to take a tour of the many types of audio gear the company makes.

Building Your Own DAW (Digital Audio Workstation): The Big Three, Plus the Really Important One

Given that the PC-based all-in-the-box solution is the best option, let's look at the hardware requirements needed. We'll take you through what you need to build your own *digital audio workstation*.

When digital audio workstations (DAWs) were first introduced in the late 80s, manufacturers generally sold the whole thing as one package. If you bought a Studer Dyaxis, for example, you'd buy the hard drive, software, and audio interface (sometimes even the monitor) from them. But now, using the all-in-the-box philosophy, you can turn your PC into a DAW by getting each element separately. This a la carte approach lets you mix and match in a manner that best suits your needs.

To build a desktop studio that's a music makin' machine, you'll need to get a PC (or upgrade your current box) with the holy trilogy of computing power:

- A fast processor
- Plenty of RAM
- A seriously big hard drive

Plus, to get audio in and out of your computer, you'll need an audio card/interface specially designed to do this (and in some cases it will do much more). Your audio card is a really important part of your setup. Let's look at the big three and the all-important audio card.

Processor Speed

This one is key. If you want to work with a densely layered multitrack mix with all kinds of filters and plug-ins, you need a CPU as fast as a Starbucks employee who gets all the free espresso she can drink. When it comes to CPU speed, the faster the better. Comparing clock speeds of Mac and PC can be confusing, because a Mac 400MHz can zip along at about the same speed as a Pentium III PC that's rated at twice the speed. If you're driving a Mac, a 733MHz G4 processor is preferable. If PC is your tool, something significantly faster than a 1GHz processor would be great. Can you get by with a slower speed? Yes, but you might not be able to record a stereo track while simultaneously playing back eight other highly filtered or edited tracks. If you need to go lower, a 266MHz Mac processor is still highly capable, as is a 500 MHz PC. Still, though, faster is better. This is such a key part of your desktop operation that if you need to spend a few more bucks on it, it's worth it.

Hot Link: Roland (http://www.rolandus.com)

Roland makes audio gear for every occasion (see Figure 8.5). And the Roland site's tutorial section is a good way to learn about audio.

Figure 8.5

Take a look at the Support section, and browse through the tutorials on Digital Mixing and Hard Disk Recording.

RAM

Did we mention the more is better rule? Someday every computer will come with a giga-byte of RAM as the standard (in fact, that day might not be too far off). In the mean time, your desktop studio should have at least 256MB, preferably in the 500MB range, and a gig of RAM is not too extreme. You want to be ready when you have multiple applications open: Your audio and MIDI program, plenty of third party add-ons, not mention your browser and your CD burning software.

The good news about RAM is that it is cheap. Buying 256MB of RAM will set you back no more than your lunch money for the month. This is a key area to spend a little more to bring your box up to snuff.

Can you get by with less? Sure—that's part of what desktop audio is all about. Pack your system with 128MB of RAM, but keep your eyes open for another 128MB chip (or more).

Hard Drive

Audio files take up a lot of hard drive space—a one minute stereo file at 16-bit, 44.1 kHz eats up 10 megs. And add another 50 percent storage space if you're using 24-bit files. So if you don't have at least a 10GB hard drive, you'll be forced to constantly back up your projects and clear your hard drive to start new projects. And if you're like most creative musicians, you're a serious audio pack rat. You'll never want to delete a take or a sample. So, everything gets saved (including those partial takes, and even all that out-of-tune stuff. You just never know). This means storage space gets filled up as quickly as a your uncle Larry at a pancake eating contest.

It's highly recommended that you dedicate a hard drive to audio only. You don't want to be storing your audio files in the same space as your software and other files. The most compelling out of a variety of reasons to do this is *seek time*. As your computer retrieves a file, searching through all that other material greatly increases seek time.

If you must use your main hard drive as your audio storage drive, at least partition that drive so the audio files are separated from everything else. However—and this is impor-tant—when you partition your hard drive it erases all the current data, so you need to do your partitioning before you start to use that new hard drive, or when you have everything backed up.

A desktop computer that's really rigged for audio work usually has one or more hard drives specifically dedicated to audio storage. Some project studio engineers have half a dozen or so hard drives, each dedicated to a project or a type of work. So when Band X walks in, the engineer simply plugs in their hard drive and starts recording.

Of course, if you're doing a lot of audio work, you'll also need to deal with archiving issues. To find out about backing up your work, take a look at Chapter 16, "Archiving."

> **Hot Link: Yamaha** (`http://www.yamaha.com`)
>
> Yamaha makes just about every kind of sound-related gear imaginable. Visit the company's site (see Figure 8.6) to check out its vast array of audio gear.

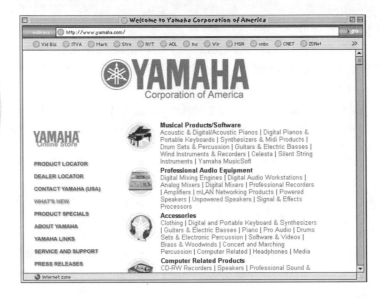

Figure 8.6

No company has a broader line of sound-related gear than Yamaha. What other company makes everything from pianos to MP3 players (not to mention motorcycles)?

The Audio Card/Interface

No matter how souped up your box is, it can't accomplish much without a way to get sound in and out. For your box to communicate with the external world, it needs an *audio interface*. This audio interface plugs into one of the ports on the back of your computer or into a slot inside.

If you don't have an audio card, you're stuck with your computer's built-in audio interface. Using these built-in audio interfaces for recording is like trying to drive on the highway with your bicycle. You might get someplace, but it won't be pleasant. Recording live sound with the built-in audio card inputs might result in audio like a vintage 1930s recording: really thin and mid-rangey—not the effect you want in most cases.

Lack of an audio card is a limitation even if you're not planning on recording an external sound source. You can import audio that's already pristinely recorded without a good card, but to do good work with it you need to be able to hear it—and that requires a card with high quality outputs.

The typical built-in audio interface on both Mac and PC is not too impressive. Many Macs come with 16-bit stereo audio interfaces built in, but shouldn't be relied on for even semi-serious recording. Likewise, PCs come equipped with a sound card, but they're usually merely functional devices that are not optimized for audio hot-rodding.

Your audio card converts sound from analog to digital—*this is a critical leap*. This A/D converter is a central component of your desktop studio; it plays a big role in determining how good your recordings sound (and that's what it's all about, isn't it?) If you're ever talking with a pro audio person and you want to seem cool, just say "it all comes down to the A to D." Most likely they just say "yup." No more discussion is needed.

The act of converting live sound (analog) to a computer file (digital) is fraught with technical difficulties. The A/D converter has a tough job. Various manufacturers of A/D units use different components, not all of which are the best for accomplishing this difficult task. The bad news is that not all sound cards perform it equally well; the good news is that even today's mid range A/Ds do a pretty good job of it.

Hot Link: The Digital Experience: Sound Cards (http://www.digitalexperience.com/cards.html)

This page contains a chart that attempts to list all the specs on every sound card made (see Figure 8.7) .

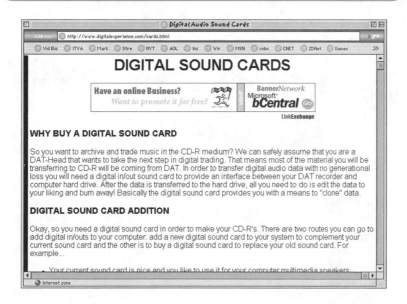

Figure 8.7

Who keeps this page updated? Whoever it is must spend some serious time keeping up with the ever-changing world of sound cards.

AUDIO INTERFACES: AUDIO CARDS, SOUND CARDS, A/D CONVERTERS

Let's clear up some possible confusion about sound card and audio card terminology.

The term *sound card* usually describes a Windows-compatible device used chiefly for basic sound operations. In their earliest days, they did little more than produce the various chimes, bleeps, and blips a computer plays. (Actually, in the very early days of Windows computers they shipped with no sound *at all*—a fact that made Mac users recoil in horror.) As sound cards grew up, they've grown surprisingly credible in terms of actual audio and music. MIDI became standard equipment: Sound cards have sound chips in them that make them minisynthesizers. They enable you to hear a MIDI song file even if you don't have a MIDI keyboard hooked up to your computer. You can't buy a new sound card without digital I/O. They've gone way beyond their role as a source for all the explosion sound effects and other wonderfully violent game sounds.

These days, the 500 pound gorilla in the field of Windows sound cards is SoundBlaster, made by Creative Labs. The best SoundBlaster is practically a studio in a box. We'll look at one of these useful units.

Okay, but why are some devices called sound cards and some called audio cards?

Hot Link: Interfacing Microphones to Sound Cards (http:// www.shure.com/support/technotes/app-soundcard.html)

Makers of the popular SM-57 microphone, Shure provides a helpful tutorial about using mics with sounds cards (see Figure 8.8).

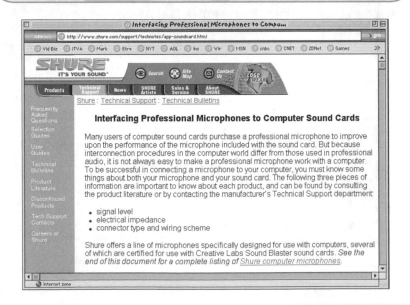

Figure 8.8

This is a well-done guide that gives helpful hints to eliminating problems like impedance mismatch.

The sound card's closely related cousin, the audio card, is dedicated to providing analog and digital I/Os for your computer. A good audio card does not need a library of sound effects onboard (although some of them have such a sample library). It's simply an interface—but an important one—between your computer's hard drive and the various sound sources that will fill up that hard drive.

In the old days, sound cards were junky little things for gamers, and audio cards were serious interfaces capable of high quality audio. But as sound cards have grown up—and audio cards are available in cheapo models—the difference has lessened. You don't need to believe someone who tells you to spend big bucks on an "audio card."

Perhaps the best term is *audio interface*, which would include the many variations of sound cards, audio cards, and also a third beast: the A/D converter. The analog to digital converter does nothing more than convert analog sound into the zillions of ones and zeroes that represent digital audio. It's a good choice for users who either don't need other add ons like MIDI or have another way to access them.

One more point before we look at some interfaces. Some cards are software specific and some will work with a broad range of programs. If you have an audio setup that's a hardware/software combination made by one company—like Pro Tools by Digidesign—the audio card is designed specifically for that program. It's like a marriage; and these kinds of software/hardware combos tend to be good ones. The designers have (hopefully) worked out all the compatibility issues.

What Is DSP?

Digital Signal Processing (DSPs) chips are like audio engines. Many sound cards are equipped with DSP capability. DSP chips provide the computing power to do the heavy-duty calculations necessary for tasks like reverb or complex delays. They perform much of the work that would tax your PC's CPU. Since these chips are doing the hard work of filtering and processing audio, they turn your computer into much more of a phat machine than if it only used its own CPU. The downside of relying on DSPs is that they tend to interface with proprietary software only, are an additional expense, and need to be upgraded every so often.

What Is Full Duplex Capability?

If you see the term *full duplex*, it means that the sound card can play back pre-recorded audio while you record new tracks. In other words, it will let you overdub. You'll need this if you want to build complex tracks from a variety of live sources (or if you want to overdub 20 tracks of yourself, which is a time-honored technique of the home-based creative musician).

JARGON

What Is Wavetable Synthesis?

Older sound cards played back sound using something called FM synthesis. The original FM synthesis sounded pretty lame. It was cheap, and it sounded cheap—very "synthesizer" sounding. Many of today's cards use an improved version called wavetable synthesis. This method uses samples of real-life recordings, and thus can sound pretty authentic.

Examples of Audio Interfaces: Sound Cards, Audio Cards, and More

Audio cards, like most of audio gear, come in a blizzard of options and configurations. So you really need to determine your needs before you go shopping. Do you need a card that gives you eight inputs and outputs? Or can you get by with two I/Os? You'll of course need more mic inputs if you're recording several players simultaneously—these inputs are analog inputs, and you'll need at least 4–8 if you're going to record a band. You'll need more digital I/Os if you have a lot of studio gear that you want to connect to your PC. On the other hand, maybe your composing style focuses on layering pre-recorded sound, so two analog and two digital I/Os may be all you need.

And while you're asking yourself questions: Do you want a proprietary card/software bundle, which only works with one program, or do you already have good software, and so you just need a card?

Be aware also that different cards are capable of handling different sample rates and bit depths. Some cards, for example, are capable of 16-bit, 48kHz recording, while others go all the way up to 24-bit, 96kHz. Of course, you pay extra for a card capable of higher resolution recording. Is it worth it? Again, it gets back to what you want to do with it and what your budget is. Remember that a CD's resolution is 16-bit, 44.1kHz, so if saving cash is your highest priority, anything above this quality is unnecessary. However, higher resolution capability sure is nice, especially since it's getting to be the standard—those cards that can only do 16-bit are starting to look dumpy. Bottom line: If you have a few extra bucks to spend for the 24-bit, 96kHz capability, go for it.

By the way, your A/D converter should always be mounted outside your computer. Internal units often have a problem with added noise due to being inside your computer.

Sound Blaster Live! Platinum 5.1 Sound Card (http://www.americas.creative.com)

The Platinum 5.1 Sound Card (see Figure 8.9) gives you more sound capability for $150 than you could have purchased for thousands of dollars several years ago.

Figure 8.9

Creative Labs is the big name in sound cards.

As mentioned, Creative Labs is the leader in sound cards, and with good reason. For $150, the Platinum gets you in the ballgame. Analog and digital I/O, MIDI, digital signal processing (good for gaming as well as effects like flanging, chorus and reverb), not to mention Dolby 5.1 surround sound capability. As a one-stop solution for a reasonable cost, it's worth it.

When should you go above the level of the SoundBlaster? If you're going to charge money to record musicians, you probably won't impress them when you tell them you bought your sound card to get good sound effects for the Kill and Destroy game. But that SoundBlaster will work beautifully for you for all sorts of demos and personal creative work.

One weak point of some of the sound cards: the mic input. (We don't mean this about Sound Blaster in particular, but about many of the cards in its category.) A quarter-inch mic input is not as good as an XLR, which is a professional-level audio connection (for more about XLR and other audio inputs and outputs, see Chapter 10, "Audio Connections.") And some sound cards don't even have a quarter-inch input; they have nothing but the lowly eight-inch input. So if you're planning on doing any recording of live sound, take a close look at the mic inputs of that potential sound card purchase: It's highly recommended to get one with XLR inputs, such as the Aardvark unit in Figure 8.10.

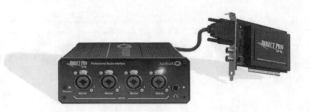

Figure 8.10

With the Aardvark Direct Pro 24/96 Computer Recording Interface, for $500, you get everything you'd need. It's capable of 24-bit, 96kHz recording, real-time DSP effects; it has MIDI capability, S/PDIF I/O, and four XLR mic inputs.

Photo courtesy of Aardvark.

M Audio DiO 2448 Digital I/O Card

As the "just get the job done" option, there's the M Audio DiO 2448 Digital I/O Card. We've seen this unit on sale for less than $100.

The DiO is equipped with optical and coaxial I/Os, as well as a stereo analog output so you can monitor what you're sending in. It can handle 24-bit audio—a nice option, although if you just need 16-bit capability, you could find something cheaper. It's designed to interface with S/PDIF equipment like your CD-R or a MiniDisc player. But it does not have a microphone input. So if you want to record live players you'll also need a separate dedicated audio converter with mic input jacks.

The advantage of the DiO is that, if you don't need mic inputs, you don't have to pay for them. And many users either don't want to record live musicians, or expect to get their own high quality mic pre amp to add to the set up. This card would be an effective inexpensive choice for them. Moral of the story: Figure out what you want to do before looking at the zillions of choices in audio interfaces.

Apogee PSX-100, shown in Figure 8.11, is a dedicated A/D converter. Its mission in life is to convert analog signal into digital signal, and it does so on a professional level. It doesn't do MIDI; it doesn't have a library of samples built in. But it's a tool that enables a home user to create a sound that rivals that of a high-end studio. What it does—A/D conversion—it does really well. In fact, this unit is an external A/D converter only; you still need an audio interface to get the audio into your computer. The PSX-100 has

- Two channels of 24-bit A/D and D/A conversion with 117dB dynamic range (that's good). And you can record at a wide variety of samples rates: 44.1, 48, 88.2, and 96kHz.
- All the most common digital interfaces: AES, ADAT, TDIF, S/PDIF (coax and optical).
- Gold-plated XLR jacks for analog and AES/EBU I/O (gold is used for increased conductivity) .

Figure 8.11

At the other end of the spectrum is the Apogee PSX-100. You're cool when you say you have an Apogee. But it ain't cheap. We've seen this one listed for around $2500.

Photo courtesy of Apogee.

The Laptop Audio Interface

It's one of the absolute coolest aspects of desktop audio: A sound studio in your laptop. In the future we'll all have one. But what about an audio interface for your portable studio? Many cards can be used on a laptop or a desktop—if your laptop has FireWire or USB, for example, you can choose from among many of the cards on the market. But if you're looking for an audio card that's small and light, take a look at the PCMCIA cards. For example, the VX Pocket by Digigram (http://www.digigram.com). It handles 24-bit audio with two I/os, and it fits in your hand.

Mac or PC?

It's the Big Dichotomy: Mac or Windows. The truth is, you probably already lean one way or the other (these things are decided at birth, aren't they?), and so we're guessing you're not going to switch, even if you're about to build a desktop audio studio. But still, a few thoughts:

It used to be that if you wanted to work with a particular software program, you had to use a Mac or a PC, because some leading programs were "one system only." But now most of the leading MIDI/audio programs, such as Logic Audio, Cubase VST, and Pro Tools, are written for both.

So don't let anyone tell you that your system must exist on one platform of another. Either Mac or Windows will get you where you want to go.

JARGON

Latency

The term *latency* refers to the short time delay between the moment audio enters your computer-based system and the moment that sound comes out the system's outputs. It ranges from a few milliseconds to over a half second. One way to avoid latency problems is to use an external mixing desk to simultaneously monitor what you're recording and the pre-recorded tracks playing off of your hard drive. More conveniently, many of today's good audio cards have been designed to virtually eliminate latency.

NOTE

The Luxury of the Double Monitor

Looking for a way to spend more money on your PC setup? There's nothing like having a second monitor. It's truly a luxury, I realize, but it comes in very handy for long projects. Most software packages offer several screens to view the same audio. With one monitor, you can toggle between your two main screens; with two monitors you can keep the screens open all the time. A nice setup option indeed. Note, with Windows you'll need either two graphics cards, or what's known as a dual head card, one with two outputs. Our favorite dual head card is made by Matrox.

EXTRA GEAR

In This Chapter:

Look at the extra gear, apart from your basic PC, that adds functionality to your desktop studio:

- Mixers, to help you route signals
- Hard disk recorders, in case you're looking at alternatives to the all-in-the-box PC workstation approach
- Microphones and mic pre amps, to ensure you're getting the best sound
- Many more shiny pieces of gear that will help drive your credit card balance into the stratosphere

AUDIO GEAR: IT'S BEAUTIFUL, AND IT WANTS YOU TO TAKE IT HOME

Gear. Goodies. Toys. I just love 'em, don't you? Really cool audio gear, fresh out of box, ready to make some wicked tracks. Those gleaming mixers with row after row of multi-colored knobs and faders. A hot microphone, maybe a big fat Neumann—you know you can capture some beautiful noise with that. And then there's the outboard gear, much of which is being replaced by software, but still: It's great to have a rack of compressors and delay units to add new possibilities to the creative process.

This chapter will look at some of these fun and shiny toys. The basic audio gear is covered in other chapters: the PC/sound card center of your system is covered in Chapter 8, "Hardware: Have PC, Will Travel"; take a look at Chapter 4, "MIDI: The Virtual Orchestra," for MIDI stuff. The gear in this chapter is the "extra" gear—equipment that adds capability to your studio. Do you really need this stuff? Well, in many cases there are ways to work without it. But do you want it? Oh yeah, you bet you do. So dust off your credit card and let's go shopping.

Wait a second. We've already made this point, but it's worth repeating: You can buy all this gear either used or new. We highly recommend looking at the used market before walking into the music store and plunking down your cash. There is a massive used market for this stuff (find places to shop for used gear in Chapter 5, "The Desktop Philosophy: Virtually Everything Should Be Virtual, Or, How Can We Do This Cheaper and Better?"). However, there's still a lot to be said for buying new gear. If you're going to spend $500 on some-thing, you want to be sure no one has spilled soda on it. All right, on to the gear…

Mixers

Mixers function like a studio's main routing section. Typically, all the inputs and outputs from each piece of a studio's equipment are connected to the mixer, enabling you to combine audio signals from various pieces of gear, and assign tracks to multiple locations. However, now the software mixers that are built into many good audio editing packages handle a lot of this routing. So many home studio setups function quite well without a hardware mixer. Still, some sound designers prefer an actual mixer; they would rather work with physical buttons and knobs instead of clicking incessantly on a computer screen.

Mackie 1202 VLZ

Mackies have cult status as home studio mixers. They're known to be surprisingly clean sounding, and they get the job done without blowing your budget. There are many different types of Mackies: The unit shown here goes for well under $500 (see Figure 9.1). It has phantom power built in, in case you get your hands on a nice condenser mic. Notice the four XLR inputs, just enough to mic a basic drum kit if you need to cut corners. And the whole thing is small enough to be carried back and forth to live gigs if that's what you're doing. Thousands of bands have been recorded with units just like this one.

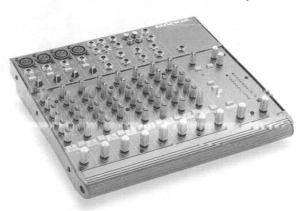

Figure 9.1

Mackie mixers are one of the most popular choices for home studios.

Photo courtesy of Mackie.

Yamaha O2R

We can vouch for the O2R (see Figure 9.2). It is one sweet console. There was a time when the idea of a digital console was only for the biggest of the big studios. You had to win the lottery to think about buying one. But units like the 02R changed that. At around $5,000, it's still pricey for the casual user, but it's cheap considering what you get: 24-bit recording, full automation, phantom power, enough inputs to record anything smaller than an orchestra, a full complement of built-in effects, and compatibility with all the digital formats. This unit sets a standard for high quality for a reasonable price.

Figure 9.2

Yamaha O2R: 40 input/8 Bus digital console, 20-bit A/D with 24-bit signal path and output.

Photo courtesy of Yamaha.

Hard Disk Recorders

Over the last several years, hard disk recorders have become complete recording solutions. They are PCs dedicated to recording and editing audio, and the best of them are full fledged audio workstations. But many desktop musicians would rather soup up the PC they have than buy a separate computer dedicated to recording. Those who prefer the hard disk recorders say that since these units are specially designed for audio work they're a more powerful tool. For more about hard disk recorders, see Chapter 5.

Tascam MX-2424

The Tascam MX-2424 is really a complete recording system in one box (see Figure 9.3). It has 24 tracks of 24-bit sound, with up to 999 virtual tracks. Record, edit, mix—just add microphones and you're in business.

Figure 9.3

Tascam MX-2424 is a 24-track hard disk recorder.

Photo courtesy of Tascam.

This Tascam unit is particularly well suited for field use. Tascam makes a point of advertising compatibility with Pro Tools and Digital Performer, among others. So you can take this unit on a field trip and record Sound Design II (for Mac) or Broadcast Wave (for PC) files and then port these files over to any number of systems to edit and mix at home. Or, you can also get a monitor for the MX-2424 (not shown in picture) to facilitate cut-and-paste nonlinear editing on the unit itself.

Mackie HDR24/96

The Mackie HDR24/96 is a good choice for those who say, "Hey, my little PC will never stand up to the rugged demands of what I need." With this unit, you save your PC for surfing the Internet; this is a CPU/hard drive dedicated to audio and nothing else. The HDR24/96, shown in Figure 9.4, (like the Tascam unit it is in direct competition with) will record 24 tracks of 24-bit audio simultaneously. With the right configuration, this unit will record 12 tracks of 24-bit, 96kHz audio at the same time—some serious audio capability. Like the Tascam, you can use a monitor with this Mackie to provide a visual reference for the unit's fully nonlinear editing.

Figure 9.4

The Mackie HDR24/96 24-track recorder. This Mackie unit is a fully functional digital audio workstation.

Photo courtesy of Mackie.

Portable Digital Studio

The portable digital studios were once funky little units that used cassettes. Now that they've grown up and become digital, there's a lot you can do with them. And their portability is a major selling point; they're perfect for taking to the gig or a collaborator's house across town.

The Roland Boss BR-8

We've seen the Roland Boss BR-8 advertised for around $700—significantly less than the full-fledged hard disk recorders (see Figure 9.5). This system records all its audio to removable Zip disks (although it can only use 100MB disks, a limitation). The unit's inputs are RCA and quarter inch (it would be nice to have XLR), and it has no waveform display.

This lack of a waveform means you have to confirm your edits by ear, which might build character but is kind of pain in the patutsi. Those complaints aside, this unit has everything you'd need to create a basic demo of your song: full-fledged, nonlinear digital recording and editing with built-in effects. And, it's considered easy to learn. If you have the budget to go several steps up in the Roland line, take a look at the VS-1880, one of the most full-featured portable digitals.

Figure 9.5

The Roland Boss BR-8 is a studio in a box.

Photo courtesy of Roland.

Korg D1600

The Korg D1600 portable digital recorder comes with a 20GB hard drive, and it's swappable, so you can easily pull drives in and out when you change projects (see Figure 9.6). It also comes with—we like this—a CD-R/RW drive and touch-sensitive edit screen. With 16 physical tracks, 128 virtual tracks, and waveform display, this unit could quite capably record the band.

Figure 9.6

The Korg D1600 has a 20GB drive, which gives it enough storage space for several multitrack song demos.

Photo courtesy of Korg.

Hard Drive

If you're going to be serious about working with sound on your PC, you'll need a hard drive dedicated to audio. Among other advantages, this enables your computer to seek and find audio clips faster. Additionally, it used to be that once a hard drive was full, a sound designer would back up the audio to CD or another medium, erase the audio on the drive, and start filling it again. But as hard drives have fallen in price, some musicians have started using the drives themselves for storage. For more about external hard drives, see Chapter 8, "Hardware: Have PC, Will Travel."

What's cool in hard drives these days is to be hot-swappable. If you have a drive like the Glyph FireWire you don't need to reboot your computer to change drives in the middle of a hot 'n' heavy session (see Figure 9.7). This drive is compatible with Macintosh and PCs (some PCs may require a host bus adapter) and enables you to record 73 minutes of 24-track audio at 24-bit, 48kHz. By our math that's well over 12 hours of 2-track recording at 24-bit, 48kHz.

Figure 9.7

The Glyph FireWire is hot-swappable, so you don't have to turn off your computer to change to a new drive.

Photo courtesy of Glyph.

There are a multitude of companies that offer high quality audio storage gear, including drives and peripheral equipment like cabling and adapters. While you're shopping, explore the options offered by Granite Digital (http://www.scsipro.com), Maxtor (http://www.maxtor.com), and Seagate (http://www.seagate.com). Be aware that not all drives are compatible with all systems. You'll need to check to see if the drive and related storage equipment works with the gear you already have.

A/D Converter

Most audio cards/sound cards come with built in A/D (analog to digital) converters. Indeed, this is their biggest purpose in life. Some really serious audiophiles choose to go one step further and get a unit dedicated to analog to digital conversion. Be aware, though, that even mid-level A/D converters are pretty good these days. And upper-level units like the one shown in Figure 9.8 are a true luxury; we include it only to whip up a frenzy of techno-lust. For more about A/D converters, see Chapter 8, "Hardware: Have PC, Will Travel."

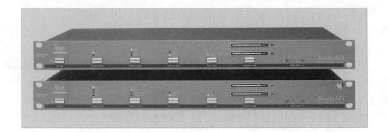

Figure 9.8

The Apogee Rosetta has a reputation as one of the best A/D converters available

Photo courtesy of Apogee.

The Rosetta does only one thing, but it does it particularly well: A/D conversion. The jump from analog to digital is one of the most perilous moments in the audio signal chain; if your studio isn't set up to do this well, it will always be a limiting factor. Mention to people that you have a Rosetta and—if they know what it is—they usually make a mental note that you know what you're doing.

But if you don't have a Rosetta-style budget, you can still get a good A/D unit. You'll find perfectly good digital converters in any number of audio cards, including those made by SoundBlaster (http://www.creativelabs.com), M Audio (http://www.midiman.com), and Aardvark (http://www.aardvark-pro.com), as well as many other manufacturers.

Outboard Gear

Outboard gear is like a desktop musician's sound palette: It enables you to color and manipulate audio in a manner similar to that of a painter working on a canvas. You can brighten things up, fill things in, and bring your audio into sharper focus. Outboard gear used to be available only as hardware, and the following section looks at physical, hold-it-in-your-hands hardware outboard gear. But realize that most types of outboard gear are now available as either software or hardware.

To learn about using outboard gear, see Chapter 17, "Mixing, Part 1."

DBX 1066

This dual-channel unit comes in handy for both recording and mixing (see Figure 9.9). Many recordists like to compress the vocals and other instruments while *tracking* (recording) to prevent distortion and provide a steadier volume level. This same compression/limiting function can help give an instrument more "punch" or presence in the final mix. A really useful piece of gear.

Figure 9.9

The 1066 comes in handy for both recording and mixing.

Photo courtesy of DBX.

Drawmer MX60

If you can afford only one piece of outboard hardware, this kind of all-in-one unit is a good solution. It's perfect for recording: It provides phantom power for mics, and compresses and brightens vocals as you lay them down, a technique favored by some recordists. Drawmer is a well-respected name in audio production.

Lexicon MPX-1

This Lexicon multi-effect processor has the advantage of dual DSP processing, so it outputs two completely different effects returns at the same time. In other words, you can use it to simultaneously create a small delay to fatten the vocal sound and a spacious reverb to add interest to the violin. It's MIDI controllable and has stereo S/PDIF in and out.

Alesis Microverb4

At right around $200, this is an affordable source of effects. It has 100 presets and allows up to 100 user-definable settings for reverb, delay, chorus, flange, pitch shifting, and more. It will also mimic the sound of the classic Lezlie organ for that rootsy sound.

Microphones

Microphones come in two main types: *dynamic* or *condenser*. Each type has its use, and the well-equipped desktop recordist has several of each in her mic cabinet.

One of the chief technical differences is that condensers require *phantom power* and dynamics do not. Phantom power is a 48-volt power supply, which is often supplied by a mixing desk; you can also buy a standalone microphone pre-amp to supply this necessary power boost. A mic pre-amp is needed for both the dynamic and condenser, as the output of mics is so low that they need a helping hand to get to usable amplitude. Experienced recordists know that the right mic pre makes all the difference. It colors the recorded sound, adding warmth and brightness—each mic pre changes a recording in its own way. If you're working with a cheap mic pre, this will always limit your sound.

Microphones are transducers, meaning that they change energy from one form to another, in their case acoustic to electric. Dynamic and condenser microphones are built differently, and hence change sound waves to electrical current in different ways. Inside of a dynamic mic is a thin metallic diaphragm and an a attached coil of wire. This coil is surrounded by a magnetic field; as the coil moves in response to sound waves, it causes electrical current to flow. Inside of a condenser mic, the diaphragm is mounted in close proximity to a back-plate. When the diaphragm moves in response to sound waves, the distance between it and the backplate changes; the amount of resulting current is proportional to the displacement of the diaphragm in relation to the backplate.

Although these underlying technical differences are good to know, there are also considerable practical differences in the way these two types of mics are used in the studio:

- **Dynamic:** These mics are durable workhorses. The can handle mild abuse and still sound good. They tend to be cheaper than condensers, and they work well in a lot of situations. They are particularly well suited to recording loud sound sources (like guitar amps). The most popular dynamic is either the Shure SM57 or SM58.

- **Condenser:** These mics are better suited to sounds that are delicate or pretty, and do a significantly better job of capturing the high end. They are a lot more expensive than dynamics, but if you want to be well equipped to record vocals, you need a condenser. Some big names in condenser mics include the Neumann U-87 and the AKG 414.

You'll also want to be aware of your mic's pickup patterns: omnidirectional, cardioid, hypercardioid, and figure 8. These pattern names refer to the shape of the spatial field within which the mic has an effective frequency response. (Translated: the area around the mic that the mic does a good job of recording.) Many microphones, especially condensers, can be switched between patterns. The pickup patterns are as follows (see Figure 9.10):

- **Omnidirectional:** This pattern picks up sounds from all directions equally. It's useful for picking up ambient sound.

- **Cardioid:** This pattern is similar to the shape of a heart (cardioid means "heart-shaped" and comes from the same Greek root as "cardiac"). It's effective at capturing what's right in front of the mic and rejecting sound that's on the opposite side. Many dynamic mics have a cardioid pickup pattern.

- **Hypercardioid:** This pattern is similar to the cardioid but its area of greatest sensitivity is focused directly in front of the mic; hence it rejects unwanted sound in front of the mic better than the cardioid. However, there's a small area of sensitivity directly behind the mic, which can cause problems if you forget about it. This pattern is useful for creating an "intimate recording," by focusing narrowly on the sound source itself.

- **Figure eight:** This pickup pattern resembles the number eight; a mic set to the figure 8 picks up sound in a circular pattern both in front of and behind the mic. This can be useful for recording a small group of backup singers with a single mic, placing singers on either side.

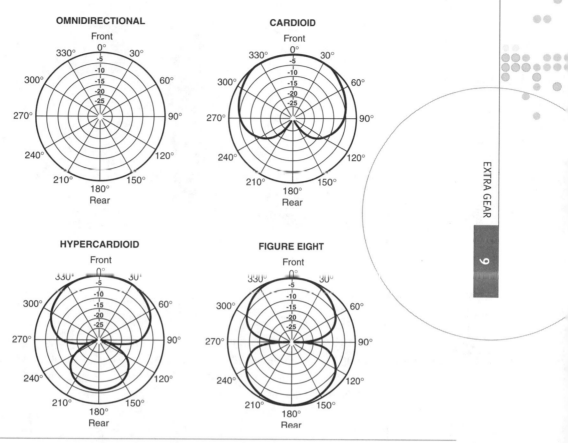

Figure 9.10

The various microphone pickup patterns. Notice the differences: The omnidirectional, for example, captures sound in a full circle around itself, but the figure eight is most sensitive to sounds originating in the front and back of the microphone.

Shure SM57

A classic, and at the right price, around $100; probably the first (and maybe the only) mic you should buy (see Figure 9.11). This dynamic mic is ruggedly constructed, with a built-in pop screen to cut down on plosives (the popping P's). You'll see musicians of all stripes using it, from rock to jazz to hip hop.

Figure 9.11

The Shure SM57 is a popular dynamic mic.

©Shure, Incorporated. Used by permission.

AKG 414

An excellent choice for vocals and strings, this condenser is one of the recording world's most popular mics (see Figure 9.12). You can switch the 414 to omni, cardioid, hypercardioid, and figure 8, giving it versatility for a lot of uses. Expect to spend around $1000 (or more) for this studio classic.

Figure 9.12

The AKC 414 is an excellent vocal microphone.

Photo courtesy of AKG.

Neumann U 87

A great microphone, part of many famous recordings over the decades, and still a highly respected choice (see Figure 9.13). It's known for its smooth, natural sound. This condenser mic in combination with a good mic pre produces some wonderful sounds. But at around $2,500, you could spend as much on this one mic as a good basic PC/software setup.

Figure 9.13

The Neumann U 87 has been used in countless famous recordings.

Photo courtesy of Sennheiser.

The PZM Microphone

The PZM mic (Pressure Zone Microphone) is a strange looking little mic. Unlike the tubular shape that most mics have, a PZM mic looks like a thin, square metal plate about four inches on each side. There's a square metal pencil shape in the middle of the plate, with a gap between it and the plate. The mic element faces the metal plate, which means it faces away from the sound source. You most typically see PZM mics mounted as foot level mics in theaters or on conference tables. They also have music recording uses; some recordists use a pair of PZMs to record a chorus, or mount them on the ceiling as drum overhead mics. PZM mics are omnidirectional, so they pick up everything in a complete circle surrounding them. These mics are great for recording ambient sounds.

Microphone Pre Amp

You might not need a separate pre amp. There's probably one built in to your audio card or mixer. But some sound designers buy a separate, high quality mic pre amp because these devices play such a key role in creating good recordings. A good mic pre amp can really improve a microphone's sound.

As a sign of how obsessed recordists can be with pre amps, some of them go for $2,500 or more. The DBX 386 Digital Tube Pre Amp is available for around $500. Notice that this unit uses a vacuum tube. This is retro technology, and highly desirable. Most mics use solid-state circuitry instead of a vacuum tube. But the tube vacuum tube provides a warmer sound and has acquired a kind of cult status.

On the high end are mic pre-amps like the Amek Neve 9089 (designed by the legendary Rupert Neve), the Focusrite ISA 110, and the Avalon VT737SP. If your life is dedicated to getting the best possible sound from a microphone, you'll want to look at a major league pre-amp like one of these.

Monitoring Systems

Those computer speakers will only take you so far. If that's all you're working with, you're not really hearing your tracks. Shopping for speakers can be a tricky thing. They are one of the most subjective areas of audio production: It's hard to say that there's a "perfect" monitoring system. You'll hear a lot of conflicting opinions based on personal taste, advertising trends, and so on. When shopping, it's a good idea to take a CD with you that you're familiar with, so you'll have a standard of reference as you listen. (And if you're spending enough, some retailers will let you bring home a pair to try them with your system.)

The cheapest way to get good speakers for your desktop setup is to hook your setup's output to your home stereo system. But it's not necessarily the best way. The critical factor in studio monitors is accuracy, rather than pleasantness. That is, some hi-fi home speakers strive for cosmetic appeal—they boost high and lows to make music sound better. Effective studio monitors (the term "monitor" refers to speakers) are designed for flat response: They represent the low end, for example, the way it really exists in your track. Working with flat response monitors means that your mixes will translate better to other listening situations—you don't want to be surprised every time you play your tracks someplace new.

Speaker frequency response is usually found somewhere in the speaker's promotional brochure, and looks like this: 20Hz–20kHz +/-3dB. These plus and minus numbers tell you how far the speakers deviate from a flat frequency response—the smaller the numbers, the better. If you see one that's +/- 1dB, that's quite good.

Studio speakers typically use a two-way design, with woofers (for the low end) from 6" to 8". Or you'll see a three-way design with woofers of 10" to 15", 1" dome tweeters (for the high end), and 3" to 5" midrange drivers. Some of the big names in studio monitors are JBL, KRK, Audix, Yamaha, Tannoy, and Urei. You'll also notice the term *active monitors*, which means the speaker has a built-in amp and active crossover (better for splitting the signal between high and low frequencies) to maximize the system. These active monitors (Meyer and Genelec are big names) generally are the best choice for the desktop setup.

The speakers themselves cost a bit more, but you save that because you don't have to buy a separate amp for them. (That also means you don't have to figure out what amp to get and deal with hooking it up. You have more room in your working space as well.)

Yamaha NS-10

The NS-10s had a long run as one of the most popular studio speaker models. Big budget studios kept a pair handy, and many home studios used only a pair of NS-10s. It wasn't that they sounded so great. It was that they became a common reference, a standard for comparison. Some engineers traveled with their own pair so they could have a familiar source of reference in a new studio.

Genelec 2029

These Genelecs are a good example of an active monitor (see Figure 9.14). Notice that these are referred to as *near fields*. An ideal studio setup has both full-size monitors and these smaller units. For a home setup, many people work quite happily and effectively with just the near fields, and perhaps a small radio-style speaker for an additional "real world" reference.

Figure 9.14

The Genelec 2029 speakers are digital input active monitors; the 1029 speakers are analog input active monitors.

Photo courtesy of Genelec.

Beyerdynamic DTT 990

Because most desktop studios have only one pair of speakers, the headphones play the critical role of an alternative monitor, in addition to enabling a musician to hear a mix while overdubbing. It's worth it to spend the cash on a good pair; expect to spend $150 to $200 for a professional pair of phones (see Figure 9.15).

Figure 9.15

After you've listened to your mix through the speakers, put on a pair of quality headphones like the DTT 990s to get a fresh perspective on the music.

Photo courtesy of Beyerdynamic.

Power Amplifiers

You've got to get juice to those speakers somehow, and that's where the power amp comes in. (Always use the term *juice* to refer to electricity to your friends—it will make you appear knowledgeable even if you hardly know how to plug in a lamp.) The power amp is often a neglected area of a desktop setup. And really, you don't have to spend a lot to get something that does the job. (To repeat an earlier point, many home users get self-powered speakers, and therefore don't need an amp for their speakers.)

Amp power is rated in relation to the amount of power the speakers draw. You'll find it listed in the amp's specs. It's determined by the impedance of the speaker load; you'll see amp wattages based on 16 ohm, 8 ohm, and 4 ohm. If you prefer to skip the math, simply get yourself a unit with 100 watts per channel for near fields in a small studio.

By the way, if you're using a home amp that has treble/bass or loudness controls, make sure they are set to the neutral position.

For a desktop setup, you don't need an amp that will power New York City. The Crown D-45 will do a good job for less than $400.

DAT Machine

We put the DAT machine last on this list not because it's a lowly piece of gear—no, anything but. It's that we have a hunch that we're moving away from this format. The DAT machine is a two-track digital tape machine. Throughout the '90s people mastered to DAT. Now that digital file formats have become ubiquitous; people are mastering directly to the hard drive and then perhaps burning a CD. DAT was also used for backup, but even that's headed for the audio graveyard. So put a DAT machine last on your list of studio purchases. However, it still comes in handy for field recordings, so if you want to record the band out at the gig, the DAT machine is a possibility.

This Tascam DA-45HR is a sweet unit, capable of 24-bit, 48kHz mastering (see Figure 9.16). Or, you can flip a switch and use it for 16-bit recording. It has AES/EBU and S/PDIF coaxial digital in and out.

Figure 9.16

The Tascam DA-45HR can record at 16-bit or 24-bit. Remember, though, that if you're going to transfer 24-bit audio into your PC, your audio card must be capable of 24-bit recording.

Photo courtesy of Tascam.

CHAPTER 10

HOOKING IT ALL UP: CONNECTIONS AND CABLING

In This Chapter:

- Learn about your computer's inputs and outputs
- Discover the basic electrical principles that govern audio connections
- Find out the inner workings of audio connections, both analog and digital
- Learn how to impress the opposite sex with your knowledge of audio cabling. (Actually, that's impossible, but in a perfect world it would be so.)

The trick to connecting your desktop studio is to do it right and forget about it. Properly done, your studio's cabling will be like your long-lost uncle—fondly remembered, but requiring no action or attention. Improperly done, your connections and cabling can turn into a minor (or not so minor) nightmare. Pops, crackles, hums, mysterious shorts, distortion—all can be caused by problem audio connections.

Few things can stymie creativity like having to stop your musical flow to figure out where that nasty ground hum is coming from. By the time you get things working again (which they would be if the connections were done right the first time), you've lost that lovin' feeling.

Depending on your audio setup's degree of complexity, you'll have varying degrees of connection and cabling challenges. You might have such a simple setup that getting things in and out of your computer is all you need—the true desktop studio. But we're always hungry for more gear, aren't we? So you may have an external mixer and some auxiliary toys that require you to deal with things like impedance mismatch and the joy of ground hum. For that you'll need to know a few basic concepts.

Hot Link: About.com Home Recording (`http://homerecording.about.com/mbody.htm`)

At some point in the sometimes tangled process of setting up your desktop rig, you might need some help. You can visit the About.com Home Recording site (see Figure 10.1) to ask a question in the site's discussion forum.

Figure 10.1

Kevin Becka's About.com guide to home recording is a great resource for studio setup. Take a look in the site's discussion forum for solutions to common problems.

CONNECTING GEAR TO YOUR COMPUTER

In the future, everything will be inside the computer—all the synthesizers, the CD burner (or whatever media storage is fashionable), all the audio filters. The audio studio of the future will be one massive desktop computer with multiple audio ins and outs for microphones (that is, until they figure out how to make synthesizers sound like singers, at which point we won't need microphones anymore).

But we're not there yet. So even the most humble PC-based audio studio is often surrounded by an array of gear. This extra gear can include a rack of synthesizers, audio processing gear, and any number of sound making tools.

This auxiliary gear must get hooked up to your computer—today's primitive PCs still cannot do mental telepathy—so let's take a look at the various interfaces. Some of these are on their way out, some are growing more popular, but it helps to know about all of them.

SCSI

Pronounced "skuzzi," this stands for Small Computer System Interface. SCSI is a popular interface for connecting any number of peripherals: CD-ROMs, hard drives, CD burners, and the like. The SCSI interface is fast and is a good choice for audio work, which requires the rapid transfer of data. Over the years, the need for data transfer speed has increased and has surpassed the capabilities originally designed into the SCSI protocol. But computer designers have made incremental additions and improvements to SCSI, hence the references to "ultrawide" and "fast" SCSI. (Some of these variations are compatible with the others, some are not.)

So, SCSI remains the fastest and most robust audio interface, but it's also the priciest, and most home users don't need SCSI's capability. By the way, one important tip to remember is that each device connected via SCSI has its own ID number, and two devices cannot share the same number. Many setup headaches are solved by checking the SCSI ID number—if you find that two devices are set to 3, for example, you've just figured out why one of them is not recognized by your computer. (Set one of the devices to an alternate number and you'll be on your way.)

USB

The Universal Serial Bus (USB) has become a standard for hooking up all manner of things to your PC: everything from PC telephones to digital speakers. It's an easy and straightforward computer port, and doesn't require you to do things like set dip switches or IRQs. As audio interfaces go, USB is comparatively slow, but you'll find many audio devices that use USB.

The USB port on the Mac replaces the serial ports that were used to connect MIDI interfaces (in pre-USB days, you typically used either the modem port or the printer port to connect your MIDI interface).

> **Hot Link: USB Implementers Forum (http://www.usb.org/)**
>
> USB is everywhere. Visit the Implementer's Forum site (see Figure 10.2) to find out more about this highly popular interface.

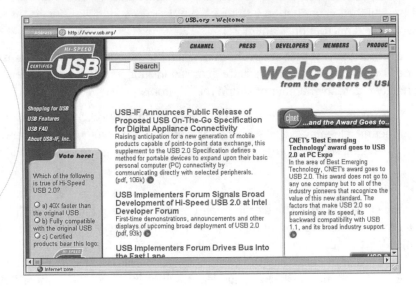

Figure 10.2

Got a question about USB? Find out about this seemingly ubiquitous standard at this site that combines industry and consumer information.

IDE

Intelligent or Integrated Drive Electronics (IDE) is an interface used on PCs and many recent Macs. It's relatively inexpensive, and its data transfer rate has advanced to the point that it supports some of the fastest CD burners, and even hard drives in array configurations. Many home-based sound designers use IDE quite happily. Its speed enables it to handle complex audio multitrack mixes, so it's a good choice for most sound applications.

FireWire

FireWire, a newer interface standard, is a popular choice among today's desktop musicians—there's definitely a buzz about FireWire. However, your computer might not be capable of this interface (if it's older, it might require a FireWire card, but its CPU speed might not be sufficient). If your computer can handle it, FireWire's speed and ease of use make it a good interface for audio work. FireWire is hot-pluggable, meaning you don't have to reboot your computer to change drives. (This is in contrast to SCSI, which should not be hot-swapped.)

Hot Link: GetAdaptec (http://www.getadaptec.com/)

Adaptec is a leading name in connectivity technologies such as USB, SCSI, and FireWire. The site (see Figure 10.3) provides information about FireWire as well as related technologies.

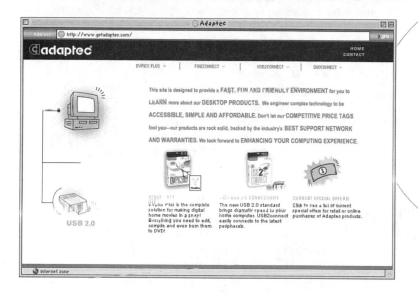

Figure 10.3

This is far from the only source for FireWire connections, but the Adaptec site is a good source of information.

Of course, if you want to connect a given piece of audio gear with your PC, its connections must match those of your PC. Attempting to plug in a FireWire device to a USB slot, for example, won't get you very far. Fortunately, you can buy adapters to adapt your computer's input slots to a greater variety of devices, although not every configuration is possible. Check with your local retailer to see if there's an adapter available for what you have in mind.

PCI

The PCI slot has become a standard interface for many audio cards. To communicate properly—or at all—with a PCI audio card, the software requires a supporting driver. (A driver is a piece of additional software added to your computer's operating system.)

For some audio cards, this causes no problems because they're directly supported from within the software. This works to your advantage in situations when you buy an integrated software/audio card package from one manufacturer, like E-Magic's Logic. This driver-software sometimes gets more problematic when using a sound card by one company and audio software from another, but that's become much less of a problem in recent years.

Be careful, especially if buying used PCI audio cards. They might not have updated drivers that support newer operating systems, such as Windows XP or Windows 2000.

The Versatility of PCI

If you have a PCI slot in your computer, you can use it to get an adapter card for most any other interface. So, for example, if you want a SCSI interface but your computer doesn't have one, you can install one though your PCI slot.

Is It Plugged In—And Turned On?

Okay, it seems obvious, but we've all done it. Before you come to the conclusion that one of your connections is faulty, check to see if each piece of gear is actually plugged in and turned on. Is the volume turned all the way down? Some musicians think they are being helpful by turning down the headphone volume when they are done—all the way to zero. Moral of the story: Check the simple stuff first.

Hot Link: Basic Electronics (`http://webhome.idirect.com/~jadams/electronics/`)

The Basic Electronics site (see Figure 10.4) explains electronics in terms that are accessible to learners at all levels.

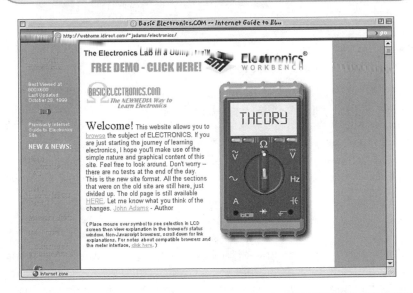

Figure 10.4

Author John Adams has made teaching simplified electronics a life mission. Take a look at the "Electronics on a Budget" article. A well-done site.

CONNECTIONS BEYOND YOUR COMPUTER

Well, it's time to face the music and talk about impedance and resistance. Let's face it, these are not sexy subjects. When Tom Cruise is escaping in his little red sports car in Mission Impossible II, we know he's not going to turn to his babe and say, "Hey, let's talk about impedance mismatch." Still though, it's an essential subject for the home studio user who wants to avoid wasting time and energy with unnecessary problems.

A Little Terminology: The Five-Minute Electrician

Desktop studio owners don't need to be master electricians, but a basic knowledge of electrical principles comes in handy. It won't be as important if you're working with just your PC, but if you have extra equipment hooked up, it really helps—all audio gear is electrical, so you want to know your amps from your watts, don't you? Let's dive in:

- *Voltage* is electrical pressure. Think of a tank of water: Just as the water exerts physical pressure on a pipe it supplies, so a voltage source exerts electrical pressure, also referred to as electromotive force. You also can think of voltage as electrical "potential." There is voltage in a battery, but that doesn't mean anything is happening. Voltage has the potential to do work, but nothing gets done until a circuit is completed. Then, current flows and work gets done. Electrical potential is measured in volts.

- *Amperes*, or amps, is a measurement of electrical current flow. The greater the current flow, the greater the amount of amps. A 100 watt amplifier draws about one amp.

- *Resistance* to this electrical flow is measured in *ohms*. All electrical *conductors* (a conductor is material that can carry electricity) have at least some resistance.

- A *watt* is a unit of electrical power. A 60-watt light bulb eats up—surprise—60 watts. The concept of volts, amps, and watts are interrelated, as follows:

  Watts = volts × amps

- *Impedance* is the total opposition to alternating current by an electrical circuit. Impedance is measured in ohms. When people talk about impedance matching, they're talking about matching the impedance of the load (the thing that draws electricity) to the internal impedance of the power source (the thing that provides the electricity). Impedance mismatch can cause distortion even when output levels are low.

- *Capacitance* is the property of being able to collect a charge of electricity. A *capacitor* is a device for accumulating and holding a charge of electricity.

- *Inductance* is the property of a circuit by which a change in current induces an electromotive force.

Hot Link: AC Electricity and Electronics
(http://www.sweethaven.com/acee/forms/toc01.htm)

If you want to dive deeper into the subject of electronics, visit the AC
Electricity and Electronics site (see Figure 10.5) .

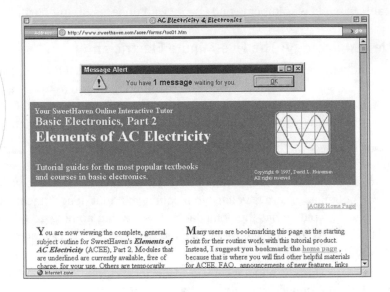

Figure 10.5

This online course takes a more advanced approach, but is still accessible to the general student.

Cabling Concepts

Now let's move out of the theoretical and go back to the real world. Specifically, let's look
at the essential concepts that aid you in handling your audio cabling. Notice that the theoretical electrical concepts play a role in helping you pick the best cables for your studio
setup. Here are the key rules for configuring your studio cabling:

- **Cables affect the quality of your audio: match cable quality.** Two cables may look
  very similar but have very different electrical properties. Factors such as resis-
  tances, capacitances, inductances, and shielding capacity may be significantly different. The key point here is to avoid mixing cables with different properties: This
  mismatch can cause headaches.

- **Don't use cheap cables.** If you can possibly spend the money for a better cable, you'll save yourself hours of hassle. There's some divine audio law that says cheap cables will suddenly short out at exactly the wrong moment. When you shop, pick from among the middle price range—you'd have to be a true audiophile to need the really high-end cables, but spending the cash to get solid mid-priced cabling is money well spent. Cable prices depend partially on capacitance and resistance: The lower the better. A cable with a lower resistance carries a stronger signal; a cable with low capacitance provides better frequency response. Look for cables with resistance under 100 ohms per 1,000 feet, and capacitance of under 100 pico-fards (pf) per foot.

- **Keep your cables as short as possible.** Those overly long cables can eventually cause ground hum. If a cable is really bunched up, it increases its inductance, which could negatively color the quality of your audio.

- **Good shielding is a good thing.** Look for cables that have foil shielding; this is highly desirable. The one bad thing about foil shielded cables is that they don't flex and bend around the studio very well. So use these for applications that don't require a lot of twisting and turning, like hooking up your outboard gear (which probably won't move around much). For cables that you'll drag around the studio quite a bit, like instrument and microphone cables, it's better to use braided and wrapped cables. It's important to look for cables with stable insulation, including a tightly braided shield that is kept snug by the outer jacket—it's less likely to become loose and short out.

- **Balanced connections are beautiful things.** This rule is important. In fact, it's safe to say if you can make all your cables balanced, you should do so. Balanced con-nections (tip-ring-sleeve) have fewer problems with interference from other cables than unbalanced connections (tip-sleeve) have. The redundancy of two signal con-nectors in a balanced connection usually results in a higher quality audio signal. But be aware that you must have a balanced signal for a balanced cable to help you. Both the signal source and the input connection must be balanced for a true balanced connection.

- **Keep audio cables away from power cables.** If the cables that carry your music are laid across the cables that carry your electricity, you may hear the problem. One of the ways studio folks keep these two types of cables apart is by using a *snake*. This is a bundle of audio cables inside extra insulation; it also helps keep you orga-nized—all your cables are tied together. By the way, if your setup is so cramped there's no way to keep the audio cables away from the power cables, at least make them cross at a 90 degree angle.

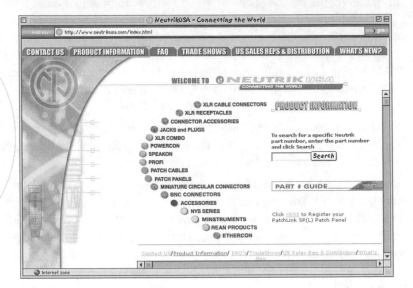

Hot Link: Neutrik (http://www.neutrikusa.com/index.html)

You'll find audio jacks and plugs galore at the Neutrik site (see Figure 10.6)

Figure 10.6

The company's motto is "connecting the world," and indeed, Neutrik is a leader in audio connector technology.

Commonly Used Connectors

Look on the back of a sound card or other audio gear and you'll usually see a row of inputs and outputs. Many of these ins and outs are described with their own mysterious little acronym—it's the audio industry's own language, although it's not as indecipherable as it looks. Here are the most common connectors you'll need to make beautiful music (or sound of any kind):

- **1/8-inch Stereo.** Though modest looking, this type of jack plays a significant role in desktop audio setups. Some sound cards use it, and you may find an 1/8-inch input on your MP3 portable. It helps to have 1/8-inch adapters handy: 1/8-inch to RCA, 1/8-inch to quarter inch, and so on.

- **RCA.** The lowly RCA analog connection is a consumer-level connection for audio work (see Figure 10.7). It's an unbalanced connection, which means its wiring is not as effective a shield against interference as a balanced connection.

Figure 10.7

The RCA plug, also known as the phono plug, is one of the most common connectors found in home studios.

Photo courtesy of Switchcraft.

- **Quarter inch.** Quarter-inch analog connections come in both the balanced (see Figure 10.8) and unbalanced (see Figure 10.9) varieties. This is a fact you may not need to be concerned with, but if you encounter an audio problem trying to make a quarter inch connection, it may be because you're combining balanced and unbalanced connections. It's helpful to be aware of whether the quarter inch jack you're plugging into is balanced or unbalanced. (And that might require looking at the manual. Bummer.)

Figure 10.8

Look at the shaft of this quarter-inch plug and notice that it's divided into three parts: tip, ring, and sleeve. This is a balanced quarter-inch plug.

Photo courtesy of Switchcraft.

Figure 10.9

Notice that the shaft of this quarter-inch plug is divided into two parts: tip and sleeve. This is an unbalanced quarter-inch plug.

Photo courtesy of Switchcraft.

- **TT.** These little connectors (tiny telephones) are most commonly used in professional studios. They are small enough so that you can fit many connections into a single patch bay; it's not uncommon to see a pro patch bay with hundreds of TT inputs. Most home setups use quarter inch jacks.

- **XLR.** A fully balanced connection, the XLR is used for mic cables and some PA connections (see Figure 10.10). Most mixing boards have XLR connections. You can easily string together XLR cables to create a single longer cable if need be, although it's more reliable to use a single long one.

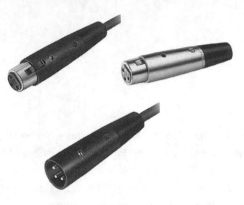

Figure 10.10

A fully balanced connection, the XLR plug is often used in microphone cables.

Photo courtesy of Switchcraft.

NOTE

The Microphone Input

A mic input is usually either quarter-inch or XLR. A microphone's output level is so low that it requires a separate amplifier to increase it: a mic pre amp. This is a critical piece of gear, which is covered in detail in Chapter 9, "Extra Gear."

JARGON

The Patch Bay

A *patch bay* is a panel with rows of jacks that allow you to access the input and output of all the gear that's hooked in to the bay. You might, for example, patch the output of your DAT machine to the input of your cassette deck. Most desktop setups never need one of these.

Hot Link: Switchcraft (http://www.switchcraft.com)

The Switchcraft site (see Figure 10.11) is a must-visit if you're shopping for audio connectors.

Figure 10.11

Connectors, jacks and plugs, cables, and patch bays: Switchcraft has it all.

Digital Connections: The Way to Go

It's highly desirable that as many of your connections be digital as possible. When sound designers talk about staying in the digital domain, they're referring to sending signals throughout the audio system without ever needing to convert it to analog. For example, consider this studio setup: a Mac G4 running Pro Tools hooked up to a Yamaha 02R digital mixer with a DAT machine and a CD burner hooked in to the console. Once you get audio into this kind of closed digital system—through a mic, or importing a sound file—it stays digital. There's no need to convert to analog and then back to digital as you move audio from device to device.

To clarify, the following acronyms aren't actually connections; they represent digital audio formats. But you'll find ports on audio gear that are referred to as S/PDIF In, or AES out. So you need to be familiar with these concepts if you want to understand the connections you'll find on a lot of good digital audio gear:

- **S/PDIF.** Pronounced "S.P. DIF" or "SPI-DIF." The Sony Phillips Digital Interface is the most common type of digital interface. It's a stereo connection, meaning you get both right and left channel information on a single cable. Your audio card's S/PDIF connection enables you to load material from many devices, such as a CD player, DAT machine, or MiniDisc. To add confusion, there's more than one type of S/PDIF interface. The most high-end SP/DIF connections use an optical signal to transmit audio data. This is very cool and is clearly the wave of the future. The S/PDIF inputs for many sound cards use coaxial RCA connections that use copper wire to transmit audio data. This is good too, but nothing's as groovy (or as expensive) as optical. By the way, the optical connector that S/PDIF utilizes is called TOS Link, because it was developed by Toshiba.

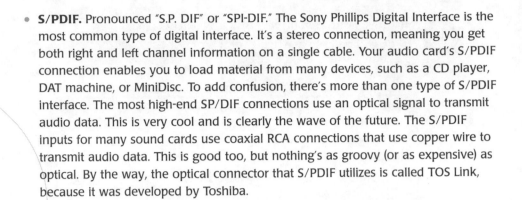

Hot Link: Connecting to a Digital Recorder (http://www.soundblaster.com/resources/)

Go to this site in Figure 10.12 and click the Features of the Digital I/O card link. Take a look at the section on connections for digital recorders: There are some good diagrams. However, don't be too concerned—connecting digital devices is really no more complicated than connecting analog devices.

Figure 10.12

If you read the SoundBlaster guide to connecting digital recorders to sound cards, you'll realize it's not a difficult task.

- **AES/EBU.** Audio Engineering Society/European Broadcasting Union, typically referred to as A.E.S. This is a professional quality digital standard. AES/EBU inputs and outputs are usually XLR. Sometimes this digital I/O is found side by side with the S/PDIF connection. AES, like S/PDIF, is a stereo signal. (There's also an AES/EBU connection that uses coaxial cable with BNC connectors, though you very rarely see this in home equipment.)

- **TDIF.** A digital connection developed by Tascam, hence the first letter in the acronym. It carries eight channels of digital audio, and uses a 25-pin connector called a DB25.

- **ADAT Lightpipe.** Developed by Alesis for use on the ADAT system, Lightpipe carries eight channels of digital audio. Other companies have adopted this protocol (for example, the Pro Tools Digi001 system has a Lightpipe I/O).

Digital Incompatibility

If you're trying to send 40kHz digital audio into a machine that's set for 44.1kHz digital, it won't work. Digital sample rates must be identical between input audio and the digital machine set to receive this input. This is because the clock rates don't match; to find out about clock and synchronization issues, see Chapter 15, "Audio Synchronization."

CHAPTER 11

TYPICAL STUDIO SETUPS: A SOLUTION FOR EVERY BUDGET

In this chapter we look at

- A ground-level studio setup, using equipment most PC users already have
- An intermediate studio setup that requires a minimal equipment budget for maximum audio capability
- An advanced desktop studio that gives you the tools to produce professional level sound design
- A home studio by a top producer, Chris Vrenna, a former member of Nine Inch Nails who works on a wide variety of music projects

EVERYONE'S INVITED

The best thing about the advances in desktop audio technology is that it puts creative tools in the hands of almost everyone. If you have access to a PC, you can build your own mini-studio. You might not get any Hollywood film scoring gigs with a desktop setup—then again you might—but you can make a lot of music.

So with even a (really) modest budget, there's a studio for you. You might be just starting out—that's fine; there's a lot you can do with even a basic setup. Often, having a starter setup just means you won't be able to work as quickly as if you had all the latest digital whirligigs. You won't have as many options—but you still might have way too many.

If you do have some bucks to spend, you can truly strike terror into the hearts of those studio owners who have oak-paneled control rooms, receptionists, and espresso machines. The music world is full of people with fair-to-middling setups (but creativity and good ears) who create product that rivals that of studios with oak paneling and espresso machines.

Moral of the story: Don't let lack of equipment get you down. The truth is that real creativity can shine with even the most modest tools.

As for equipment, if you can't afford it this year, just wait. Audio hardware and software keeps getting cheaper and cheaper. I would not want to be an audio equipment manufacturer.

This chapter takes a look a three setups, from the most basic on up to something that could turn out professional-level product. There's a solution for everyone.

Hot Link: TechTV: Build a $1000 Music PC (`http://www.techtv.com/audiofile/`)

Take a look at TechTV's guide to building a studio on the cheap (see Figure 11.1). Actually, the tutorial gives tips on going even lower than the headline suggests.

Figure 11.1

The TechTV guide to building a desktop studio gets you started with minimal cash investment.

BUT WAIT, THERE'S ONE THING YOU NEED NO MATTER WHAT

Important note: For each of these setups, we consider access to the Internet to be a given. If your home studio isn't hooked into the Web, you've just set yourself back 10 years. You're losing out on the richest source of sounds—and software, and production ideas, and musical collaboration—ever created.

That Net connection should be the fastest you can afford. You want to be able to surf quickly and download even faster. If you're shopping for software, it's great to check out a half dozen possibilities without having to wait for paint to dry. And when you see the 30-day trial download, you don't want to be discouraged by the 3.3MB file size. So get yourself a broadband connection: DSL, cable, or whatever flavor of fast Net connection they sell in your part of the planet.

The musical collaboration that the Net facilitates can't be stressed enough. Say you have a cool track, but it really needs an exotic oboe part to fill it out. With just your PC, SoundBlaster sound card, and a Radio Shack microphone, you won't be able to record a high fidelity exotic oboe part (or much of any kind of oboe part). But you can e-mail your file to that wild oboist who lives in Vancouver, have her lay down a bunch of alternate tracks, and e-mail it back to you. She can also e-mail the file to a few of her composer friends, who might give you suggestions for improving your piece (especially that 13-minute tribute to Abba in the middle—are you sure you want to leave that in?).

Our point is whether it's for collaboration, downloading, or learning, a Web connection—a fast one—is a vitally important part of the desktop recordist's setup.

Hot Link: Build It for Less (`http://www.audio-recording-center.com`)
Visit the Build It For Less site (see Figure 11.2) for some sound guidance about audio recording setups.

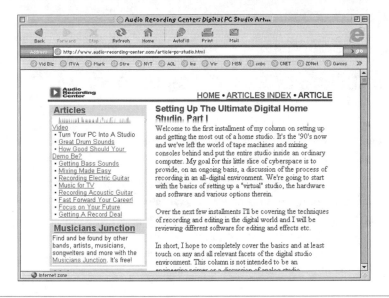

Figure 11.2

The Audio Recording Center site has some great info on setting up a desktop studio with a minimum of cash.

Setup 1: The Basic Desktop

This first setup offers basic music composing/production capability even if you don't have much to spend. In fact, most of today's computers are equipped at this level practically right out of the box, with the exception of the software. And the price of an entry-level audio/MIDI program is pretty modest; some of them are even available as freeware. Although this first setup is perfect for a beginner, there are many quite experienced musicians who work efficiently and productively with systems much like this one.

Here's what you need:

- PC with a full complement of audio software
- Good audio card with both analog and digital inputs and outputs
- CD burner
- Net connection

Whoa. This ain't much, is it? But it's more than you might think. Take a look at this modest list and notice the key part: "a full complement of software." To be creative with hardware this basic, you'll need audio software with recording/editing and MIDI composing capability. For example, if you have Cool Edit Pro you'll be able to splice and dice audio files, have multitrack layering and mixing tools, and be able to do some advanced MIDI doodling.

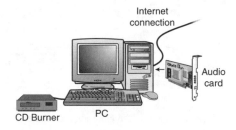

Figure 11.3

This basic desktop setup is, well, pretty basic.

Of course, you won't be able to record a live performer. So to get sound and music to work with, you'll need to rely on importing files digitally, either by downloading from the Web or by ripping from a CD. Maybe a friend has a library of samples she can e-mail you. This is the kind of setup that is made for a program like Acid, the program that helps you loop and layer until you've developed the ultimate dance/techno masterpiece.

You could also download a software-only synthesizer such as the Yamaha YXG50 SoftSynth. This would enable you to create some of your own sounds, and would aid in playback of any MIDI files you imported.

Hot Link: MusicPlayer (http://www.musicplayer.com)

Got a question about your home setup? Click the Forums link on this site (see Figure 11.4). The site itself covers a lot of bases, but the Experts Forum has an impressive aggregation of gurus.

Figure 11.4

Query the experts at the MusicPlayer site about audio gear and techniques.

To spice things up, you could download a DirectX plug-in that lets you add crazy ear-catching digital effects, or something simple like AcousticVerb, a DirectX plug-in that provides the sound of a natural concert hall. Or, you might try ProDelay, a VST plug-in that does all manner of echo effects.

Obviously this basic setup is limited. It really wouldn't be enough to create, for example, a song demo that you could shop to publishers (although for some genres, notably electronica, it would be sufficient for this purpose). But you could lay down a basic chords/melody/texture song demo for your bandmates. And you could burn your mixes to CD, or save them as WAV files to play off the hard drive.

Little Computers with Big Abilities

The Saul Zaentz Film Center in San Francisco is a top-flight production studio; when they were mixing the Oscar award-winning movie *The English Patient*, the facility had multiple Macintoshes networked together. This allowed a variety of sound editors/designers to work on sound effect and dialog editing at the same time. It was an exceptionally high tech setup, but really, each of those Macs was just a computer with a good audio card and software—a similar setup as this Basic Desktop we've just described. And there they were, doing some of the biggest budget audio work in the country.

Hot Link: Home Studio (`http://www.homerecords.se/environment.htm`)

This small Swedish studio bills itself as a pro studio, although its name is Home Studio (see Figure 11.5). It's set up with a 24-track Pro Tools system and has kept the homey feel: Both the kitchen and bathroom have mic connections, and when your session is done, Kerstin will cook you one of her specialties. Show me the L.A. studio that will do that for you.

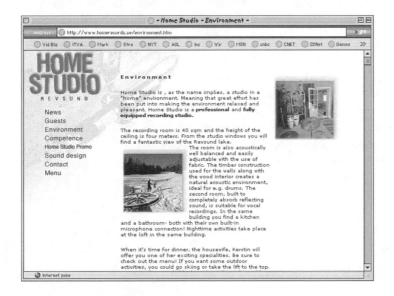

Figure 11.5

This unusual little studio is a good example of how the boundary between home and pro studios is getting progressively blurrier.

Setup 2: Ready to Groove

What's amazing about the following home setup is that, not that many years ago, this much capability would have cost tens of thousands of dollars. And now it's available for a fraction of that. Though not deluxe, it's enough for any number for projects, from musical to company presentations to theatrical/film sound design.

Here's what you need:

Everything from setup 1: A PC with plenty of software, a good audio card, CD burner and a Net connection. Plus:

- An external hard drive
- MIDI interface
- A MIDI keyboard or sound module
- A good microphone
- Headphones
- Good Computer Speakers

The setup in Figure 11.6 is the first step up from a complete starter kit, but really gets you in the game. With this setup you could create a good songwriter's demo of your newest tune. In a pinch, you could mix your band's demo sufficiently to give to club owners to help you get gigs. Preferably you'd do the recording itself elsewhere, but if you wanted to push the boundaries of your system (and your band is small) you could record and mix a basic debut CD with this studio.

PART II   LET'S START BUILDING

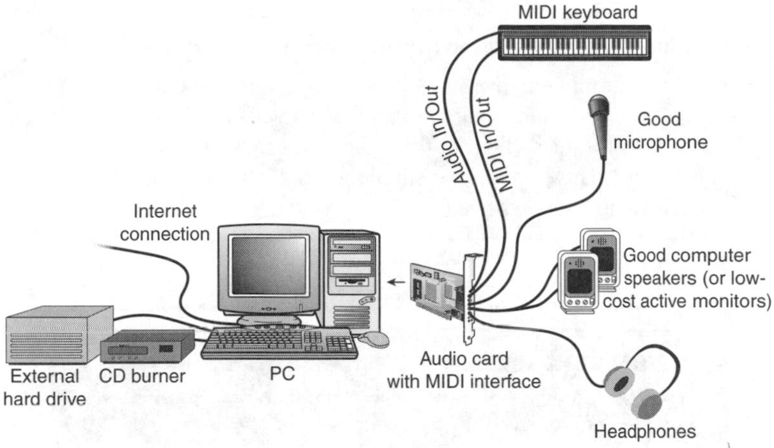

Figure 11.6

Setup 2 is found in project studios around the world.

Your CD burner would enable you to burn the discs yourself—just make sure you get some good labeling software to make it look nice. Find out more about labeling software in Chapter 21, "CD FAQ, Pt. 2: Before and After The Burn."

This system would enable a kind of poor man's overdub, allowing you to layer new parts as you listen to the prerecorded tracks. You could play or sing along to the prerecorded tracks as you listened on your headphones (plugged into the sound card). You would be musician, engineer, and producer all at once, but that's okay; many have done the same thing with stellar results.

Keep in mind if you're setting up this basic studio, you want a sound cardwith several inputs and outputs—don't get the most stripped down model you can find. You might have a friend who comes over with an extra MIDI keyboard—or a really good microphone—and you'll want the inputs to accommodate that. (On the other hand, if you don't have sufficient inputs, you could still connect one additional MIDI module at a time and lay down new tracks in a multitrack fashion. Creating can be slow with less gear, but it's still possible.)

> **Hot Link: Gravacao E Edicao (`http://www.homestudio.com.br/`)**
>
> This home studio equipment list has the feel of a well equipped home setup: Cakewalk is the main program for *gravacao e edicao* (recording and editing). As for mics, they list three: an AKG 414, a Shure SM57, and a Shure SM58. The computador should get the job done; it's a Pentium III 600 with a 30GB hard drive (see Figure 11.7) .

Figure 11.7

Here's another professional studio that calls itself a "Home Studio," but this one is in Brazil.

If you have multiple MIDI modules (and that's a beautiful thing), you can daisy-chain them together so that they all play even if your MIDI interface is such a cheapo it only has one MIDI in and out.

The external hard drive may feel like a luxury—and it is—but having a drive dedicated to audio saves a lot of headaches. If you're going to get serious, it's a practical necessity. And with some systems (like some Pro Tools configurations) it's a requirement.

The last list item, good computer speakers, is bit of an oxymoron, like jumbo shrimp. There really are no computer speakers that make audiophiles put down their copy of *Sound and Video* and shout for joy. But the point here is to use minimal cash to get your monitoring (remember, "monitor" is studio lingo for speakers) above the level of what's built in to your computer, which in most cases is heinous. You're not going to do any truly artful mixes when listening to computer speakers, but you will at least *hear* what you're doing, which is more than can be said for that little bleep-blip speaker on your PC.

And really, adding a pair of low-cost active monitors (they come with their own amp built in) would be a major step up for this home rig.

Setup 3: Practically Big Time

Building a home studio like setup #3 won't be cheap. Spending what's necessary for such a setup means either that you're a professional (or want to be), you'll be charging to use it, or you're a very serious hobbyist. However, if you take the time to learn how to use the equipment properly, you'll be able to turn out some beautiful sounds.

Here's what you need:

Everything from the first two setups: A PC with plenty of software, a good audio card, CD burner, Net connection, external hard drive, MIDI interface, MIDI keyboard or sound module, microphone, headphones. Plus:

- Mixer (but be aware that more and more musicians are working without one; see discussion)
- Amplifier
- Quality speakers
- Outboard gear
- DAT machine
- Sampler
- More microphones, preferably a pair of high quality condensers
- High quality microphone pre-amp
- Acoustic treatment

Oh baby, baby. With this much equipment—and the skill to use it artistically—you wouldn't be *practically* big time. You'd *be* big time. This list is the core of even the most high-end studio. The difference between the desktop setup and the big budget studio is that the big studio will have six pairs of Neumann microphones, one pair of which is specially enhanced, and they'd use them in a room designed by an acoustician flown in from Dallas, and there would an espresso machine. The home user would have only one pair of Neumanns, just some acoustic baffles to deflect noise, and an overused Mr. Coffee machine.

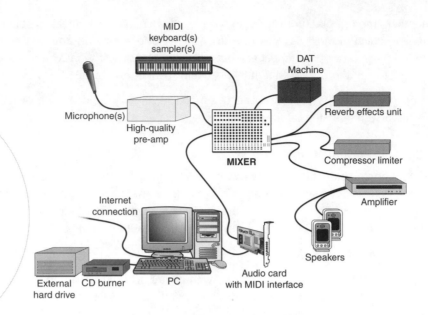

Figure 11.8

With a desktop studio like that in setup 3, you're ready to create some sweet audio.

But is there an audio difference? Put someone who cares in the mixer's seat of that desktop setup, spend plenty of time tweaking and mixing (you can take more time since the studio clock isn't ticking), and then listen carefully to the finished product. In some cases you won't be able to hear any difference at all.

The piece of gear that helps setup 3 go several rungs up the production ladder is the mixer. Nothing big, perhaps just a 12-channel Mackie. The real brains of the setup remains the PC, and all the critical recording, editing, and mixing is done within this box, but a mixer enables you to route signals with greater ease and sophistication. It gives you more choices for combining your outboard gear, MIDI modules, and microphones (and helps set up a monitor mix for the headphones). Also, many of today's prosumer mixers come with built-in compressors and effects units, which add new colors to your palette.

However, the mixer (which can be a major expense) is an item that even upper-level home sound designers are now working without. We wouldn't be surprised if external hardware mixers gradually go the way of the Brontosaurus. A mixer's most important functions—providing inputs and outputs and aiding signal routing—are often done less expensively and just as effectively by an audio card/software combination. If you have a sound card with, say, 12 inputs and outputs, or even just 6 inputs and outputs, you could plug everything into the card and do all the routing with software. Before you make the leap to buying a mixer, think about spending more on a sound card with extra inputs and outputs, and getting a audio program with a built-in mixer—which most of the better programs have.

Prosumer is one of the vague terms you'll run across in music gear catalogs. A piece of gear that's referred to as prosumer is considered nearly professional quality, but is priced for the consumer market. It's hard to say exactly what that means, but generally speaking, it means the manufacturer has put more bells and whistles on it, and for audio gear, it should have S/PDIF inputs and outputs.

Connected to your mixer is an amplifier, which powers your speakers. (But also remember that you can buy active monitors—speakers with amplification built in—to avoid the expense of a speaker amp.) The speakers provide an element that sometimes gets forgotten in the desktop world: an accurate monitor. To mix, to artfully record and edit music, you need to hear what you're doing—really well. It's tough to make accurate and precise adjustments to the acoustic guitar's reverb level if you're listening on so-so computer speakers.

Hot Link: Le Home Studio (http://perso.club-internet.fr/krem)
This home studio is in France (see Figure 11.9). Staffed by Phillipe Genestie and Remy Katan, they're ready for business.

Figure 11.9

This studio's motto is "Come with your ideas...leave with a CD!"

The most deluxe desktop setups have full-size monitors as well as near fields, which are smaller speakers placed close to the recordist, and hence are less affected by room acoustics. It's also ideal to have a third speaker setup, a really small beat-up pair that maybe your dog gnaws on. This multiple monitor setup provides a variety of listening perspectives. Music sounds a little bit different (or a lot different) on every pair of speakers; you want your mix to sound good on the sweet speakers as well as the 4-inch Radio Shack specials.

You might be surprised to see outboard gear on this list. You can certainly work without this hardware help if you need to cut costs. These tasks—like delay or compression—can be done with software, and done much more cheaply. Still, it's nice to have a Lexicon or other hardware effects box to add another dimension to your mix. It can be convenient to not have to route everything through software.

Hot Link: Tweakheadz (`http://www.tweakheadz.com`)

Rich the Tweakmeister's site is a must for those assembling their own audio setup (see Figure 11.10) .

Figure 11.10

It even describes how to get some scary samples out of a squeaky chair—now that's home ingenuity.

Next on our list is the microphone preamplifier, often called a *mic pre*. A good mic pre makes all the difference. It adds color to the sound of your recording, boosting dimensions like warmth and brightness. A good mic pre in combination with a high-end mic—positioned properly—is what makes great recordings sound so ear-catching. (Good musicians help too, but you can always fix their problems in the mix, can't you?)

Hot Link: Baffles for Sound Separation (`http://www.clearsonic.com/`)

With the right acoustic treatment, a home environment can sound similar to a pro studio. Visit the ClearSonic site (see Figure 11.11) to explore some of your options.

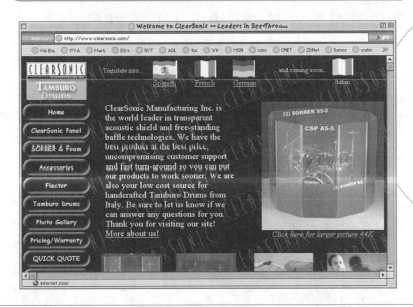

Figure 11.11

If you're brave enough to record a full drum set in your living room, look at ClearSonic's line of acoustic baffles.

A DAT machine appears on the equipment list, although the days of the DAT machine might be numbered. In a world dominated by digital file formats and CDs, we'd be leery of investing in a DAT machine unless you're really serious. But if you work with a lot of collaborators, the need for a DAT will come up.

As for acoustic treatment, this is usually the desktop recordist's downfall. It's not likely that your bedroom, your living room, or your basement can be turned into an acoustically perfect environment. But you can get part of the way there with the help of a carefully placed acoustic baffle or two. Some home-based sound designers actually use the flaws in the home environment to create interesting recordings. Try recording the vocalist in the bathroom for that boxy reverberant sound, or out in the garage to add some serious room tone.

Hot Link: Acoustical Solutions (`http:/`
`www.acousticalsolutions.com/`)
Click the recording link to find out about sound proofing your home setup.

A PROFESSIONAL'S HOME STUDIO: CHRIS VRENNA

As a former member of Nine Inch Nails, drummer-composer Chris Vrenna has been making music on the computer as long as anyone. He now has a solo career under the name Tweaker. Vrenna gets called on to add his mixing and programming skills to an eclectic smorgasbord of music projects, including Smashing Pumpkins, Weezer, and Hole. He was also hired to compose an original soundtrack for a game by Electronic Arts called *Alice*, a gothic version of *Alice in Wonderland*.

Vrenna (see Figure 11.12) is the ultimate desktop sound designer. His home setup, with racks full of gear surrounding his computer, puts all the sounds of modern music at his fingertips: retro, techno, pop, electronic, and plenty of sounds he calls "whacked."

Figure 11.12

Producer Chris Vrenna takes a highly creative approach to working in his home studio.

In an interview for this book, Vrenna talked about his home setup: the hardware, the software, his working space, and what it all means to his creative approach.

His space is modest: a 13′ × 16′ room for equipment, with an adjacent smaller room for overdubs. He describes his computer setup as "nothing cutting edge, but solid." Indeed, his computer, a Mac 9600 with a G3 upgrade card along with a Mac G3 233, is nothing that causes a gasp of techno-lust. But, he says, "If it ain't broke, don't fix it." He makes the point that you can spend a bundle to buy the newest computer only to see it drop by half the price. "You can only chase technology's tail so long before you've lost so much money you don't care anymore," he says.

He uses two 15-inch flat panel computer monitors, which enable him to keep his Mix window and Edit window open at the same time. These monitors are mounted over a Yamaha 02R digital mixing console (see Figure 11.13). Because his console is digital, once he records audio, it stays completely in the digital domain.

Vrenna's main audio program is Pro Tools. He uses it for all recording, editing, and mixing, as well as his MIDI programming. He uses Cubase software as an interface with his numerous software synthesizers. Vrenna is a major fan of Cubase's software synthesizers, and he also gets a lot of use out of virtual synths like Rebirth and Kobolo.

He has so many MIDI modules that he must use both his Mac printer *and* modem port to get them all connected. He's particularly fond of modules that can sound like vintage analog synthesizers, such as the Nord Lead II, the Roland JP8000, and the Yamaha A1NX.

His main sampler is an EMU E6400 Ultra, which, he says, "has been totally upgraded with everything you can get for it." He also uses the Kurzweil K2000, the rack version. He's really enthused about his EMU Virtuoso 2000: "It has the best orchestral sounds I've heard."

He has a digital drum kit set up in his overdub room—not surprising since he's a drummer. He uses the kit for practice and to occasionally layer in a percussion track.

Working at Home Versus Working at a Studio

When Vrenna produces an album, he does the main tracking at a high-end recording studio, but he adds parts in his home studio. "We'll record drums and a big guitar setup in a studio, and then we'll come back here and do vocals, guitar, and synth overdubs," he says. "It's very quiet, it's peaceful, and to be realistic if you're talking about expense, as a producer I don't feel right spending a band's money on an expensive studio for basically one microphone and one microphone pre amp.

Figure 11.13

Notice the Yamaha O2R digital console on the right side.

"It's good for me that Pro Tools is my main software of choice because it seems that it's becoming much more of the standard than all the software brands out there," Vrenna says. Because Pro Tools is used at so many facilities, he can move projects seamlessly from home to studio. He'll bring his own hard drive with him to a studio, record the artist to the drive, and then bring the basic tracks home to fill out and tweak as obsessively as he wishes. When he's finished creating the music, he'll burn his Pro Tools session to a handful of CD-ROMs. He'll FedEx those CDs to the mix house—a facility with all the studio toys known to Mankind—which will import the files into their Pro Tools software and create a polished final product.

Often, the music travels back and forth on hard drives. "I did one remix for Weezer and they sent me the whole drive with everything on it."

The Low Cost of Audio Technology

"My other rig is an 001," says Vrenna, referring to the lower cost Pro Tools rig. "The beautiful thing about an 001 is, it's a $750 piece of gear that will run on anyone's G3 and will play 24 tracks. If you want you could get an Apogee Rosetta [A/D converter] for a thousand dollars, get a really good A/D converter and your stuff would sound really good. Or, for less than $2000 you can get a blazing G4 and a 24-track Pro Tools rig."

The Relationship Between Technology and Music

"You can record your album on a four-track cassette, and if it has something to say that kids can relate to and it's a good song that makes you want to listen again and again, it doesn't matter," Vrenna says. "I hope that's what everyone realizes: You don't have to have every piece of gear in the world.

"*Pretty Hate Machine* (an early Nine Inch Nails album) was done with a Mac plus—the one with the little black and white screen built into it. We used an EMAX 1, an Oberhiem expander, and a Prophet VX. That was the entire arsenal of gear that Trent [Reznor] owned when we did *Pretty Hate Machine*. We made every sample in the EMAX. This just shows you don't have to have all the gear to feel like you can do it. It's all about creatively working with the materials you have.

Figure 11.14

Vrenna has the numerous racks of outboard gear; the quarter inch patch bay in the middle helps connect it all.

"The Beatles were on the technological edge at their time. No one ever tried to combine two four tracks—that was groundbreaking. And now everyone's on the edge of technology given our time period. It's just that technology is super cheap and super readily available to every person on the street.

"So what the focus comes down to is: What do you do with that technology? If every single person can buy a Digi 001 for $750 and create sound just like the big studios can do it, that doesn't mean that music is worse. All that means is that maybe that kid with $750 will make a better song than the guy with the $40,000 system in his million-dollar studio.

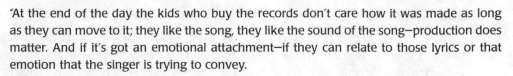

"At the end of the day the kids who buy the records don't care how it was made as long as they can move to it; they like the song, they like the sound of the song—production does matter. And if it's got an emotional attachment—if they can relate to those lyrics or that emotion that the singer is trying to convey.

"For the first Alanis Morrisette album, she recorded all of that on ADAT, and then they mixed it at Glenn Ballard's house. And I hear the snobs say 'Yeah, it sounded like it was recorded on ADAT. It sounds thin.' I'm like, *yeah*—tell the 16 million kids who bought it that it sounds too thin."

PART **III**

THE JOY OF RECORDING: HOW TO RECORD AND EDIT WITH YOUR DESKTOP AUDIO STUDIO

CHAPTER **12**

HOW TO RECORD AND EDIT

In This Chapter

- Learn the importance of setting levels
- Look at desktop editing techniques
- Delve into the wide world of microphones
- Learn various techniques for recording
- Find out about overdubbing
- Take a look at some troubleshooting tips

TAKE ONE: ROLLING

All right, you're ready to go. You've got your recording software set up, you've got room in your hard drive, and you've got a live microphone. Now you want to actually record some sound. It's time to lay the foundation of your audio mix. Cool.

But before you click the Record button, you've got to do something really important: set the record levels. What's important here is to not set the levels too high or too low. To do this, you'll need to look at your input meters as the sound plays. Ask your singer to sing, or keep playing your keyboard, and take a look at the meters.

Recording at the level shown in Figure 12.1 is a problem: if you record audio with the levels set this high, all your audio will be distorted. In the old-fashioned world of analog, some distortion was okay. In particular, the distorted electric guitar practically defines hard drivin' rock. But digital distortion is another animal. If you distort a digital recording, it's like…game over. It's just ugly. So if your input levels are too hot (and make sure you're checking the instrument's loudest passage), you must decrease the level going into your computer.

Figure 12.1

This input level is too hot.

On the other hand, you might see a level that looks like the one in Figure 12.2.

Figure 12.2

These input levels are too low.

Although this low-level input doesn't create as many problems as levels that are too hot, it's still not optimal. You're not taking advantage of the full dynamic range of your digital recorder. If your input levels are this low, it's best to increase them.

Strive for just the right level. As you monitor the audio you're about to record, listen for the loudest points. Adjust your input so that these peaks are close to your recorder's ceiling—as high as possible without distorting. You want the input to peak close to 0dB, with allowances for sudden spikes in levels.

When you're done setting the levels, you're ready to click Record.

The Recordist's Trick

Some producers go into record even while setting the levels. It's a psychological trick to help the talent. She thinks there's no pressure—she's not really recording yet—so she's free to give her best performance. Anything you can do to relax the performer is usually a good idea. When it's all said and done, all the technology in the world is useless without an emotionally persuasive performance. Conversely, a great performance can overshadow some minor technical problems.

What's a Transient?

A *transient* is a momentary rapid increase in volume, often a short spike that's so quick you won't see it in the input meter. For example, the impact of a snare drum causes a transient. Be careful with transients; even though they're momentary, they can cause distortion.

Record at CD-Quality Resolution—At Least

When you set your record preferences, choose to record at 44.1kHz, 16-bit—or better. You might say, hey, that eats up a lot of hard drive space. And you'd be right. But it's worth it. Even if your mix is going to be reduced down to a lowly MP3 file (which has only a small fraction of the fidelity of a 44.1kHz, 16-bit file), the rule is to record at high quality. After an audio file's resolution is set, you can't improve it. If you record sound at, say, 32kHz, 16-bit to save disc space, and later convert it to a higher resolution, you're not actually improving the sound. You're just creating a file that faithfully reproduces 32kHz, 16-bit—but eats up more drive space.

Today's audio software/hardware often goes as high as 96kHz, 24-bit. If you want to go that far, that's fine. I've often heard engineers admit they can't hear the difference between 44.1 and 48, and that anything over (such as 96kHz) is a waste. On the other hand, I've heard audiophiles swear by 96kHz sample rate.

As for bit depth, there seems to be agreement that 24-bit is noticeably better than 16-bit. But remember, the final medium is probably CD, which is 44.1kHz, 16-bit; if you record at this resolution you can burn to CD without conversion. So, if you're looking for a simple but good solution, record at 44.1kHz, 16-bit. (Note to future humans reading this book: Yes, I realize that 44.1 kHz, 16-bit is primitive by comparison to your 387kHz, 64-bit holograph recording, but hey, we have not yet developed the third ear you have.)

As you record, you might see the sound's waveform being drawn (if your software is capable of this). When you're done, you'll have a wave file that looks like Figure 12.3.

Figure 12.3

This is a graphic representation of a sound file drawn by audio recording software.

Look at the screen drawing of the sound wave, with all the little squiggles up and down as the sound changes shape. It's pretty weird when you think about it: It's actually a drawing of…sound. On the other hand, it's not weird at all—this drawing reflects the laws of nature. When the sound wave's amplitude is higher, the drawing is larger; when the amplitude is low, the drawing reduces down to a little squiggle.

EDIT UNTIL YOUR FILE IS UNRECOGNIZABLE

The graphic drawing of a sound wave greatly facilitates editing. When editing with reel-to-reel tape, you have to rock the tape over the heads and listen for an edit point—and having a graphic realization of sound is one small step for man *and* a giant leap for mankind.

It makes it that much easier to cut, paste, twist, bend, and shape sound until it bears no relationship to the original. That is, the software gives you the option—you might not choose to use it. The trick is to use all these tools and maintain the humanness of the music. Unless you're producing techno, in which case, go for it.

But wait. Before you touch that file, there's something very important you must do: *Rename the file.*

Some software editing functions are *non-destructive*; that is, they don't change the original file, but they keep track of your edits and play the results of your changes. Other edits actually do change the original sound file. To protect your original sound file, find your editing software's Save As function and rename this original. That way, you'll always be able to get back to the original if you've performed 15 edits and suddenly realize you'd like to start over. It's at this point that the beauty of nondestructive editing becomes apparent. No matter what you do to that poor sound file, the original is safe on your hard drive. That's a good thing.

To perform an edit function on a sound wave, you first must select it (see Figure 12.4). With Pro Tools (most editing software does this in a similar way), this is as simple as clicking and holding on a given point with your mouse, and dragging to the right or left to select as much of the sound wave as you'd like.

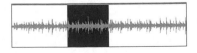

Figure 12.4

A sound wave with a selection made for editing.

After you've selected that section of audio, you can do any number of things with it. Maybe this moment of sound was the singer's only good performance of a phrase in an otherwise forgettable take. After you've separated it from the rest of the bad take, you can select it, type in a new point in time—one that will join this phrase with other good takes—and click Return (see Figure 12.5). Some software allows you to simply "grab" the audio with your mouse and place it where you want. Moving sound files is as easy as that.

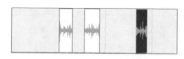

Figure 12.5

This sound cue's middle section has been cut and then pasted a few seconds later in time.

That's an extremely common type of edit, but it's only one of many that you can perform on this selected cue. You could also

- Turn it up or down in volume
- Equalize it to enhance some area of the frequency spectrum, from the bottom of the low end to the upper edge of human hearing (and above, for that matter)
- Loop the sound, turning it into a continuous bed
- Reverse it, making it play backward for that freaky "Blair Witch" effect
- Change its pitch, putting it in a higher or lower register

Or, you could change the length of the sound without changing its pitch (see Figure 12.6). This is one of the most technologically amazing edit functions enabled by modern audio software. The amount of math this takes—the software must algorithmically alter the ones and zeros that make up this digital cue—is staggering, and today's software does it in the blink of an overcaffeinated eye.

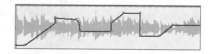

Figure 12.6

This short sound cue has been stretched to several times its length. We have now over-edited it so much that it is completely unrecognizable as the original sound recording. We desktop recordists are now happy.

RECORDING GOOD SOUND: USING MICROPHONES

Okay, we know we can get sound into the PC, and we know we can edit it until it's an example of audio insanity. But let's go back a step and take a closer look at the recording process itself. To get a good sound into computer, you have to understand using microphones. Simply recording basic audio and editing is pretty straightforward. But if you're looking to create true sound design or music production, you'll need to understand something about the art of the microphone.

The first rule of using microphones is to actually use a real one. That is, you probably got a little plastic one with your PC. Or you've probably seen little desktop mics on sale at computer stores. Just say no. These are not good things. These little fake mics will indeed pick up sound, but are best thought of as a way to create unusual and exotic effects than a tool to record anything you'd want to hear. These little mics add noise to your recording, and record a very narrow frequency spectrum—you lose the rich lows and the nice clean highs.

Or, Skip Recording Altogether

It's entirely possible you'll do absolutely no live recording in your desktop studio. Instead, you may spend the money to record in a high-end studio and then take the audio files home to edit and mix obsessively in your (free-of-charge) home setup. This is common practice in desktop/project studios around the world.

Hot Link: Microphone University (http://www.dpamicrophones.com/index.htm)

And you thought using a mic was just a matter of pointing it at the singer. Heck no—being a true expert takes time. Browse though Microphone U. to learn about everything from placement tips to mic construction technology.

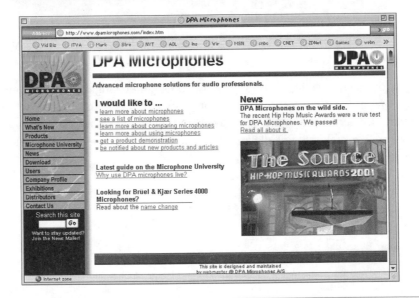

Figure 12.7

This online tutorial is a good source of information about microphones.

So, get yourself a good mic. The single most popular choice is either the Shure SM57 or SM58. You won't spend much more than $100, and you can't go wrong. These mics are industry standards. I've seen them used on the Letterman show, and I've heard that legendary guitarist Eddie Van Halen uses one to mic his guitar amp. Is there a better role model for us to follow?

The Shure SM57 and SM58 are dynamic mics. Unlike condenser mics, they require no phantom power and are really durable—they take a beating and keep on working. They work well in any number of situations; if you can only get one microphone, one of these is a good choice.

The SM57 will do the job for you, but if you can afford it, it's really sweet to have a condenser mic in your cabinet. They do a much better job of recording sound that's quiet or delicate (like a vocalist's intimate singing), or a really pretty sound. A condenser more accurately records those all-important higher frequencies. The condenser mics of choice for many studios are made by AKG and Neumann; old standbys include the AKG-414 and the Neumann U-47 and the U-87. (The Neumann U-87 is arguably the best mic ever made. It sounds good on just about everything.)

(By the way, you can always tell if someone just bought a Neumann without really knowing anything about it if they pronounce Neumann as "Norman" or "Newman." It's pronounced "Noy-min." Getting the pronunciation right goes a long way toward seeming cool in the studio.)

Okay, You've Got a Microphone, What Do You Do with It?

Actually using the microphone is one of the most upper-level arts in the recordist's trick bag. It probably deserves a book unto itself. But there are few basics that will get you on your way.

Remember not to run your vocal mic cable over the power lines. This is one of the easiest things you can do to avoid problems.

First, the environment in which you're recording colors the sound almost as much as the mic itself. If you're in a big, reverberant space, your recording will have a ringing, echo-ey sound. If you're in a dead room—one with no hard surfaces to bounce sound waves around—you'll get a more intimate recording that emphasizes the sound source itself. Either one of these may be good or bad, depending on the feel you're going for, but realize what we call The First Basic Truth of Recording:

If it's recorded that way, it's going to sound that way.

Audio history is littered with semi-tragic situations in which recordists in a hurry or in a noisy environment or lacking the proper equipment said—foolishly—"I'll fix it later." Oh no you won't. The famous phrase, "We'll fix it in the mix," is really the road to hell. Oh sure, if it sounds thin you can add some bottom end, or if it sounds dull you can brighten it. But these efforts are uphill battles. The point is to not be satisfied with your recording until the basic recording itself sounds good. And then you can filter or otherwise equalize a sound with much better results.

A microphone is like an ear with no brain attached. That is, our ear hears the sound of a space and filters it according to our perception. That air conditioning vent that you've stopped paying attention to—the mic picks it up loud and clear. And that ever so small traffic sound? As you brighten and compress the recording in the mixing process, those tiny traffic sounds are as noticeable as King Kong on the Empire State building.

Hot Link: Neumann Microphones (`http://www.neumann.com/`)

Ever the leader in microphone technology, Neumann has introduced yet another advance in recording: the digital microphone (see Figure 12.8). The unit contains its own A/D converter. So all you need is a hot PC, some good software, and one of these units, and you're set to make great recordings. However, you don't even want to look at the price.

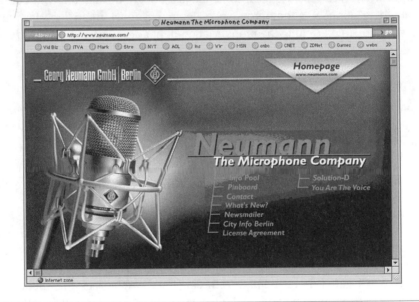

Figure 12.8

The Neumann digital microphone creates techno-lust in many audiophiles.

Simply put, be sure you get a quiet environment. You can add echo or noise later, but subtracting it is a major headache.

Record with a Highpass Filter

A highpass filter lets all frequencies above a user-determined frequency pass, attenuating the low end. This can be a helpful technique for eliminating low-end rumble in a noisy recording environment. Use it carefully though, because losing too much of the low end can make audio sound thin.

Some recordists prefer it if both the microphone and sound source are stationary during recording. They place the microphone about five to eight inches away from a singer—and keep both as motionless as possible. An amateur singer will want to bounce and jump around. This makes the final mix much more difficult—volume levels change unpredictably, and even a difference as small as a few inches can significantly change a vocalist's sound. So recordists who prefer the stationary approach place a mic on a stand and never let the singer hold it. And once they find the singer's best position, they keep him there, perhaps even marking his spot with tape. Other recordists give the singer a handheld mic, and allow her to move at will. For some singers this freedom is critical, and if it means you need to work harder in the mix to make the volumes consistent, that's okay. Some singers "work" the mic, playing it more closely in certain passages for greater intimacy. Ultimately, getting the best recording involves doing what's necessary to get the best performance from your musicians.

As you're recording, listen for plosives. These are little gusts of wind that come from a vocalist's mouth when she sings a word that includes the letter P (and sometimes other letters, such as B, T, and D). For example, trying saying this sentence with your hand in front of your mouth:

When I say P it can Pop.

Notice the small gust of wind you feel when you pronounce the letter P. This small gust turns into a major popping/thumping sound as it hits a microphone. These little tornadoes can completely destroy a recording. They can distract the listener from the music itself. (On the other hand, a really small one is nothing to worry about—this really becomes a judgment call at a lower level).

The Homemade Pop Filter

Placing a pop filter in front of mic is a good way to eliminate popping P's. If you're feeling cheap you can make your own. Take a nylon stocking and stretch it over a hanger, bending the hanger into a circular shape just big enough to protect the mic. It takes a bit of arts-and-crafts adventurousness, but it's a great thing to have handy. Or, if you're not that do-it-yourself, you can buy ready-made foam pop screens. Either way, you're going to need one if you're serious about recording vocals.

Finding just the right mic placement includes a bit of mystery. There's no manual that specifies exactly the right position to place a mic to record every sound source. Yes, you should place a mic five to eight inches away from a singer, but that's only a rough guideline, really no more than a starting place. Sometimes you'll want the singer right on top of the mic. Move the mic a little to the left or the right and the difference can sound remarkable. It's amazing when you start experimenting.

> **Hot Link: Critical Distance and Microphone Placement**
> (`http://www.shure.com/support/technotes/app-critical.html`)
>
> This site is hosted by Shure, which makes sense when you realize that the company makes some of the world's most popular microphones (see Figure 12.9). This site covers a technique for finding the "sweet spot," the optimal mic placement.

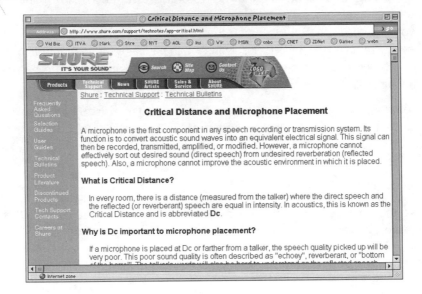

Figure 12.9

The Shure site offers some helpful tips on mic placement.

And that's the recordist's keyword for mic placement: experiment. You never know what will happen. Some big studios employ assistant engineers to move the mic around as the head engineer listens. They know that somewhere, within the few feet around the sound source, is exactly the right place to put a mic to get the desired effect. This is the sweet spot, and it's worth hunting for.

Phase Problems

When you use two microphones to record a single sound source, phase problems can occur. If two sound waves of equal amplitude and frequency start their cycles at different moments in time, they cancel each other out, partially or totally, because the peak of one wave may occur at exactly the same moment as the valley of another wave; if you combine these two signals you get silence. These two sound waves are referred to as *out of phase*.

When you record one sound with two mics, both mics are capturing a sound wave of equal (or close to equal) frequency and amplitude. But if one mic is two feet away and the other is six feet away, these identical sound waves are captured at slightly different moments, which can cause lesser or greater degrees of cancellation, depending on placement. You can check for this by combining the output of both mics. Pan them both mono inside your recording software. If combining the two mic signals makes the music sounds weak or "hollow," you have a phase problem. It's best to reposition your mics to eliminate this. Mics that are very close together—like the classic XY pattern—don't have a problem with phase because they pick up sound at essentially the same moment.

Roughly speaking, placement of directional mics (that is, cardioid, not omnidirectional mics) can be referred to as *on axis* or *off axis*. So a sound source is placed either within a mic's area of greatest frequency response or outside of it. A sound source that's miked on axis sounds brighter and more present; an off axis mic technique adds more of the ambient room tone. Again, it's worth experimenting. There are dozens of interlocking variables that will change the sound, from how reverberant the room is to that day's barometric pressure to how beat up that particular mic is.

Producer Chris Vrenna

Chris Vrenna, a former member of Nine Inch Nails, whose credits include Weezer and the Smashing Pumpkins, talks about recording:

"At the end of the day, it's all about how it was printed. It's all about how well that sound was recorded—to whatever medium you're recording to. The kingpin of anyone's studio is the A/D converter. If you've got that analog going in good, once it's digital— you're done.

"A good mic pre amp, a good DI box, a decent compressor, and very good A/D converter are necessary."

You'll also want to use the *proximity effect* when placing directional mics: The closer a mic is to a sound source, the more bass frequencies it picks up. This can be quite helpful in warming up a voice, or in adding some fullness to a thin-sounding voice.

The list of possible mic placements contains as many positions as the Kama Sutra, but you want to at least be aware of a timeless classic: the XY stereo pair. In this method, two mics of the same model and make are placed with their capsules as close together as possible, at an angle between 90 and 135 degrees in relation to each other. The midpoint of the two mics faces the sound source, and the mics' outputs are panned hard left and right, respectively. The beauty of this method is that there's little worry about phase cancellation and it provides an excellent stereo image.

Hot Link: Sennheiser Microphones (http://www.sennheiserusa.com/)
Sennheiser makes a well-respected line of microphones (see Figure 12.10).
The Sennheiser 421 is a classic choice for miking drums.

Figure 12.10

If you're going to record drums a lot, it's quite handy to have a Sennheiser 421 in your mic cabinet.

Recording Different Instruments

Because the desktop studio is typically more of a mixdown/production tool than full recording facility, you might not find yourself recording the whole group. But what the heck, you might drink one too many Lattes one day and invite the entire high school marching band over. If so, here are some tips on miking a variety of instruments:

- **Brass.** Put the mic a foot or so from the bell for a very upfront sound, or a few feet back to help it blend in with other tracks. If the brass player (or any player) really starts wailing, you may need to use the pad function on the mic or in your software. This attenuates gain by around 20–30dB.

- **Woodwinds.** Instruments such as saxophones, oboes, and clarinets can be a challenge because the sound can come out of different places depending on how it's fingered or how many holes are covered. Try to find a position about a foot away that points toward both the bell and the player's fingers.

- **Guitars.** The electric guitar (bass, lead, and rhythm) can be really easy to record if the player is going direct (see "Recording Direct," later in this chapter). If not, the classic approach to recording electric guitar is to put a dynamic mic in front of the guitar amp's speaker. You can start by placing it so close it's almost touching, and then move it back according to how you like it. Acoustic guitar can be a tricky animal to get recorded. It requires a good condenser mic, usually placed about six inches to a couple of feet away from the guitar. Try to keep the guitarist from moving.

Hot Link: Beyerdynamic Microphones (http://Beyerdynamic.com/ frequency.html)

Take a look at the frequency response charts at the Beyerdynamic site, shown in Figure 12.11. These charts tell you how accurately each of the company's mics captures sound across the lows, mids, and highs. The MCE 86/86 model, for example, is flat through the mid range, meaning it neither boosts nor cuts this range. However, this mic adds about a 4dB boost as it moves toward the high end, making it a bright mic.

Figure 12.11

Each microphone colors a recording in its own way, as you can see from the frequency response charts at the Beyerdynamic site.

- **Drums.** In the spirit of the pared down desktop studio, let's look at miking a drum kit minimally—but realize that it can be done very elaborately, with a cabinet full of mics, one on every piece of the kit. With drums, it's important to optimize the kit itself: Is the snare drum tight enough? Are the tom-toms tuned properly? There are a half dozen questions to discuss with the drummer before even thinking about mics. After the kit itself is tweaked, place an XY stereo pair a few feet above it. Place a mic a few inches from the snare drum, but take care not to set it in the drummer's line of fire. Add a mic to the kick drum—use a dynamic mic; it can take the punishment (an Electro Voice RE-20 would be a good choice here). This three- or four-mic setup can produce a credible sound if you have a good sounding drum kit, with a good player, in a good sounding room, and take the time to experiment with mic placement.

Recording with EQ and Compression

Many recordists prefer to record *flat*, that is, without any EQ to enhance the recording. They like to boost highs or lows later, during the mix, when they can tweak obsessively and listen to each setting at their leisure. However, don't be afraid to experiment with adding a boost to a given frequency if you feel the sound needs it as you're recording. The same is true of compression. You can record a more consistent input signal by compressing your recordings by, for example, 3–6dB. Realize though that once you record with EQ and compression, those elements can't be changed later. The concepts of EQ and compression are covered in more depth in Chapter 13, "The Recordist's Tools."

Hot Link: The Mic Setup Page (`http://www.oade.com/tapers/micsetup.html`**)**

The Oade Audio site, shown in Figure 12.12 has lots of good photos demonstrating mic technique.

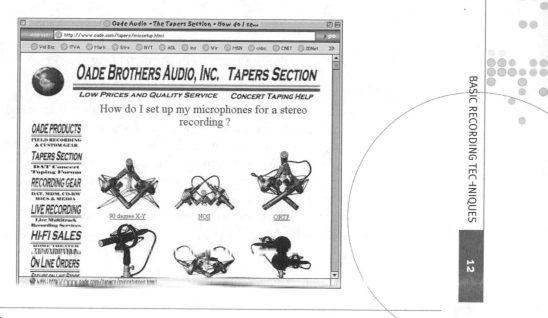

Figure 12.12

Learn more about using microphones by visiting the Oade Audio site.

RECORDING DIRECT

You don't have to use a microphone to record live sound. Many instruments (like your synthesizers) have a direct audio output that can be plugged into your sound card or mixer. Some purists look down on this approach—they feel it lacks the color and authenticity of miking an amp. But recording direct can produce a cleaner sound by bypassing the sometimes distorted components of an amp. Recording direct also eliminates having to worry about other sounds in the room—when you go direct you of course pick up only the instrument itself.

You might want to buy a DI (direct insertion) box—they're not too expensive and can add color to your audio palette. You can find simple DI boxes, or you can pick up a processor/DI combination unit that will color and filter your electric instrument in strange and wonderful ways. Typical DI boxes include settings like "Super Fat Marshall Stack," or "Ultra Clean Chorus."

THE OVERDUB: LET'S ADD STILL ANOTHER TRACK!

Overdubbing is the process of recording additional tracks while listening to the already recorded tracks. Modern live recording is based on the overdub. Without it, music as we know it would not exist. Once the overdub was invented in the '60s, music production became exponentially more sophisticated, allowing musicians to add and tweak—and tweak and tweak—until they reach a degree of perfection that's impossible to reproduce in live performance.

This is one of the reasons that some bands don't sound as good in concert as they do on CD. While recording the CD, they had the luxury of doing take after take, overdubbing each musician's part until it's perfect. But when you play live, it's live—mistakes and all.

To overdub in your desktop studio, you'll need to set up the following:

- A way for the musician to hear the already recorded tracks, called the *monitor mix*. You could use your speakers, unless you're recording with a microphone, in which case the musician must wear headphones to keep the monitor mix away from the microphone. (If you have numerous performers at once, they all need headphones, which means you'll need to buy a *splitter box* to split the headphone signal to many musicians.) As a helpful extra, it's a good idea to send some reverb into the performer's phones, so that her voice doesn't sound so dry.

- The pre-recorded material must be routed to the performer in sync mode, which is called various things in various software packages. The point here is to ensure that the singer's voice and the pre-recorded material are in correct relation, timewise. With analog tape machines, this meant that the record head was used as the play-back head, so that the singer's performance wasn't laid on tape a fraction of a sec-ond late. With software, this mode is sometimes referred to as the input mode, although you'll need to check the manual (oh no!).

- You'll need to start to monitor the pre-recorded and the new material as the singer is laying it down. It helps to keep the old material a little lower volume than you normally would so that you can focus on the singer.

It's at this point that you need to listen as intently as you can. Overdubbing is about per-fection, but perfection that sounds human. The wonderful advantage to overdubbing with a PC is that you can keep doing takes until the singer turns green in the face. You'll need a way to keep track of each one of those takes, making notes as you go as to which take was good for which phrase. Later, when the singer is done, you can spend hours (or days) piecing together each of these takes, attempting to assemble a take which will radically change the future of music as we know it—or at least be on pitch throughout most of the verse and chorus.

Hot Link: Overdubbing Techniques (http://www.record-producer.com/)

Click on this site's Technique link to find a complete tutorial about overdub-bing (see Figure 12.13) .

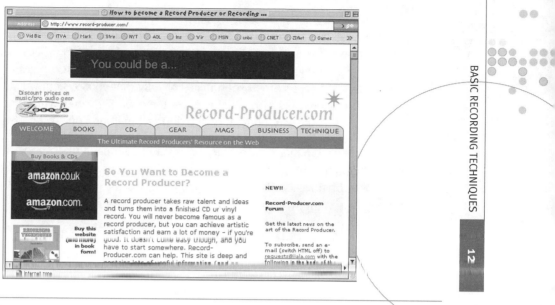

Figure 12.13

Learn more about overdubbing at the Record Producer site.

BUT I'M NOT GETTING ANY SOUND!

Yup, it's frustrating. The singer's there, ready to sing her heart out, but when she starts to sing, you don't hear even the smallest hint of sound coming through the system. Nothing. Nada. Silence. It has happened to every single audio engineer in the history of the world. Don't sweat it; it's a part of life. (Although the musicians do get impatient after a while.) Here are some possible fixes:

- **Check your cables.** Try replacing the cable with one you know—for sure—is working. If there's still no sound, you know it wasn't the cable's fault.

- **It might not be plugged in.** It's hard to look suave after you've been trying to get levels for 10 minutes, only to discover the cable isn't even plugged in (or plugged into the wrong place). Oh yeah, and is the piece of equipment turned on?

- **Take a look at your software.** Is there a little mute button selected? Are you really in input mode? Are the volume faders up at a high enough level?

- **Check out the audio card's preferences.** Somewhere, deep in the preferences, there might be a box checked that guarantees silences at just this moment.

- **Are the speakers actually making sound?** Maybe you wouldn't hear anything right now even if all your PC's software and hardware were aligned with the Seven Planets—because that little knob on your speakers is turned down. Or, in the case of headphones, the little volume knob near the input jack might be down. Try playing a pre-recorded sound cue to verify that your system will actually make sound (you could also use this to set the overall volume, which you may have turned all the way up to 10 when you first realized your system was silent).

When recording a musician or vocalist, it's a good idea (a really good idea) to get things set up before they get there. It helps if there's no one waiting while you figure out why you can't hear anything. It also creates a better mood for the musicians if things are up and running when they walk in—and a good mood means better results.

C H A P T E R **13**

SAMPLING

In This Chapter:

- Learn the theory and terminology of sampling
- Discover where to get samples
- Look at a sampling of samplers
- Learn various sampling techniques

SAMPLING IS WHAT'S HAPPENING NOW

To say that sampling is a hot topic is an understatement. Within the world of music it's close to being a tidal wave, a cult movement, a way of life. It's a method of creating music and it's a style of music itself. It's used in home studios and in big budget facilities, in London and Los Angeles and Dubuque, Iowa. It's been around for many years but each year it keeps getting bigger.

But wait. What is sampling? If you're not a member of the sampling crowd it's easy to be confused about it—there's a terminology tangle in sampling. The term *sample* is used in digital audio to mean more than one thing.

When you're talking about digital audio theory, a *sample* is a tiny snapshot a digital recorder takes of a sound wave. A typical recorder takes 44,100 samples per second; this is referred to as a sample rate of 44.1 kHz.

But when you talk about sampling in music creation, the word *sample* means something else altogether. In this case, a sample is a short digital audio recording, sometimes as short as 2 to 5 seconds, sometimes just a short burst of sound less than a second. These short digital recordings come from several sources. They might be snippets of sound taken from a CD of a major artist. They might come from a CD specifically loaded with musical and other sounds intended to be used as samples; these discs contain everything from helicopter sound effects to drum 'n' bass patterns to someone's granny yelling "let's dance." Or, you might get your samples by recording them yourself, grabbing a mic and capturing a car honk or a guitar riff, then editing it to a tight little 1.8 second sample.

(Confusingly, each of these musical samples has…a sample rate. Your snare drum sample might be at 44.1 kHz sample rate—so the same word means two different things in one sentence. Couldn't they have called samples—the short digital recordings, not the audio theory term—something else?)

Hot Link: SampleNet (`http://www.samplenet.co.uk/`)

The SampleNet site is a great place to visit if you want to build a library of samples (see Figure 13.1).

Figure 13.1

The library of samples available at SampleNet is all free: free of charge and free of copyright concerns. Time to start downloading.

So sampling is a way of making music, but it also can be thought of as a style, or an element of style in several genres. There's a long list of artists who have used sampling as a significant element in their styles; Beck and Chemical Brothers come to mind. These artists have taken a dozen or hundreds of samples, layered them, mixed and matched them, often blending them with live musicians, to create fresh new ear-catching musical sounds. Hip Hop and techno artists are particularly fond of sampling, but at this point musicians from most genres use sampling at least somewhat. A traditional rock 'n' roller might grab the snare sound from a Van Halen album to replace his drummer's snare sound (which creates the need to get permission from the copyright holder).

Probably the most sampled musician of all time is James Brown. More musicians have grabbed little snippets from his records than from any other. An entire generation of rappers has used snare-kick-guitar-sax-vocal samples taken from the Godfather of Soul.

Which illustrates the basis of sampling as an art form. Sampling takes the old and makes it into something new. Some critics say it's a form of creative exhaustion—if sampling musicians were really creative, they would develop something all their own. But then, artists have always built on the past. Beethoven took a musical style he learned from Haydn and pushed it forward. The Rolling Stones took basic American rhythm and blues and gave it a new feel. So the fact that sampling merely reuses already created material is criticism that, to my ears, falls flat. Additionally, many musicians create their own samples. In this case, sampling is about manipulation and creativity, using the technology to create something new from an existing clip.

Hot Link: Tweakheadz (`http://www.tweakheadz.com/samples.html`)
The Tweakheadz site (Figure 13.2) is a great resource for musicians interested in sampling.

Figure 13.2

You'll find a collection of free and for-sale samples at the Tweakheadz site, plus a wealth of info about sample tweaking techniques.

What's unique about sampling is that, when it draws upon earlier music, it actually grabs *the recordings themselves*. Previous generations of musicians listened to what came before and imitated and developed by ear; a sampling musician uses the actual performances of other musicians. This wasn't possible until very recent technology made it so.

Without the dazzling editing and manipulation tools made possible by digital audio technology, sampling couldn't rise to the creative level that it does. So, it's a music making method that is particular to our time period.

Hot Link: Rarefaction (http://www.rarefaction.com/products.html)
Before you call your sample library complete, visit the Rarefaction site (Figure 13.3). There are some wildly creative sounds there.

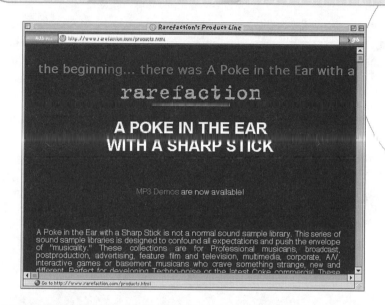

Figure 13.3

When it comes to sampling, these west coast sound designers are inspired artists. Their royalty free sample library, called A Poke In the Ear With A Sharp Stick, is an ear-bending trip through the strange and the different.

How a Sample Is Born

Okay, our creative sampling musician—let's call her Rachel—is working on a rude little track. She's got the drum and bass pattern grooving, and she's written the melody. But she decides she needs some kind of guitar riff, a hot guitar sample, to set up the main hook. Something really memorable to surprise and perk up her listener's ears. Where is she going to get it? She could

- **Get a sample CD.** If she has a few bucks to spend, this is a good way to go. Rachel can buy a CD with a clearly organized library of sounds and choose from among the disc's dozens or hundreds of guitar sounds. Not only are the recordings professionally done, all the riffs are already edited down to easy-to-use samples.

- **Sample from a CD or video.** Rachel has a CD put out by one of her friend's bands, The Flying Turkeys. She really doesn't want to listen to that Flying Turkeys CD, but (after asking permission to use it) she could load in one of the songs to her computer and look for an interesting guitar riff. Because Rachel always layers and manipulates the sounds she samples, it doesn't matter whether the source music is really hokey. She knows there's no way to separate out the various instruments from a mixed song, so she listens for a section where the guitar is "clean"—where the drums and bass stop and the guitar plays all by itself. She cuts a 3.2 second sample from this section.

- **Do It Live.** She's really not a guitar player, but Rachel can strum a single chord. So she hooks a microphone into her sound card and records several different strums. She listens back and picks the best one, editing the most interesting take so it's just the strum itself, exactly 3.2 seconds long in this case. It sounds a little too bright, so she runs it through her software's equalizer to turn up the low end. She then reverses the strum so it plays backward, and then adds a canyon-like echo.

 Hot Link: Kid Nepro (`http://www.kidnepro.com/`)
You'll find new sounds for many synthesizers at the Kid Nepro site (see Figure 13.4).

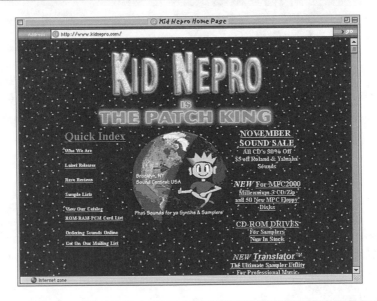

Figure 13.4

This Brooklyn, NY-based retailer sells thousands of sounds for many different models of keyboards.

Tweak and Tweak Some More

At this point, Rachel has a whole bunch of guitar samples. None of them seem perfect by themselves, so she layers them, putting one on each track, aligned on top of each other so several play at one time. This layering creates a sound greater than the sum of its parts. The guitar sample from the sample CD sounds the best, so she uses it as her foundation. The Flying Turkeys sample sounds highly processed, but she processes it even more, adding a flange effect and running it through a DirectX plug-in that gives it a retro sound. The sample she recorded herself sounds out of tune with the others, so she uses a detuning plug-in to raise the pitch—there, that's about right.

Rachel listens to the whole thing together. Hmmm…doesn't sound like a guitar anymore. It sounds sort of like a cross between a cat screech and an alien invader spaceship explosion. But it's got possibilities. She decides to cut up just a small snippet of it, just about a third of a second, and use it as—hey, why not?—a percussion part. It's got a real "pop" to it, and if she layers it in with the snare drum, it might sound really cool. And, she could layer it with three or four snare samples, reverse it, and then…

Sampling and Copyright

When it comes to copyright law, the truth about sampling is straightforward. You cannot sample any copyrighted recorded work and make it commercially available unless you have permission from the copyright holder. You might have heard that you don't need permission for a sample under seven seconds, or if it's just a drum sound, it's okay. Pay that information no attention. If the work is copyrighted, you need permission for commercial use.

Take the group DNA, who did a sample-driven remix of Suzanne Vega's "Tom's Diner." The group put out just 500 copies of it—but it became a major hit, getting heavy radio play in many countries and selling millions. The group got a cease and desist letter from Vega's record company, and lost its royalties. Or consider the case of Richard Ashcroft, singer for the Verve and songwriter of "Bittersweet Symphony," on the charts in '97. He was informed that "Bittersweet Symphony" contains a small string sample that someone else owns the copyright to—and lost all the royalties to this commercially successful music.

Hot Link: Sampleheads (http://www.sampleheads.com/)

The Sampleheads site is a great site for, well, sampleheads (that is, a musician obsessed with sampling—and there are a lot of us). If you're one, stop on by this popular site (Figure 13.5) .

Figure 13.5

Here you'll find retail sample libraries for just about any musical style, including a collection by jazz drummer Peter Erskine.

Incorporating Samples in Your Mix

Once you have your samples, how do you actually put them in your song?

This is where the sampler comes in handy. Samplers are devices specially designed to record, play back, and manipulate small bits of audio. Unlike synthesizers, they don't have any sounds of their own (although some come with accompanying libraries of samples). But they have all manner of pitch shift/phase/flange/weird 'n' strange effects tools to help you change a perfectly normal sound into something that's unrecognizable (many synthesizers have built-in effects too, so the line between samplers and synthesizers gets a little blurry).

Organize Those Samples

Searching for that guitar sample you created two weeks ago, you look into the folder and realize...you have 37 samples, all with the word "guitar" in the title, but which one is the keeper? And you spent four hours tweaking it. This is a great creativity killer, so find a way to organize your samples. Not only will it save you time—and efficiency keeps that creative flow going—but you'll need to assemble your samples into groups to assign them to your MIDI module. Your organizational method depends on how you work, but there are a couple of basic methods. First, you'll invariably create several versions of that vocal sample, so figure out a way to designate your final version; call it "snare-final.wav" or something similar. Second, create subfolders with descriptive names (and even dates) so the drum samples don't get mixed in with the woodwind samples, and vice versa.

But you don't need an actual sampler to sample; you could record small bits of audio onto your PC and manipulate as we just saw Rachel do. Yes, samplers are particularly good at sound manipulation, but samplers are also helpful in playing back samples in response to a MIDI message. The sampler holds the individual samples ready for playback, and when it receives the proper MIDI message (which you assign), it plays back the sound. If you just want to put in an occasional riff sample, you don't need to use a sampler; you could just place the sample visually using your editing software. But if you want to use, for example, a snare sample that repeats through a three-minute song, you certainly don't want to go through and place every snare hit manually. Just put it in your sampler and send it a MIDI Note On message on every backbeat. And your sampler's sound bending tools enable you to change the snare's pitch, or give it more bottom end, or morph it into a completely new sound.

Hot Link: Sound Dogs (http://www.sounddogs.com)

You can find samples from the Sound Dogs site (Figure 13.6) on this book's companion CD.

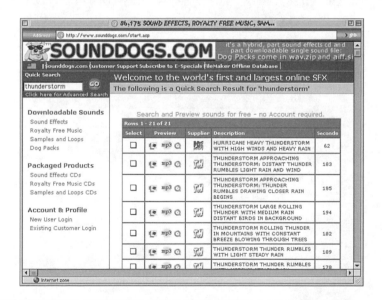

Figure 13.6

An enormous online sound library—you can buy and download individual sounds as you need them.

Hardware Samplers Versus Software Samplers

Like most of today's audio gear, you can get either hardware or software versions of samplers. Both have their advantages and disadvantages.

Not surprisingly, the software versions are significantly cheaper. You can usually buy a software sampler *and* a computer upgrade for less than the cost of a hardware unit. A hardware sampler needs its own hard disk and RAM, and ideally will have a CD-ROM drive. And many hardware samplers have famously tiny displays that make you scroll through multiple screens to edit parameters. However, the hardware units do have some warm fuzzies: They don't put extra stress on your PC's CPU, they spare you the setup headaches associated with virtual samplers (let's see, does this program work with my sound card?), and some units have a lot more output jacks than your sound card. Occasionally it's nice, too, to reach out and twist an actual hardware knob instead of doing all that dragging and clicking. And in terms of cost, have you looked at the used market for hardware samplers?

But on balance, software samplers give you more for less. As computers get ever more powerful, the hardware sampler is going to be a rare beast—you won't need this extra piece of metal and plastic. If you can keep your studio contained in your PC, do so.

Hot Link: Sound Ideas (`http://www.sound-ideas.com`)

If a specific sound effect has ever been recorded, you'll probably find it in the Sound Ideas library. Visit the company's site (Figure 13.7) to find out about its massive selection of sounds.

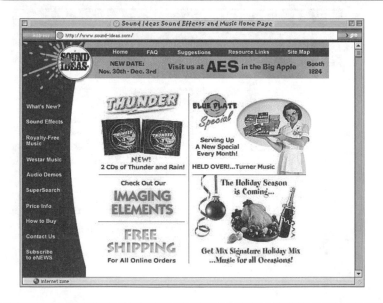

Figure 13.7

Possibly the largest sound effect collection available, the Sound Ideas library includes everything from classic Hanna Barbera cartoon sounds to presidential speeches to movie effects from Lucas Films.

The Many Shades of the Software Sampler

Virtual samplers come in many flavors. Some of them work as plug-ins, some of them are standalone units, and some are available in either configuration. The prices vary just as much. You can spend around $40 or you can spend well over $600. Or, you'll find some that are shareware or even freeware. As you might expect, the plug-in samplers are on the cheaper end. But in this case that doesn't mean you get less—many plug-in samplers are just as good as the standalone programs. The insider's truth about software samplers in general is that you can get a lot without shelling out too much cash.

Hot Link: FXPansion (`http://www.fxpansion.com/`)

The disadvantage of the plug-in samplers is that they only work with the programs they're designed to be plugged into. You're not going to be able to use a Pro Tools plug-in with Cakewalk, and vice versa. Many of the soft-samp plug-ins are VST, but—this is good news—there's software you can get to make VST plug-ins work with DirectX programs. Made by FXPansion, shown in Figure 13.8, it's available in three different levels of capability.

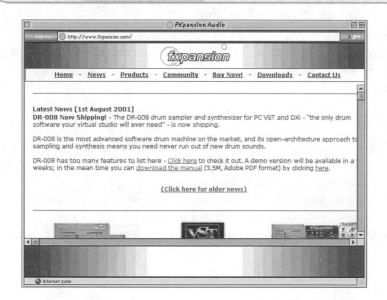

Figure 13.8

The site is worth touring around; the company makes a wide selection of plug-ins and effects software.

JARGON

What Is ADSR?

ADSR stands for *attack*, *decay*, *sustain*, and *release*, the four parameters that shape the *envelope* of a sample—that is, four factors that determine how it sounds. The *attack* setting defines how fast an envelope opens: a fast attack like 10ms (milliseconds) is typical for percussion sounds; an attack time longer than a second or so gives instruments a subtle start like that of a string section. The *decay* setting defines the amount the envelope will decrease after the envelope has opened; you can set the decay to make the attack appear more or less pronounced. *Sustain* defines how long the envelope stays open; if it's set to a length shorter than the sample itself it will cut off the sample's end. *Release* defines how long the envelope takes to fade out after the sustain period has passed: If it's set to a longer value, it creates a natural fade; an extremely short release time stops a sound abruptly, which is useful for isolating one sound from the sound that immediately follows it. You may also see the acronym *EG (envelope generator)* used in conjunction with ADSR. An EG is the device used to shape the ADSR settings.

A Sampling of Software Samplers

Desktop musicians get excited about software samplers because they can be wildly creative tools. With their ability to twist and expand and shape audio, making music clips sound like nothing most normal people have ever heard, they are a sound designer's most colorful palette.

With time, it's likely that the functions of soft-samps will be incorporated into the main record/edit programs. The upper level programs, like Cool Edit Pro or Cubase, already have a mega-toolbox of sound design tools built in to them. Looking to the future of audio software, it's probable that even the most basic off-the-shelf programs will have the sound design capabilities that you'll find in today's soft-samps. What separates the soft-samps from the built-in tools of a main record/edit program is level of sound design sophistication. The tools in, for example, Cool Edit Pro will get you cruising at 5000 feet, but the shape-blend-mix tools in a good soft-samps explore the audio equivalent of deep space.

Hot Link: BitHeadz (http://www.bitheadz.com)

Stop by the Bitheadz site (Figure 13.9) to explore the company's high quality software synthesizers.

Figure 13.9

This company makes the highly respected Unity DS-1, a killer soft-samp.

Reaktor (Windows or Mac)

Native Instrument is a big company in audio software, and Reaktor is one of its flagship offerings. If you love tweaking audio, you've got to be careful with Reaktor—with as many choices as it offers, they may find you days later, trying to add just one more morph effect to that 16-track layered sound cue you've been working on.

Reaktor provides you with hundreds of pre-set ways to manipulate sound—a good idea, since booting up the software and looking at its many faders and knobs might be daunting for some. So you can pick from its pre-sets that have been optimized for loops and drum samples or whatever, or you can just start twiddling on your own.

Reaktor is a multitimbral sound design tool, meaning it enables you to play back multiple instrument sounds—patches—at one time. So you can layer 15 sample Instruments (its terms for a sound manipulation scheme) at one time, or 7 if you're in stereo mode. The software enables you to set a different MIDI receive channel for each Instrument, and if you have that many physical outputs, Reaktor will play that many of its freaky patches at one time.

JARGON

What's a LFO?

An *LFO*, low frequency oscillator, is a device that outputs a control signal you can use to change the character of a sound. Most all samplers have LFOs built in. LFOs can modulate volume and pitch to create a variety of effects, including vibrato, tremolo, and wow. You can vary the LFO setting while listening to how it colors the sample, experimenting with various settings until you like what you hear.

And the Reaktor sounds do get freaky. It offers seemingly endless choices for morphing and waveshaping, pitch shifting and time stretching, filtering and vocoding. The software does a complex spectral analysis of your audio, meaning it studies the amplitude and relative phase of various frequencies across the full spectrum of the signal. This enables the software to break a sound cue down into a dazzling array of variables, allowing it complete control of playback rate, pitch, and other sound-changing specifications.

Hot Link: SampleCell (http://www.digidesign.com)

SampleCell, a popular virtual sampler for Mac and PC, was first introduced more than 10 years ago. Soft SampleCell 3.0 no longer needs the dedicated hardware of earlier versions. It now uses your computer's CPU. Check it out at the Digidesign site (see Figure 13.10).

Figure 13.10

SampleCell has been a popular tool among desktop musicians for many years.

The Native Instruments company has come up with a cool way to facilitate sharing among Reaktor users. On its Web site it has posted dozens and dozens of user-created patches. You can download another musician's setting, put in your own audio, and you get the benefit of hours of work by another creative sound designer.

What Is Multisampling?

If you sample a guitarist playing middle C, and then pitch that note up an octave, it will not sound like the guitarist playing an octave higher—it will sound like middle C pitched up an octave. To truly re-create the guitarist's sound an octave above middle C, you must sample her playing that actual note. This process of sampling an instrument across the complete register is called multisampling. As you might guess, it's extremely time consuming. When you buy a commercially produced sample CD, all this work is done for you.

GigaStudio (Windows)

You can get this leading software sampler in three different configurations: the no expense-spared GigaStudio 160, which is capable of 160-note polyphony (remember, *polyphony* is how many notes will play at one time); GigaStudio 96, with 96-note polyphony, or the much cheaper GigaSampler.

The good thing about GigaStudio is that umpteen sample libraries have been designed for it. If you want symphonic sounds, pick up one of the many CDs chock full of orchestral samples. It's just as easy to get a library of classic rock, indigenous instruments, or Star Treky-strange stuff. In effect, once you have the software installed and a shelf of sample CDs, you have the audio world at your fingertips. Just load and play.

You can take these sounds and run them through GigaStudio's filters to change amplitude and pitch, filtering and layering the sounds with the program's straightforward interface. Although it has a full complement of sound design tools to contour audio, it doesn't have quite the depth of, say, Reaktor. But it's easily used by less experienced users, and has a sound library large enough for professional use.

> **Hot Link: Virtual Sampler (http://www.virtualsampler.de)**
>
> Made by Speedsoft, Virtual Sampler is available as either a DirectX or VST instrument, and is one of the least expensive highly capable soft-samps (see Figure 13.11). It's capable of 64-note polyphony and 16 discrete outputs. Windows only.

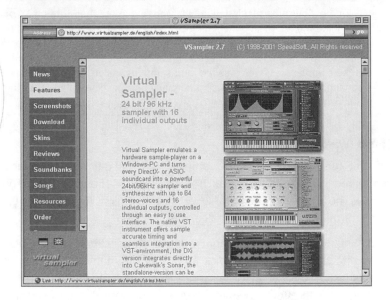

Figure 13.11

Speedsoft's Virtual Sampler is a multi-faceted software sampler.

Stella 9000 (Mac)

This soft-samp is part of a larger group of Mac software, the Kobolo Studio9000, which contains three virtual synths and a software drum machine. If you had the whole group you'd have a serious software orchestral at your disposal.

The Stella9000 is available as either a VST plug-in or a standalone program. Its user interface puts everything in one window—something to be thankful for when you're deep in a sound design session and don't want to scroll around to change parameters.

The 9000 is 8-note polyphonic, which is nothing to write home about, but its filter section is deep. You can blend the output of a mind-boggling array of parameters in lowpass, bandpass, and highpass filters. For example, one of the 9000's menus offers a 2-pole, 4-pole, and an 8-pole, a notch filter (which lets you specify a very narrow frequency) with two 4-pole filters. This, in combination with the 9000's other ADSR manipulation tools, guarantees that the sounds coming out of it sound nothing like the sounds going in.

Hot Link: Steinber's Halion (http://www.steinberg.net/)

Near the top of the user interface is a graphic display of envelope parameters (see Figure 13.12). This enables you to intuitively change a sample's attack, decay, sustain, and release. A little lower on the interface, you can decide which frequencies to enter for the various filter settings. By using the keyboard, you can hear what that sample sounds like at a different pitch. Note that many of the parameters have a bypass option; this enables you to quickly turn a filter on and off, so you can hear if you like the sample better with your settings or without.

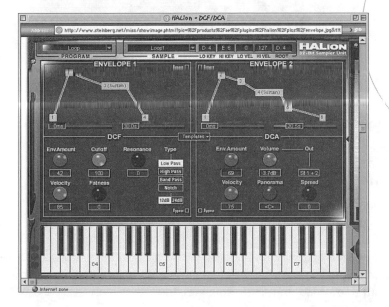

Figure 13.12

The Halion soft-samp's graphic user interface enables you to intuitively change its parameters. Made by Steinberg, it's available for Mac and Windows.

The Hardware Sampler

When it comes to hardware samplers, three big names are Akai, E-Mu, and Kurzweil. The Akai S6000, for example, gives you all the sampling firepower you need: It has a full range of filters, LFOs, and envelope contouring tools, and most conveniently, it provides you with 16 analog outputs. This means you won't have to worry about outputting all of your samples through your soundcard's limited outputs, as you do with a software sampler. And this Akai is 32-channel multitimbral, 64-voice polyphonic output, so you could build your entire song with its output—many have done so.

In response to those who say that samplers' visual displays are too small, Akai has built this model with a large removable front control panel, so you don't have to squint at a 5″ screen (see Figure 13.13). This unit has been advertised for $2500.

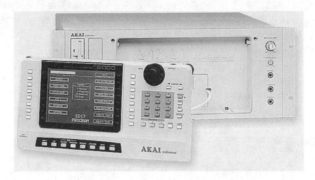

Figure 13.13

The Akai S6000 has a large monitor to facilitate sample editing and manipulation.

Photo courtesy of Akai.

SAMPLING TIPS AND TECHNIQUES

Okay, you have your samples, you have your sampler, you're ready to dive in. You have a fresh little snippet of audio all ready to be manipulated, but where do you start? The answer, really, is that there is no answer; the only limit is your own imagination, and the number of filters and effects your sampler offers. Get in there and play. Even veteran tweak heads often don't know what they're about to do before they do it. However, you might start with a few tried and true techniques, tricks that most everyone who's worked with samples has tried. You could:

- **Cut it down to size.** It sounds obvious, but it's the first step: Cut the audio immediately before and after the sound you want. This is actually a really important step. You're deciding precisely how much of that violin riff you want—do you want all of that note, or just part? What part?

- **Normalize.** This lifts the amplitude of the sound to its maximum level before distortion—in effect it makes the sound its loudest and most present. But be careful. If you're going to increase the sample's high or low end at a later point, you may want to lift the sound's amplitude only 90 percent or so; if you're all the way to the limit and you increase the high end, the high end will distort.

- **Loop.** It almost goes without saying that you'll loop your sample. But how? Do you want to do a straight loop, simply repeating, or do you want the tail end of the sample to overlap with the front as it repeats? Or perhaps some variation of the two.

- **Distort.** We just recommended watching out for distortion, but forget it. Who are we anyway? The sample sounds too clean, it needs some grunge, some edge. Look for the distortion button and crank it up.

- **Play it backward.** This one is far from original. It's been done so often, and it's often the first thing people go for. But it still sounds cool. The classic use of a backwards sample is to begin something; at its most cliched use, a backward cymbal with reverb is used to start a phrase.

- **Layer it, and then layer it some more.** Again, this sampling technique has been used untold times, but it remains one of the best methods for creating interesting audio. You never know what something will sound like when it's layered with something else, or with a changed version of itself. Try layering a sound with a reversed version of itself, or shift the copy back various amounts of time in relation to the original. And try fiddling with the relative volume: Which layer should be louder, and by how much?

- **Run it through a frequency filter.** Cut off all the bottom end, or make it sound mid-rangey and telephonic, or give it a dark sound by filtering out all the highs.

- **Time compression or expansion.** A sampling classic. You can stretch a sample by about 15 to 20 percent before it begins to take on a new identity.

- **Pitch shift.** You can move a sound up or down into a new register, and then combine it with the original. You could build a complex chord this way, or just make the music sound strange.

- **Add an effect.** It's with effects you go off the deep end: tremolos, delays, chorus flanging, several effects in combination with each other.

And remember when you experiment: No one has ever worked with this exact sample with exactly the same set of sound design tools, intended for the piece of music you're working on. It's yours—there is no right or wrong answer except what sounds good to your ears.

CHAPTER 14

DJ NATION: GETTING STARTED AS A TURNTABLIST

In This Chapter

- Learn about the history of the DJ
- Find out how desktop audio has merged with the turntable
- Discover the equipment you need to get started as a DJ
- Explore fundamental turntable techniques

LONG AGO, IN A GALAXY FAR AWAY

Take a trip back in time, all the way back to 1970, to a nightclub in New York City called the Sanctuary. The crowd there approached dancing with a spiritual fervor, and they wanted the music to be one seamless non-stop groove that kept going all night long.

The man driving the crowd to its heights of dance ecstasy was Francis Grasso, one of the earliest and most influential DJs. Not that he was the first to spin records at a social occasion—that had been done at innumerable high school sock hops. And the practice of playing records in clubs went all the way back to France during WWII, when the Nazis banned live music in nightclubs. The French, themselves gripped by the need to keep dancing, invented the disc spinning nightclub, hence the term *discothèque*.

But Grasso did more than spin records. Spurred on by the nightly Sanctuary crowd—responding to the crowd like a jazz improviser—he created a fluid musical line from the likes of James Brown, Isaac Hayes, Motown, soul, and R&B, filling it out with Latin and African grooves. Grasso played the turntables as musicians play their instruments. He developed a technique he called "slip-cueing," in which he placed a felt pad between the vinyl and the turntable, allowing him to keep the disc stationary over a revolving turntable. He had a gift for choosing just the right moment to let go, starting a musical phrase so it meshed with the one playing on his second turntable.

Hot Link: DJ Magazine (`http://www.djmag.com`)

DJ magazine covers the spinning scene from LP reviews to club schedules (see Figure 14.1). It encourages readers to vote for turntablists to include in its list of Top 100 DJs.

Figure 14.1

DJ magazine enables readers to for vote for their favorite DJ.

Grasso and the other DJs in the nascent disco scene further developed the concept of DJ as musician through the early '70s. They used the pitch controls in turntables to shape musical phrases, allowing them to meld two disparate beats. The mixing of the music, the way one track was melded and combined with another, became its own form of music composition.

For many large clubs, both in Manhattan and across the country, replacing the live band with a DJ made economic sense. As the crowds got ever larger, the record labels began to understand the potential of catering to this audience. By the mid '70s, new releases geared for these dance clubs—in a style called disco—were hitting mainstream radio stations. Disco built to a frenzy with the 1977 box office hit *Saturday Night Fever*, before it collapsed under its own over-inflated weight a couple of years later.

But turntablism wouldn't die with it. Outside of Manhattan, several economic strata lower in the Bronx, a twin form of the art had been developing throughout the '70s. One of its earliest practitioners was the legendary Joseph Saddler, otherwise known as Grandmaster Flash. Flash was a wickedly skilled platter artist, existing somewhere between musician and performance artist. He finessed his cross fades so smoothly that it seemed the music was composed as one piece. He was expert at quickly rotating a record by hand so that a single word or phrase would repeat. He could twist it back silently or—in one of turntablism's major moves—forward, so that the audience heard a scratching sound. Although he's not the official inventor of scratching (that honor goes to Grand Wizard Theodore) he took it to a new level, whipping the vinyl back and forth in the tight little patterns that defined early hip hop.

He was an early beatbox practitioner. Some of the hot New York dance clubs hired a live drummer to play along with the DJ. Flash's variation on this was to use a drum machine, filled with a bank of rhythmic fills, which he used to segue between music cuts. And he would dance along with the beats, turning away from the turntable, spinning with hands behind his back, even using his head or feet to play the turntable.

It was Flash and other Bronx-based DJs who started the practice of vocally pattering over the beat, creating spontaneous free verse with a syncopated rhyme scheme—the foundation of rap. (Just as disco was dying, the first rap hits, like "Rapper's Delight," were released.)

Grandmaster Flash's early '80s release, "The Adventures of Grandmaster Flash on the Wheels of Steel," was a proclamation that something new was happening. It was a recording made by a musician playing...a turntable. Recording in real time—no edits, no overdubs—he put all the early DJ techniques into one seven-minute document. It was a hip-shaking collage that included music by the Sugar Hill Gang, Queen, and Blondie, as well as a Flash Gordon radio play. It turned the whole notion of the forward movement of music on its head. It wasn't a new style of chords and melody, it wasn't a new beat, it wasn't even just a new instrument—it was a radical rethinking of what it meant to make music. And you could dance to it.

The DJ was born.

Hot Link: DMC World (`http://www.dmcworld.com/`)

Stop by the DMC World site (see Figure 14.2) to spin your own online club date.

Figure 14.2

DMC's mission is no less than a complete overview of the DJ universe. The site offers an online mixing set up that allows you to spin a virtual club session.

What Exactly Is a Remix?

Originally, the term *remix* meant something straightforward: The first mix wasn't too good (maybe the guitar's too loud), so let's do it again. By the early '80s, a remix meant a club version. Producers used the master tapes of current hits to create dance club versions that were longer and usually more drum-driven. By the early '90s, with the advent of samplers and digital recording, anyone could create a remix of a hit—no access to the original masters was needed (although permission is still required for commercial release). Today's remixes often use completely re-composed rhythm tracks, and take creative liberties with the basic song. A snippet of the lead vocal might float by, followed by a variation on the instrumental solo at a different tempo. Because these remixes are usually longer and have a heavy beat, they are well-suited for the dance club.

THE DJ AND THE DESKTOP

Fast forward to today, some 20 or so years after Grandmaster Flash's seminal "Wheels of Steel" release. Because that was two decades ago, and we know that nothing in pop culture lasts 20 years, the DJ must be a thing of the past, right?

Wrong. Not only is DJing still with us, it's bigger than a crate full of 4,000 records—and keeps getting bigger. In hundreds of cities across the U.S. and throughout Europe, you'll find DJ-driven clubs. You'll see spinners on the front cover of magazines (*Time* asked if turntables are the musical instrument of the future) and you'll see magazines dedicated to DJing. The platter-spinning culture is referenced in TV and print ads. The National Academy of Recording Arts and Sciences now awards a Grammy for Best Remix.

After going through many permutations, through acid house and drum 'n' bass, from Euro pop and NY disco, jungle, hard rock, and techno, gaining adherents from the rave movement to mainstream dance clubs in suburban malls, turntablism has emerged as a genuine art form. It is, arguably, the musical activity that most accurately reflects modern life, in that it takes fractured snippets from so many different places and combines them into one (hopefully coherent) whole.

But what, you might ask, does turntablism have to do with desktop recording? Think back to Grandmaster Flash's drum machine—a forerunner of today's desktop musical instrument. As turntablism has grown stylistically, it has grown more sophisticated technically. Today's DJ craft now not only overlaps with desktop audio technology, it has merged with it.

Hot Link: Global Groove Records (`http://www.globalgroove.co.uk`)

Shopping for music to add to your DJ collection? The Global Groove site (see Figure 14.3) caters to both U.S. and European customers.

Figure 14.3

Based in England, Global Groove has an extensive selection of dance club vinyl. The site has a server in both the U.S. and Europe to accommodate customers on both continents.

Of course, the DJ's art has always been a marriage of music and technology. From the turntable itself to the mixer to the very idea of using prerecorded tracks, the music that DJs make is all about the technology they use. Look at the modern DJ's setup: turntable, mixer, synthesizer, sampler—almost the same arsenal as a desktop sound designer. And if you look at the setup of the most forward-looking spinners, you'll see the final merging of these two disciplines: a PC with audio software.

Now that it's happening, this merging makes perfect sense. Both the DJ and the desktop musician use prerecorded material to a greater or lesser extent. Desktop composers' works are often layered with samples from prerecorded works; the DJ's set is built on existing vinyl. Both setups offer a lot of music-making capability for a limited budget, and both tend to be compact and portable. Although musical training enhances both skills, neither requires it. And both sets of gear are a natural fit in the other's world. A DJ can use a PC to great advantage in a live show, and often uses one to create a remix; a desktop composer can use a turntable as a musical source, in combination with live musicians, MIDI, or samples.

The technology itself is beginning to merge with products like Final Scratch, which allows a DJ to run a set from a PC (more on that in a moment), and devices like Pioneer's CDJ-1000, which enables a disc spinner to scratch while staying the digital domain.

Hot Link: The Pioneer CDJ-1000/The Beatnik Mixman DM2 Digital Music Mixer (`http://pioneerproDj.com/prodj/turntables.htm`)

In this digital age, it's amazing that vinyl records are still used for anything—and they probably won't be too much longer. Technology such as Pioneer's CDJ-1000 (see Figure 14.4) enables you to DJ using CDs instead of records. While you're exploring new DJ technology, take a look at the Mixman DM2 Digital Music Mixer, made by Beatnik (`http://www.mixman.com`). The DM2's hardware controller enables you to manipulate digital audio files as if you were using a DJ rig—definitely the wave of the future.

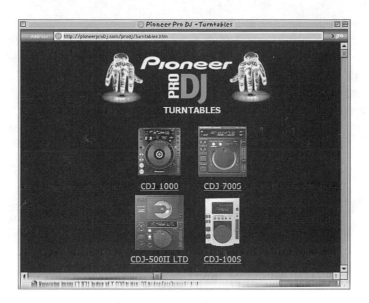

Figure 14.4

Made by Pioneer, the CDJ-1000 allows you to DJ with CDs instead of with vinyl albums.

Turntablism and the U.K.

When it comes to DJing, the U.K is a major hotbed of activity. The Brits are devoted to the dance club, and London is where some of the world's most cutting-edge DJs practice their craft.

The Gear You'll Need

Like building a desktop audio, you can spend a lot or not that much in gathering a DJ rig (translated: check out used DJ gear). Often a club will have its own turntables; you simply bring your own vinyl, headphones, and perhaps a fresh record needle. But the real spinners, of course, have their own equipment. Here's the run down:

- **Turntables.** The Technics 1200 series turntable is the instrument of choice, but there are other choices, notably Pioneer and Vestax. Naturally you'll need a turntable with variable speed—you want to vary the speed of music as you're crossfading between tracks. It's a standard DJ trick to modify the deck so that it offers a greater varispeed range than it had off the shelf.

The critical part of your turntable is the cartridge, which is the mechanism at the end of the tone arm that holds the needle, otherwise known as the *stylus*. Many DJs bring their own cartridges to a job (if not their entire rig). The big names in cartridges are Shure, Ortofon, and Stanton, but there are plenty of contenders. Each manufacturer offers a blizzard of choices. Shure, for example, makes different types based on various DJ styles—categories include Club/Rave, Dance, and Turntablist Expression; the difference is in the amount of use and abuse it's able to take, among other things. And don't forget to pick up a slipmat, which allows the record to spin as your finger holds it in place. In a pinch, a record's inner sleeve works fine; just cut out a small hole and keep spinning.

- **Mixer.** This doesn't have to be a fancy mixing desk; something small will do. Just be sure it has an input channel for everything you want to run into it. Maybe that's just a couple of turntables, but you also might have a sampler or a CD player. Realize that the little Mackie you bought to record your band is not perfect for DJ work. A turntable mixer needs a special crossfader that allows you to blend the music from both decks. If you're going all out, look for a mixer with EQ settings, which help you vary the high and low frequencies of your mixes.

Hot Link: Gemini (`http://www.geminidj.com`)

Although most clubs have their own sound system, if you're looking for your own amplification, Gemini's plug-and-play amp-speaker system makes life simple (see Figure 14.5).

Figure 14.5

Gemini makes the full DJ rig.

- **Headphones.** Phones enable you to hear the incoming song while the current one is playing over the speakers. You need to get the vinyl cued to exactly the right point so you can drop it into the play on the perfect beat. It's important to get a pair you're comfortable with—you're going to spend hours in them. (However, be aware that not all turntablists use headphones—this is a choice that depends on your individual approach.)

- **CD player.** A lot of DJs use a CD player to play back special collections of loops they've edited, or maybe some wild samples. You definitely want one with variable speed.

- **Drum machine.** When you're equipped with a beatbox, you're ready to create true pandemonium. Maybe you'd like to drop tom tom loops over a long crossfade, or mute the turntables altogether for a short percussion jam.

- **Effects processor.** A multi-effects unit like those made by Lexicon or Roland allows you to add reverb or delay to any element in your mix.

- **An effects pedal.** Your hands are busy—really busy. But what are your feet doing? The really swift DJs are jazzing up the mix with an effects pedal.

- **A mic.** The best DJ's read the crowd, picking up the mood and playing with it—talking to the crowd is an important part of the performance art. Besides, when you do your own bongo solo (you do play bongos, don't you?) you want the crowd to hear it. A classic like the Shure SM58 will do the job cheaply.

- **Sampler.** One particularly slick trick is to create samples from the songs you'll be playing, triggering playback from your sampler at inspired moments in your set.

Hot Link: Vestax (http://www.vestax.com/)

A big name in the DJ world, Vestax makes everything needed to be a working DJ. Their site (see Figure 14.6) is a complete turntablist's catalog.

- **A crate (or several) of vinyl.** It's pretty strange that this art form that's so popular in the digital age uses...vinyl record albums—an analog medium if ever there was one. Who would have thought that these black lacquered plates would be so hot in the 21st century? Yet it's not uncommon for a working DJ to have a couple thousand or more. The secret here is to have a collection that spans many worlds. Even if your favorite music is techno, to be hot you need everything from the Bee Gees to the world beat percussion stylings of Babatunde Olatunji. And don't ever show up without a copy of the Village People's "YMCA." At the square clubs, it's still thought of as a fun dance tune; at the hip clubs, it's so incredibly passé it has ironic appeal. Plenty of tunes fall into this category—you need to have them in your collection.

Figure 14.6

Vestax makes everything from turntables to DJ mixers, and also hosts the Turntable Extravaganza, a worldwide DJ competition.

- **Laptop.** Having a PC still puts you ahead of the curve, but we'll soon get to the point where it's de rigueur. Take, for example, Richie Hawtin, a.k.a. Plastikman, one of today's premier turntablists. In his live performances Hawtin uses a laptop running Final Scratch software (www.finalscratch.com). Hawtin has transferred more than 1,000 songs onto his computer—the vinyl sits safely at home when he's out in the club (no more lugging all those crates around). With Final Scratch and a vinyl record that's been specially cut, he can play any of his computer files using his turntable. If he speeds up the turntable, the song playing off the computer's hard drive speeds up; if he starts to scratch with the turntable, the song plays back in corresponding scratch patterns.

What this means is that the DJ's art can ascend still higher, aided by the creative opportunities offered by the PC. Imagine being able to automate aspects of your club mix while you continue to mix and scratch on top. And eventually, of course, that PC will be connected to the Internet, which would offer any DJ with the bandwidth (and permission) access to any cut that's been digitized.

Hot Link: Richie Hawtin (Plastikman) Tour Calendar (http://m-nus.com/calendar/)

Could you keep up with a typical month for superstar DJ Richie Hawtin? It starts in Madison (that's in Wisconsin), goes to Denver, San Antonio, Calgary (that's in Canada), New York, Birmingham (that's in England), Malta (that's in the Mediterranean), Amsterdam, Istanbul (that's in Turkey—Turkey?), Frankfurt, Dublin, San Francisco, Los Angeles, back to England, and ends in Paris. Does he get jet lagged?

techtv
tip

Tone Arm Weight

Finding the perfect tone arm weight is a topic that DJs obsess about. Different mixing techniques require more or less tone arm weight to keep the needle steady through vinyl acrobatics. You can adjust the weight using the adjustable wheel on the tone arm: the higher the arm, the more weight. You also can adjust how far forward the cartridge sits on the tone arm: the further forward, the greater the weight. If that's not enough, some DJs tape a coin or two to the tone arm for more weight. However, the greater the weight, the greater the wear on your vinyl, so it's a real balancing act.

An Important (Groove) Technique

There are as many ways to be a DJ as there are to be any kind of instrumentalist. Some spinners create an ambient groove, closer to creative sound design than a foot-tapping dance groove. And if you've ever been to a big rave party, you may have seen a "chill out" room, where the DJ lays down a laid-back groove for those who want a break from dancing. There are even a lot of different approaches among dance club DJs—the suburban dance club spinner puts out a different groove than the urban club turntablist. But one skill that's central to the DJ's art—though it's not used all the time—is keeping the music on the beat from song to song. It's sort of like learning to draw for a painter. Your paintings might be very abstract, yet the basic skill of knowing how to draw realistically is great foundation. So let's look at keeping a consistent beat going.

Modern popular music tends to be four beats to the measure. You can feel it by tapping your foot in time with the music. Four foot taps is one measure. These four-beat measures are themselves grouped into 4, 8, or 16 measure patterns. When crossfading from one song to the next, skilled DJs listen for these 4, 8, or 16 bar divisions—the real pros just feel it. As one 8-bar groove pattern is ending, that's exactly the right moment to bring in the start of the next 8 or 16 bar pattern from the incoming song.

This is important because, if people are shaking their groove thing to what you're doing, you want the songs to segue in a rhythmically coherent way. If you fade out the outgoing song 5 measures into a 8-bar phrase, and fade in the incoming song 3 measures into a 16-bar phrase, it won't feel right to the dancers. It will force them to move in awkward ways.

But it's harder than it sounds. Let's go through the steps:

- **Find the new cut's entrance.** While a song is playing in your left turntable, locate the beginning of the next 8-bar phrase in the vinyl on your right deck. Don't use the start of the song, but someplace interesting in the middle. The section you choose must mesh with what will be playing on your left deck a minute or so downstream. Use your headphones with the mixer's PFL (pre-fader listen) button depressed so the audience doesn't hear your cueing efforts.

Hot Link: Fabric (`http://www.fabric-london.com/`)

Okay, so you live in Iowa but you want to hear what's cool in London. Stop by the Fabric site (see Figure 14.7) to listen to current DJ favorites.

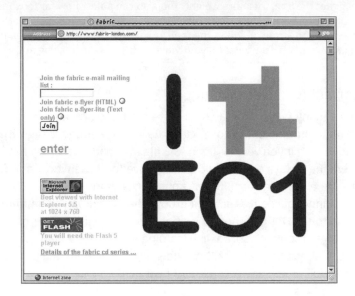

Figure 14.7

This London dance club has a mock tape deck at the bottom of its site; click Play and hear what the DJs are spinning these days.

- **Position for playback.** On your right deck, rotate the record counterclockwise one complete revolution back from the new phrase's start. (Your slipmat lets you do this while the turntable is spinning.) Make sure you undo the PFL button. When you're ready to start the new phrase, don't simply let go. The record will take too long to get to speed. Instead, give the vinyl a subtle push—but not too much; that will disrupt speed too.

- **Play the crossfader.** With your right hand ready to play the right deck, your left hand is on the mixer's crossfader. At just the right moment, you pull the crossfader over to the right, giving the incoming record a subtle wrist flick to put it in play. At this moment you hope for the best. If the club gods are smiling on you, one song moves perfectly into the next.

Have you done all that? Remember, a DJ might spin a long set, so that means maintaining an unbroken rhythm non-stop for hours—considerable concentration is required. And you do so while people are asking you to play that remix, you know, the one from a few years back that Trent Reznor did with, oh, whoever it was…

Volume Levels

It's standard DJ procedure to start at less than maximum volume level. When the club is empty at 10 p.m., approximately 75 percent of volume is appropriate. Gradually push it up to full volume over the course of a couple of hours as the space fills with bags of water (bodies) .

Techniques of the Rich and Famous

For DJs who work all over the world, commanding a five-figure salary for one evening's work, keeping a perfect and compelling rhythmic groove going is something they do in their sleep. On top of this foundation they do all sorts of rhythmic theatrics, like laying in weird samples at the right moment, two-turntable scratching, or using varispeed to create ear-catching effects. In short, creating a complete remix on the fly.

Pulling together this kind of show takes night after night of practice. It requires you to not only mix and match many techniques, but to create your own techniques, to develop a method of blending and bending music that is distinctly yours. As you're creating your own style, you'll need to know the following techniques:

- **The Two-Song Mix.** This is basic to the DJ's art. Although you need to move seamlessly from one cut to the next, you'll sometimes want to let one track float over another for an extended period. But really using this to artful advantage entails much more than a slow crossfade. Are the two records in tune with each other? If not, it might require varispeed (and a musician's ears) to get them in tune. The real artistry of the two-song mix, which might last anywhere from eight bars to a few minutes, is in choice of songs. You want to choose two songs that work aesthetically and technically with one another. Laying one bass line over another is tough, and laying one vocal over another is close to impossible. This means knowing your collection, song by song, really well.

Hot Link: Miss Moneypenny's (http://www.moneypennys.com/)

What are you waiting for? This weekly English dance party is looking for DJs to spin (see Figure 14.8). According to its ad, "The DJs are carefully selected for their musical selection and technical abilities, not for any perceived celebrity status."

Figure 14.8

If you're looking for a European DJ gig, check out Miss Moneypenny's.

- **EQ manipulation.** A standard DJ trick is to turn down all the bass on a track (in the 75 to 350Hz range) before it comes in, and then ease the bass back in so it regains its bottom end power over several measures. EQ is also used to create variety on a repetitive section; for example, turning down the mid and high range so a track is just a low end boom for several phrases, then suddenly restoring these higher frequencies so the track "comes back to life."

- **Transform.** Many mixers have a line/phono switch on each channel, enabling you to switch between your turntable (phono) and a CD or other line level input device (line). If there's nothing coming in line level, switching between the line and phono setting turns that deck's music off and on. You can use this to rapidly cut in and out of a track that you're laying over a foundation track. The goal is to use syncopation to create an interesting hip-shaking effect.

- **Two copies.** Having duplicate copies of the same album allows you to create all sorts of effects. For example, synchronize their beats and then gradually vary the speed of one of them to create a weird phasing effect. Or play one exactly a half beat behind the other. Place the crossfader so that you hear both, then move the volume of one up and down, which adds a rapidly varying delay effect.

- **Fills.** Find a percussion-only section of one song, and lay a melodic or vocal fill over it from another song, or from your sampler. This can be a very musical effect, and can also create some pretty funny mixes. (Try voice samples of any U.S. president over a hip hop rhythm bed.)

- **And of course: Scratching.** Running an album back and forth under a record needle creates that "wacka-wacka" sound famously known as scratching. This technique is more critical to a DJ who's spinning hip hop than techno music. With hip hop's more pronounced sense of syncopation, many DJs use the scratching technique to introduce a new song rather than trying to layer one cut over another. They are "dropping beats" in rather than mixing beats. Good scratching takes considerable manual dexterity—and a really musical feel—because you're scratching back and forth over a single beat or phrase; you don't want to move an inch or two extra, because it starts to sound sloppy. And you need to stay exactly in time with the beat to keep your groove driving.

Hot Link: Turntablism (http://www.turntablism.com/)

The Turntablism site (see Figure 14.9) is an online gathering spot for spinners of all sorts.

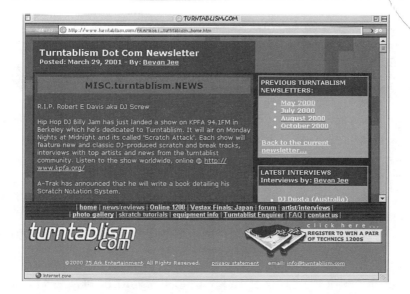

Figure 14.9

Turntabalism.com offers tutorials on technical skills such as scratching, as well as Forum for aspiring and working DJs to share ideas.

The Art of Programming

Under all the flashy techniques—scratching, EQ adjustment, exotic samples—is the DJ's most persuasive tool: the music itself. The music is what moves the audience the most. And for many DJs with modest technical skills, playing the right music in the right way is how they become major crowd pleasers.

Indeed, for some DJs, creating the playlist, choosing and ordering the songs, takes on an almost spiritual dimension. When they decide to move from Donna Summers to Lords of Acid to Li'l Louis, that's their way of making a musical and artistic statement. If you can make your statement in a way that keeps the audience shaking their booty all night long, they'll think of you as a good DJ.

First, be aware of an underlying technical concern: tempo, or beats per minute (bpm). Laid back music like reggae saunters along at 80 bpm; hard groovin' house music thumps along at 140 bpm. Many DJs slowly ramp up the energy level using accelerating bpm rates. They move up in steps, playing cuts in the 85 bpm range when the club opens around 10 p.m., accelerating in gradual waves until somewhere around 2 a.m. they're spinning an intense 140 house groove. (You also need to be aware of your music's bpm range if you want to lay drum loops over it.)

Ideally, your set will have an "arc," an organizing theme that moves and builds through many songs. Maybe your theme is love, and you play a series of songs with darker and darker approaches to this universal human emotion—or vice versa. Conversely, it's dramatic to suddenly interrupt your arc and play a surprising cut, something that's completely out of context. Use peaks and troughs to create excitement.

You want to strike a balance between entertainment and education. The old favorites are really entertaining, and will get even a too-cool crowd up and moving. But if that's all your playing, you might as well go spin in the suburban mall (which is actually not a bad job). To rise above that level, you need to mix in some lesser known—but cool—stuff with the chart toppers.

The only absolute rule is respond to the audience. This is the central tenet of a DJ's craft. It's all about flexibility and sensing the room's energy. The music is prerecorded but your performance is not—otherwise the management might as well buy a five-CD changer and push Random Play. Even the crowds at the same club will vary from night to night. Keep your feelers out. If the crowd is hipper than thou, play some vintage Skinny Puppy. If you sense they just want to dance, break down and play those Top 40 dance numbers in your crate. Develop an intuitive feel for the mood level in the room; ride the crowd's energy but don't try to force it. If they're not ready for 140bpm, you'll be playing it for an empty dance floor. But that might be the perfect time to play your slow dance numbers—and don't be too proud to do that. Like traditional musicians, the best DJs have a very authentic give-and-take with each crowd they play for.

CHAPTER 15

AUDIO SYNCHRONIZATION

In This Chapter

- Learn about SMPTE Time Code
- Find out about MIDI Time Code
- Discover how Word Clock provides a single timing reference for your digital devices
- Learn about combining the various sync methods

LET'S ALL GET TOGETHER

In the world of audio, *synchronization*, or *sync*, refers to the technique of getting one or more devices to run in tandem. Your need to deal with sync issues depends on the complexity of your setup. If you're just using a PC with audio software and a single MIDI keyboard, sync won't be of much concern for you. However, if you have three or more pieces of gear, including equipment such as sequencers, a mixer, and maybe an ADAT, proper sync is a crucial factor in getting things to work right.

For two or more tape machines to be in sync, they need to have interlocked transport speeds; when one speeds up or slows down, the other must do the same. In the digital world, for two devices to transmit data from one to the other, they must be connected with a single timing reference. The digital data flowing between devices must arrive at precisely the right moment. No two machines run or clock at precisely the same rate without a common sync or timing reference, even if made by the same manufacturer on the same day in the same factory. (Machines are more like people than we think they are.)

The concepts of sync and timing reference are important in many situations, both in the music world and the video/film post production environment. When a sound designer lays in sound effects in relation to a scene in a video or film, the sound effect of a door slam must coincide precisely with the door slam we see onscreen. Musicians use sync to get an ADAT machine to play in tandem with a MIDI sequencer. Or, when digitally routing music from an A/D converter into a digital recorder, they must ensure that these devices have a common timing reference.

Hot Link: Society Of Motion Picture and Television Engineers (http://www.smpte.org)

Learn all about SMPTE-based synchronization issues at the site of the group that invented it (see Figure 15.1).

Some of the most prevalent terms you'll encounter in audio sync are *SMPTE time code, MIDI time code (MTC), MIDI sync,* and *word clock.* SMPTE has been around the longest, and has been used to synchronize audio tape machines for decades. MIDI time code and MIDI sync, as the terms suggest, are used to send timing information to MIDI devices. These sync methods are widely used because so much studio gear now accepts MIDI data. Word clock is necessary for digital-to-digital signal flow, which means it's the big dog of today's audio studios.

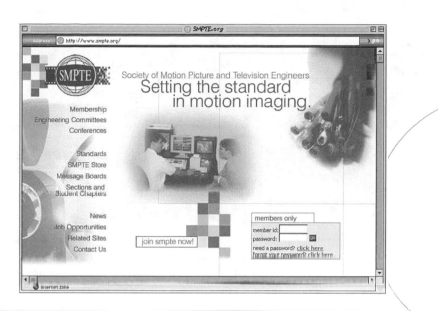

Figure 15.1

This is the group that invented the ever-popular SMPTE time code standard. A serious bunch of folks.

No matter which sync method you're using, in either a tape or non-tape configuration, one device is the master, and all other connected devices are slaves. The *master* device sends SMPTE, word clock, or MTC to its various slaves, which either makes the various *slave* devices play back synchronously or provides them a common timing reference.

That, in a nutshell, is the story of audio sync. Beyond that you get into details—and the world of audio sync abounds with detail. Different audio setups use completely different sync configurations, and sync causes its share of headaches. The Pro Tools manual contains words to the effect of "achieving sync between recording devices can be daunting." Very true words. But it's nothing a user who does a little bit of studying can't handle.

In the future, sync will be a non-issue. In some not-too-distant year your entire audio-video-MIDI workstation will be in one self-contained computer. Sync issues will disappear because your entire system will be one device, one hyper-cyber PC that can handle it all. But we're not there yet. Many desktop setups have an array of free standing audio gear that must run in tandem. These devices must be precisely synced.

Hot Link: Digital Timepiece (http://www.motu.com/)

Many studios use MOTU's Digital Timepiece to sync their equipment. Learn about this popular piece of gear at the MOTU site (see Figure 15.2).

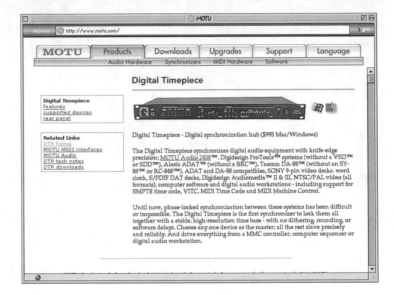

Figure 15.2

Mark of the Unicorn's Digital Timepiece is an all-purpose audio synchronizer. And while you're at the site, take a look at the company's MIDI Timepiece AV.

SMPTE Time Code

Even though we desktop sound designers are PC-based, let's go back to the world of tape for a moment. As mentioned, sync between one or more tape machines is achieved using SMPTE (Society of Motion Picture and Television Engineers) time code. A recording engineer records, or *stripes*, time code onto one track of a multitrack tape machine. This machine is the master. As the master outputs SMPTE to its slaves, these slave machines chase, locate, and follow the master. The slaves' transports stay locked with that of the master. When the master slows down ever so slightly, the slave slows down the same amount. If the master stops, the slave stops.

Drift

If two machines that you thought were synchronized start to lose sync, that's referred to as *drift*. The sound and the picture start to disassociate from each other, or the MIDI and audio are no longer at the same tempo. Sometimes the drift is subtle—but if there's a problem with sync it tends to get worse as the program plays. If it gets really bad it's referred to as *freewheeling*. That may sound like a cool term, but it describes two devices that are running without reference to each other.

By continuously reading SMPTE, the slave monitors the master's tape position using time increments of 1/24th of a second to 1/30th of a second, depending on the type of SMPTE used. These time increments are called *frames*. SMPTE time code assigns an *address* to each frame. These eight-digit addresses looks like this:

00:00:00:00

The four sets of zeros represent, from left to right, hours:minutes:seconds:frames.

A musician recording with a synched tape machine can pinpoint exact moments in a song by using that moment's time code address. Perhaps the song's first chorus happens at exactly 00:00:57:15 (57 seconds, 15 frames). The musician can fast forward up to that cue point to listen or begin to record. She may decide to lay in a guitar sample at that point, and after laying it in, shift it by a few frames (each frame typically being a 1/30th of a second).

Within SMPTE, each frame is divided into 80 equal bits. Consider the time division that's going on here. With each frame representing 1/30th of a second, and each frame divided into 80 equal parts, that means that each of those 80 equal parts is exactly...1/2400th of a second long. You can't even wink in that amount of time. However, you will encounter audio software that enables you to shift cues by sub-frames. And, amazingly, it can make a difference in the way things sound.

Hot Link: Lucid (http://www.lucidaudio.com/store/)
If you want to find out more about one of Lucid's clocking devices, you can download user's guides from the site (see Figure 15.3).

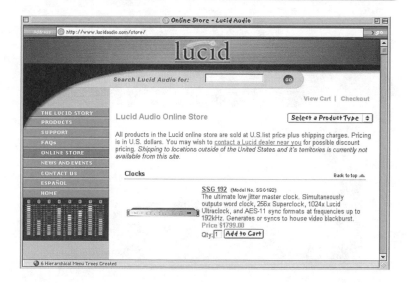

Figure 15.3

At the Lucid online store, you can browse through a variety of digital clocking units and download users' guides for the units you're considering.

Jam Sync

Many SMPTE generating devices are capable of *jam sync*. If a SMPTE generator is receiving time code, and it drops out, the device can use jam sync to keep outputting time code to keep all of its slave devices in sync for a short period or continuously, depending on the configuration. In the jam sync mode, a SMPTE generator is able to extrapolate from the code it's been receiving to keep the devices locked. Jam sync, by the way, would be a great name for a band.

You might run across two acronyms that refer to how SMPTE is encoded on to tape, LTC, and VITC:

- **LTC, longitudinal time code.** This refers to time code striped onto a linear tape machine. You'll see this term most commonly in audio manuals. A desktop audio setup is sometimes slaved to a tape machine using LTC.

- **VITC, vertical interval time code.** This is the method video production houses use. It uses the same address method as LTC, but it is encoded into the video signal itself. This makes it possible for high-end video equipment to read the code at very slow and even still frame speeds, which facilitates editing, among other advantages.

Hot Link: Aardvark (`http://www.aardvark-pro.com/`)

Aardvark makes a popular brand of studio sync devices. Explore the company's product line at their site (see Figure 15.4) .

Figure 15.4

Aardvark makes a full line of studio synchronizers. Check out the Aardvark Aardsync II.

MIDI Sync

MIDI has its own synchronization protocol designed to keep all of the devices in a MIDI system in reference to a master timing clock. With *MIDI sync*, one device is the master and the following units are slaves. The master is typically your MIDI sequencer, sending messages to the various synths, MIDI modules, and studio machines it controls. These sync messages are sent in real-time over MIDI cables. Like all sync mechanisms, MIDI clocks respond to tempo changes. So slaves slow down or speed up in response to the master—hence the master and slave move in sync.

MIDI sync is not a replacement for SMPTE. Rather, it is sometimes used in conjunction with SMPTE. You could use SMPTE to synchronize a sequencer to a multitrack tape machine. The sequencer, in turn, would use MIDI sync to keep a bank of MIDI synths locked together (more on that in a moment).

Hot Link: Synchronizing in the Digital Age (http://www.eqmag.com/ columns.html)

This article from *EQ Magazine* does a good job of exploring sync issues, and if you visit the EQ site (see Figure 15.5), you'll also find a user forum that contains posts from users dealing with many of the gnarly problems associated with studio sync.

Figure 15.5

The *EQ Magazine* online forum about digital sync issues is a great resource. Read the posts from users who have a wide variety of equipment.

MIDI sync contains timing clock messages transmitted to all slave devices at the rate of 24 pulses per quarter note (24ppq). When a MIDI slave reads one of these messages, it advances its internal clock 1/24th of a quarter note. Many MIDI sequencers further subdivide this clock rate so that events are recorded with greater resolution, for example, 1/480th of a quarter note or 1/960th of a quarter note (and many MIDI apps go way higher). Also included in MIDI sync data are start, stop, and continue commands, which the slaves respond to by—you guessed it—starting, stopping, and continuing.

You can use MIDI sync's Song Position Pointer (SPP) messages to find exact locations in your song. SPPs provide this convenient service by monitoring how many 16th notes have gone by since the start of the song. Let's say you stop your MIDI song in the middle, make an edit, and then click Play again. When the sequencer starts, it sends your synthesizer a message that tells it at what point in the song—how many 16th notes from the start—to resume playback. The synth, if all is well with the world, responds to this message and begins to play from exactly this point.

Hot Link: Sound on Sound's MIDI and SMPTE Time Code (http://www.sospubs.co.uk/)

Get feedback from fellow studio sync users at the Sound on Sound site (see Figure 15.6).

Figure 15.6

Go to this site and click the Recording Technology link to post a question about your sync snafus.

MIDI Time Code

Let's say you have a tape machine or other external recorder with audio tracks on it—your live musicians' tracks. You want to synchronize this recorder with your synthesizers—your MIDI tracks. In this instance you could send SMPTE from your recorder to a SMPTE converter, which would convert SMPTE to MIDI time code (MTC). This MTC would in turn drive your MIDI sequencer, synchronizing your MIDI tracks with your live tracks.

MIDI time code allows SMPTE data—hours, minutes, seconds, frames—to be encoded into MIDI data. It can then be transmitted over MIDI cables; there's no way to send SMPTE itself over MIDI cables.

Because MTC, like SMPTE, provides an absolute time reference, it's the desired choice for some projects. Maybe you're writing the music for a short film. You've got a full MIDI music track as well as some carefully created sound effects, which you play back from your MIDI sampler. Everything is in perfect sync with the film or video, until the wild-eyed filmmaker decides the song must go 3 percent faster. The music still sounds fine, but those sound effects from the sampler no longer sync with the film's picture.

Background Applications

Some MIDI and audio sync problems are caused by running other software applications in the background. It's best to stop these while you're in the midst of a critical record/playback situation.

This is where MTC comes in handy. Using a sequencer driven by MTC, you could build an event list of SMPTE cues. You could trigger these cues at absolute moments in time in relation to the film's picture—that man's gasp happens at exactly 00:08:13:15 into the movie. (That's 8 minutes, 13 seconds, 15 frames.) Problem solved.

Fortunately, many of today's audio interfaces have SMPTE-to-MIDI conversion built in. This is a very common method of studio sync. It's undoubtedly happening even as you read this. An SMPTE time code sync track from the audio master is being converted into MTC and routed into whatever device is driving that studio's MIDI gear, which is keeping the MIDI tracks in sync with the audio tracks. It sounds—*voilà*—like five horn players, when in reality there's one real horn player in sync with four tracks of MIDI horns.

MIDI and Audio Logjams

As audio and MIDI data moves though your desktop system, in and out the various ports/processors, they have the potential to conflict with each other. Even though MIDI occupies only a tiny amount of bandwidth in relation to its bandwidth-hogging brother audio, your PC has its limits. In this case you might experiment with increasing the audio buffer size or thinning out your MIDI data. Companies, such as Emagic and Steinberg, have designed a range of hardware devices that address MIDI timing problems.

> **Hot Link: The Distribution Box (http://www.aardvark-pro.com/)**
>
> A distribution box enables you to send word clock to several devices from one clock source. Take a look at the Aardvark SyncDA (see Figure 15.7) to see an example.

Figure 15.7

Aardvark SyncDA distributes word clock to all the devices in your studio, ensuring a single time reference.

Word Clock: Digital Communication

Synchronizing in an all digital environment is a completely different task than synchronizing analog machines, or a combination of analog and digital machines. To get the internal clocks of one or more digital devices to be properly synched, they must be connected to a single timing reference known as *word clock*.

Word clock does not give you locational or positional reference like SMPTE or MTC does. Rather, it ensures that two digital machines have a common timing reference. Two or more digital devices must have a common timing reference for digital data to flow properly between them. For digital machines to communicate with each other, they must have a common source of word clock.

Remember, a *word* in digital audio is made up of 16 bits (or more if the bit resolution is greater, as in 24-bit audio). Each one of these bits represents a measurement of an audio signal's amplitude in a brief moment in time.

As the zillions of digital words moves from one digital device to the next, each must arrive at its destination at exactly the right moment. If this process is inaccurate by even a tiny fraction of second, it results in *jitter*, a problem caused when samples are not interpreted in perfectly even amounts of time. These irregularities in word clock timing can cause pops, clicks, distortion, and indistinct stereo imaging.

Prevent jitter and other nasty digital audio problems by making sure all your digital devices are referenced to a single word clock source. There are two ways that word clock is typically set up:

- **The master clocked system.** This method is most often used in high-end production facilities with many digital machines to sync. You'll also see it in home setups that are fortunate enough to have a lot of digital gear. With master clocking, one device is the master and all other devices are the slaves (just like with SMPTE and MTC).

The master device—often a dedicated word clock generator—sends word clock based on its own internal clock to the word clock input of all the slave machines. Word clock is sent from one master to many slaves using a distribution box, or "distro box." Some word clock generators have multiple outputs that many devices can be plugged in to.

- **The self clocked system.** This method is often used to sync setups with three or fewer pieces of digital gear. When sending data from one digital device to the next, word clock is embedded in the bitstream itself. So if, for example, you're copying audio from a DAT deck into a hard disk system, the DAT deck generates word clock, which is read by the hard disk system. Think of it as a one-on-one master-slave relationship. Some desktop musicians use this fact of digital audio life to chain a series of digital devices together. Word clock is sent though the daisy chain, each device reading it in turn from the previous—and all ultimately slaved to that original source deck. But be aware that any problems at one point in the chain will be passed downstream.

The Crystal

Inside a digital sound card is a crystal-controlled oscillator. This oscillator provides the clock signal that determines that sound card's sample rate. Because nothing is perfect, this oscillator wobbles ever so slightly. This wobble causes clock jitter—some samples arrive a little late, some arrive a little early. The less jitter there is, the more focused and clear is the stereo image the card sends out its D/A converter. If you spend more on a sound card, you should theoretically be getting a card with lower clock jitter levels.

Hot Link: The BNC Cable (http://www.hosatech.com/)

You want cables? Hosa has cables. Surf the company's site (see Figure 15.8) to look at the many types of cables that you might need to complete you studio sync. By the way, if you want to look at the common digital connections, refer to Chapter 10, "Audio Connections."

Figure 15.8

The 75 ohm BNC cable is ideal for carrying word clock signal. The cable shown is made by Hosa.

Photo permission of Hosa Technologies.

TODAY'S STUDIO AND THE GREAT SYNC STEW: WORD CLOCK, SMPTE, AND MTC

If you get confused about digital sync, you're not alone. Even the most experienced techs sometimes scratch their heads about the wide array of sync possibilities.

Many feel that the self-clocking word clock method, daisy chaining a number of digital devices together, is considerably less desirable than master clocking. Others use it in home studios with no problems.

But the greater confusion arises because in today's desktop setups, the various sync methods are used *in combination*. It's not as if, as technology has advanced, the old has fallen away and the new is clear and obvious. In the transitional time period we're in, even mid-level setups are using SMPTE, MTC, and word clock at the same time. The questions quickly multiply. Which input and output should I use? How do the various sync methods synchronize with each other?

The answer to these questions depends on the particulars of your setup. One musician's problem-free sync configuration is another musician's jitter-filled nightmare. However, these tips can help:

- Rule 1 for digital sync is that to transfer data digitally from one device to the next, they must be set at the same sample rate. That machine at 48kHz sample rate cannot receive digital data from a machine at 44.1kHz sample rate.

- Here's another big one. Realize that even among sync systems, one is the master and one is the slave. You may have a device that outputs word clock, and another device that outputs SMPTE, but if they themselves are not synced together, you're in trouble. Rule of thumb: Word clock is king. So make the device that outputs word clock the master, and slave the SMPTE generator to it. The SMPTE is, in turn, sent to a MIDI time code generator. So everything locks because it's all based on one word clock source.

- Not all clock generators are created equal. Many A/D converters have word clock generators. Some send out rock solid clock that keeps everything lined up precisely; others work well with some gear and not so well with others. It helps to ask around to see if one unit tends to work better with the setup you have.

- If you're not getting sync in your setup, isolate the various parts to locate the problem. Maybe you have four different digital devices slaved to one master, and you think there's a problem with word clock—you hear clicks and pops. Or maybe your synths sit silent even though you're sending them MTC. Either way, try breaking down your system into basic components. Will one digital device successfully send signal to one other? Is the MTC problem caused by something with the MIDI system, or is the MIDI system itself not getting time code?

- Your MIDI synths are still not responding to sync. Did you enable the Receive sync mode?

- Word clock travels from device to device through cables. The cables themselves might be the problem, especially if you're using the cheapest cables you could find. Get digital cables, designed to carry information at higher frequencies than audio cables. Look for 75 (omega) cables.

- When all else fails—and it just might—don't be afraid to look at the manual or, better yet, call an experienced tech person.

CHAPTER   **16**

ARCHIVING

In This Chapter

- Find out about current practices in audio archiving

- Look at the various methods of audio data backup, from CD-RW to DVD-R

- Discover the excitement of proper archive labeling and storage!

NEW PROBLEMS, NEW SOLUTIONS

In the bad old days of analog tape, there was no archiving as we know it. All the musicians' performances were stored on the master tape on which they were originally recorded, usually a 2-inch tape designed for 24-track tape machine. After this multitrack tape was mixed down to a stereo master, and vinyl albums were cut, both tapes were put up on the shelf. All the Top 40 hits of decades past are stored in temperature-controlled libraries, where shelf upon shelf of tape reels sit quietly. Somewhere, the Rolling Stones are stored next to the Monkees, and Bruce Springsteen is stored next to the Talking Heads.

But in today's digital world we're operating with a completely different setup. We have our main hard drive, the repository of all those zillions of ones and zeros—our music in digital form—and when it gets stuffed, we have to clean it out. When your last six songs have eaten up 19GB of your 20GB hard drive, you have to copy those 19GB of audio files to another medium. This enables you to erase them off your hard drive so you can fill it again with another 19GB of audio files.

Your archive media—CDs or DATs or storage discs—becomes the final resting place of your music. If you ever need to work on it again, you must restore that information onto your hard drive.

So, the central question for today's desktop musicians with a hard drive bursting with audio files is: What medium do I copy my files to? What's the best one? What's the cheapest and easiest to use? Like anything in modern audio, you have a variety of options—in this time of season by season change, we're always dealing with a confusing conglomeration of yesterday's, today's, and tomorrow's options.

So let's look at the options. Realize that there is no single "right" backup solution, just the one that fits best with your system.

CD-R/CD-RW

Did we just say there is no right one? Well, for most home desktop users, this is as close as it comes. It's got some serious advantages over the other options: It's cheap, it's easy to use, and many musicians already have a burner. If you're creating your own music, you need one anyway; this is what you burn your mixes to when you're done. And if you don't have a burner, you can get one for less than $150, even less if you're a good shopper.

When you're done with your session, simply drag your files over to a CD, make sure it's in data not audio mode, and click Burn. It typically takes no more than several minutes. The limitation of the CD is that it does not hold any more than 650MB. But what if you have a 3GB session you want to back up? Most desktop musicians, who are used to working with limited equipment, say, "So what?" They simply burn as many CDs as they need, dividing the session in to as many separate folders as they need.

Important: It helps to have a clear and logical system when you start dividing your 4GB session among a half dozen backup CDs. Sure, if worse comes to worst you can always just sort through it later, but if you have a system and stick to it, your archiving process will be considerably easier. The type of system you'll need will depend on your overall system's configuration. Maybe you'll always want to back up the rhythm instruments in one folder, the lead instruments in another. Or perhaps it will be tracks 1–5 in one folder, tracks 6–10 in another. As long you're not simply grabbling and dragging, you're ahead of the game.

Hot Link: Data Compression (`http://www.aptx.com/FAQ/`)

This page from the APT Web site talks about audio data compression techniques, which are used for audio storage, among other applications (see Figure 16.1).

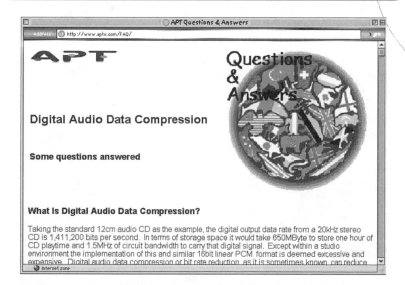

Figure 16.1

One audio data compression program for the desktop market is Zap, made by the German company Emagic.

As for whether you want to use CD-R or CD-RW blanks, you can make arguments either way. Yes, the CD-RW blanks let you write and then write again later, adding material to one disc to make your librarian duties simpler and better organized. But the CD-R blanks tend to be cheaper, so some users prefer to simply grab a fresh CD-R.

We go into more detail about burning CDs in Chapter 20, "CD Burning Overview," including burning data CDs (there is a major difference. You don't want to burn a music CD as a backup).

Higher Resolution Equals Higher Storage Needs

So you decided to record at 96kHz, 24-bit—that's great, but it's going to take a lot more storage space. For every minute of stereo audio at 44.1, 16-bit, you'll need about 10MB. For every minute of stereo audio at 96kHz, 24-bit, you'll need around 25MB.

DAT Backup

This is good choice for a higher end user with some fat audio files to back up. For example, the Glyph 12 GIG DAT Backup Drive allows you to archive several days of heavy duty work in one gulp (see Figure 16.2). If your studio is really busy—which typically means you have paying clients—you don't want to be backing up an 18GB session with CD-R. Using CD-R's 650MB increments, you'd be sitting there for a while.

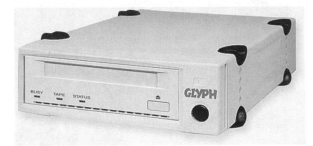

Figure 16.2

The Glyph greatly simplifies large archiving jobs.

Photo courtesy of Glyph.

The other nice feature about this option is that the software enables you to automate the archiving process. You can schedule archives to run one after the other by themselves, or run archives in the background as you keep mixing. You can even ask the software to archive the project you're currently working on, but only archive those elements that you haven't already backed up. For the power user, these options make all the difference.

Hot Link Retrospect by Dantz (http://www.retrospect.com)

Dantz's Retrospect archiving software will work with both Mac and Windows (see Figure 16.3).

Figure 16.3

Made by Dantz, Retrospect archiving software is a popular choice for data backup.

However, you pay for the convenience of a DAT backup. Not only are the individual DAT tapes much more expensive than CDs, but the archive drive itself is quite pricey. For the price of the DAT backup drive you could buy a CD-RW drive and enough discs to last for years.

The Redundant Term: DAT Tape

The acronym DAT stands for digital audio tape. Yet people refer to "DAT tapes." So what they're really saying is "digital audio tape tapes." Strange but true.

Removable Storage Disc

A variety of options fall into this category. They range from the practically obsolete like the venerable floppy—at 1.3MB it's only good for storing small files like MIDI—to the zip disc, which at 250MB is still on the skinny side (although a major manufacturer of a standalone DAW uses it for backup). The leader in this option is the Jaz drive, offering a hefty 2GB of storage (also available in the 1GB option).

This option makes sense for the "in between" user. It doesn't have the capacity for the power user—if you're archiving 10 to 15GB at a time, you don't want to be doing it in 2GB increments. But it does offer the speed of drag and drop backup for the desktop user who wants to back up in larger increments than is possible with a CD-R. However, it's still more expensive than the CD-R. We've seen the 2GB Jaz (http://www.iomega.com/jaz/) drives advertised for about $275, with a 2GB disc going for $125 (see Figure 16.4).

Figure 16.4

The Jaz makes backing up 2GB of audio files as easy as drag and drop.

Hard Drives

This option is a twist on traditional thinking about hard drive backup. Instead of finding another medium to back up their hard drives, users who chose this option simply buy another hard drive. This option is on the expensive side, but it looks like it will grow ever more popular in the years ahead, for the following reasons:

- **The effect of gravity on computer gear prices.** Hard drives just keep getting cheaper and cheaper. While you'll see an 100GB drive advertised for around $225, that price is dramatically lower than it was just a few years ago. At the rate we're going, at some point we'll see something like a 400GB drive which fits in your hand for less than $100. And someday…

- **Convenience and speed.** The buzzword these days is *hot swappable*, meaning you can change hard drives without even turning off your computer. So working on multiple projects—or getting access to archived material—is just a matter of plugging in a new hard drive. Finding those guitar tracks you laid down six months ago is a no brainer.

- **Extra peace of mind.** This one's minor but it's a nice feature. When you back up to a CD or a DAT, then erase the material off of your hard drive, there's always a little fear: What happens if this disc goes bad, or there's drop out in the DAT? With multiple hard drives you don't need to worry about this (then again, hard drives crash, so nothing's perfect). In a way the hard drive method is a return to the good old days of analog tape: Instead of archiving material to a separate medium like a CD, the hard drive itself—which is where the tracks are recorded to—becomes the storage medium.

DVD-R

This option is a bit ahead of the curve but coming on fast. It's quite likely that it will over-take the CD-R as backup method of choice for the desktop musician. The first recordable DVD unit hit the market at a cool $17,000. By 1999 you could pick one up for around $5,000. A visit to the Pioneer Web site (http://www.pioneerelectronics.com) in the fall of 2001 finds the DVR 7000, a DVD-R/DVD-RW unit, on sale for $2,000 (see Figure 16.5). For the average desktop studio, take a look at the Panasonic or Toshiba rewriteable DVD drives for about $500. Or get a CD-R, CD-RW, DVD+RW SuperDrive for around $600.

Figure 16.5

When you have a recordable DVD unit in your studio, no one can doubt that you are cool human being.

DVD-RAM (one of several DVD formats) is gaining popularity as an archiving method among desktop musicians. It's thought of as a "bit bucket"—you can dump your files to a DVD-RAM disc in 4.7 GB increments. As the drives and blank media fall in price it will gain popularity. We've seen a blank DVD-RAM disc advertised for about $30, but expect this to fall dramatically. We go into more detail about DVD in Chapter 19, "DVD Audio and Surround Sound."

techtv tip

Save to Multiple Backups

If you want a fail-safe archive, back it up twice—or more. It's unlikely that the CD-Rs you burn as backups will have any problem, but if what you're archiving is your musical masterwork, it sure is nice to have a double backup.

Online

Okay, this option is just a twinkle in a futurist's eye, but it's on its way. The current online storage options, like Freedrive.com and Myplay.com, are practical only for storing small files like MP3s. They really aren't a reasonable place to store your album's audio elements. The problem of course is bandwidth: By the time you upload 150MB of files with a dial-up modem connection, you'll be reminiscing about the good old days in 2015. However, if the files you're storing are small (like MP3s), the online storage services give you mobility. You can access your files from any PC with a Net connection, without needing to lug around a hard drive.

But there will come a day when we have the bandwidth and the file compression technology to simply dump our 150GB files into an online storage locker. The idea of having to buy static media—discs and cartridges—to store audio will seem really silly. Someday...

OKAY, SO YOU'VE CHOSEN A BACKUP OPTION. WHAT ELSE SHOULD YOU KNOW?

It's not enough to have a good backup system. You have to use it. Sounds obvious, doesn't it? But as most creative musicians will tell you, backup is pretty low in the fun category. Programming a tight little kick 'n' snare rhythm is what it's all about, but backing up your data...let's do it tomorrow.

But delaying that all important backup creates potential problems. First, if your drive is packed to the gills it may operate more slowly; it must search through more data to find the file you've just requested. More importantly—much more importantly—a drive that's not backed up flaunts the great mysterious law of hard drives: If it's not backed up, it's more likely to crash.

So do yourself the favor of establishing some kind of archiving schedule. Maybe it's whenever your drive is more than 40 percent full, or whenever you finish a song. At the very least, it's a good idea to back up after you've recorded something that's irreplaceable. You don't want to lose that once-in-a-lifetime vocal performance to a computer crash.

Hot Link: The Back UPS Pro (http://www.apc.com/products)
A backup of a different kind, this unit is an uninterruptible power supply/surge protector (see Figure 16.6). The UPS units are available as either a true sinusoidal power supply or a stepped transformer power supply. The stepped type is cheaper and is fine for your PC, but to provide a safety net for sensitive audio gear like microphone pre-amps, the true sinusoidal power supply is your best choice.

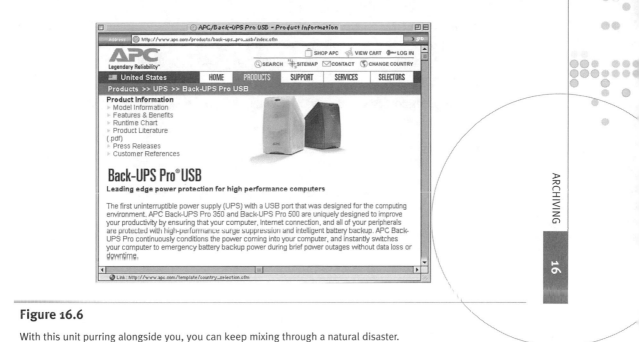

Figure 16.6

With this unit purring alongside you, you can keep mixing through a natural disaster.

THE RAW EXCITEMENT OF LIBRARY WORK

All right, let's say you're a model citizen of the computer nation, and you back up regularly. But there's one last part of the archiving process—which may be even less fun than backing up itself—that's important for complete audio happiness.

Once you've archived, label your archive. Taking the time to clearly label your backup media is time well spent. You might feel like you hardly need it. After you work on Ted's guitar tracks for six day's straight, scrawling "ted gtr" on the CD seems like all you'll ever need—you're *never* going to forget that session, are you? But after three more whirlwind guitar sessions with Ted (that guy always takes a long time, doesn't he?), you'll wonder which backup goes with which session. Which session was the reggae stuff, and which session was that open-ended jam thing?

So develop a way to label your media that concisely lists all the relevant details. The key elements to list are date, project, and personnel/instruments involved, but the particulars depend on your situation.

The important last step in backing up is finding a way to store all these clearly labeled archives so you can find them with no searching. In other words—careful, you're about to see the dreaded word—creating your own library. Typically the easiest way to do this is to work by date; simply line up the discs on a shelf, adding projects chronologically. If you know you're going to have several shelves full of backups, it's worth investing in a software program that helps you track them by date or perhaps keyword. Doing this will not only save you headaches, you'll always know where those hard-groovin' percussion tracks are stored.

By the time you've set up your library, you've reached a kind of organizational nirvana, and you may want to sit quietly and simply enjoy it. Don't be alarmed by how neat and efficient it seems; there will always be enough chaos in your life.

Seriously though, the advantage to being this organized is this: Those 20 minutes you spend looking for last month's archive could be spent making music. And what would you rather do?

Now, where did I put that CD...

P A R T **IV**

CREATING YOUR SOUND: HOW TO MIX USING YOUR DESKTOP STUDIO

CHAPTER 17

MIXING, PART 1

In This Chapter

- Learn about the many tools used in mixing
- Look at routing signal through a mixing desk
- Find out about audio compression and limiting
- Discover how to use equalization to improve your sound
- Look at often-used audio effects like reverb and delay

FINALLY, IT'S TIME TO MIX

The music has been recorded, the tracks have been layered, the samples have been painstakingly created. Now it's time to put it all together. It's time to take all those separate elements and blend them into a single, heart-stopping, mind-blowing finished track. It's time to mix.

The act of mixing all your musical elements into a polished finished product is a process that entails dozens and dozens of decisions. How much reverb should the vocal have? How loud should the bass be in relation to the other instruments? Should you include all of 12 of those percussion tracks you laid down, or choose between them—and how?

When the mix is done, your song is done. This is your final product. If you're a musician, this is what it's all about. While you hope the music itself will sell your song, the music can only sing as well as the mix. As you know by listening to the radio, even a forgettable piece of music can sound impressive with the right mix. On the other hand, imagine your favorite radio hits with a guitar that's too loud, or with an audio effect on the flute track that's distracting. You couldn't snap your fingers to it the way you do.

So, this process of combining all the elements into a finished product—creating the final mix—is a critically important process. People take hours and hours on it—and then decide to spend still more hours.

The big advantage of mixing in your desktop studio is time. You have as much as you want. No expensive studio clock is ticking away as you twiddle with the EQ. You're free to experiment and listen, and then experiment again. You're free to create a final mix, then (free of charge) go back and start again from scratch. If you decide that the vocal is too flat, you can stop everything and re-record. Make the most of this advantage to dig more deeply into the process.

And remember, mixing is fun. Rushing it is a shame. The tools of mixing are in themselves musical instruments; they offer as much creativity and opportunity for expression as a Steinway grand. Whether you're mixing the album that's your life's work, or just layering samples for the heck of it, don't forget to enjoy yourself. Take your time, pay attention, keep an open mind, be creative. And have fun.

Changing Mix Styles

Mixing styles have changed over time as much as music itself, perhaps even more. Try listening to a piece of music from an earlier decade not for the song, but how it's mixed. Notice that in comparison to, say, the '50s, today's mixes have a much wider frequency range: richer lows and more high end presence. Listen, too, for how effects like reverb and delay are used. Some time periods and styles use these in more obvious ways than others; the pop music of the '80s tended toward heavy effects use. And listen between genres. Notice that a Top 40 rock hit tends to have a more self-consciously polished sound, while hip hop sometimes has a more raw production quality. The question for your mix is: What style do you work with, and what are the standards of that style? What do you need to do mix-wise to make your music relate to that genre?

Hot Link: Soundcraft (http://www.soundcraft.com/)

As part of its sales efforts, the Soundcraft company's Web site offers a wealth of information about mixing consoles and the craft of mixing (see Figure 17.1) .

Figure 17.1

At the Soundcraft site, click on the Learning Zone link.

TOOLS FIRST, THEN TECHNIQUES

Mixing is a vast subject that could easily fill its own book (make that a *series* of books), but to break it down, we'll look first at the tools of mixing (that's this chapter), then we'll look at the techniques of mixing, in an actual mix (that's next chapter). The tools and techniques are of course completely inseparable, but hey, every mix starts by looking at things that will later be completely blended. So let's start looking at our various elements.

A mixer's basic tools are the mixing desk itself and the essential building blocks of modern audio: EQ, compression, and effects. If you know your way around these essentials, you're ready to mix. Other than that, all you need is years of experience and you can create great mixes. (Whoops, that last part might have been discouraging. But hey, mixing is a highly detailed art, and no art form can be mastered without continuous effort. However, there's a degree of satisfaction at many points in the learning process, so let's put our fears aside and plunge boldly ahead.)

The Mixing Desk: What the Heck Are All Those Buttons?

Knowing your way around a mixing desk is important for recording as well as mixing, but it's absolutely critical for mixing. And it doesn't matter that your mixing desk is software instead of those big hardware monsters: The concepts are the same. If anything, a software mixing desk is a bit more complicated, because it can be re-configured by the user in many more ways than a hardware desk.

Although every software mixer is a bit different, the good news is that they all use the same concepts. One particularly important bit of lingo is the term *bus*. A mixing desk's bus is like a school bus: It's a way to send your signal to various places. Maybe you want to bus the channel with the guitar track to a reverb unit. So you would use that channel's *bus send* to assign its output to the reverb unit. A mixing desk's *stereo bus* is its master output; all the channels sent to the stereo bus are mixed into a single stereo image. When you assign a channel's output to the stereo bus, you're combining it with all the other channels, a typical part of a final mixdown.

Let's look at a software mixing desk. The Pro Tools desk shown in Figure 17.2, like any desk, has faders and pots to control audio signal flow.

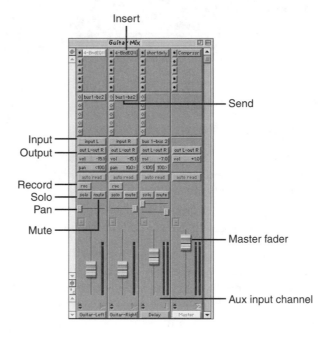

Figure 17.2

The Pro Tools mixing desk.

The components you need to know about on the Pro Tools desk (and almost all desks) are as follows:

- **Input.** Controls where the channel is getting signal from; possibilities include mic input, line input, or input from a bus send.

- **Output.** Controls where that channel's signal goes to; it defaults to the stereo bus, or you can bus the channel's output to another channel in the desk to filter or process it.

- **Level.** This fader controls the relative amplitude (loudness) of that channel's output.

- **Send.** Allows you to send that channel's output to various places. You can, for example, bus the channel's output to another channel to filter or process it.

- **Insert.** Allows you to put an effects filter or other processing application in that channel's signal path. In this case we're using an EQ filter to brighten and fill out the bottom end of the guitar track.

- **Pan.** Controls left-right placement within the stereo image. In this case we've panned the guitar hard left and hard right (all the way in each direction, for the widest stereo placement).

- **Rec.** Allows you to put the channel into record ready.

- **Solo.** If you want to hear just that channel, click Solo.

- **Mute.** If you want to silence that channel, click Mute.

- **Aux Input.** This channel has a different function than those with the guitar. It's used as the destination of the other channel's sends (outputs from those channels). Notice that this aux input channel is getting its input from bus send 1 and 2. Look over at the guitar channels—their output is being bussed on bus send 1 and 2. So the guitar track's output is being sent to this aux input. In this instance, this aux input channel is being used to add delay to the guitar sound, to give it a fuller sound. You might also use an aux input channel to *sub-mix* a section of the song. For example, for a drum sub-mix you'd send all of the drum channels to an aux input (or two if it's a stereo sub-mix) to create a master fader that controls the drums.

- **Master.** This master fade controls the mix's overall amplitude. In this instance we've put a compressor in its signal path to even out any volume variations in the music.

The beauty of a virtual mixer is that you can re-configure it with a few mouse clicks. Do you need a few more tracks? Just go to Add tracks and decide which kind you want. (Of course you may still be limited by your system's resources.) You can easily save your settings, down to the last volume tweak, and call them up several months later. And automating various elements of the mix, like an effect send or a pan position, is as easy as drawing it in. The software mixer is one of the sound designer's best friends.

Oh, one little secret about mixers you might as well face: It really helps to look at the manual. Unless you're a master, they aren't intuitive, and the differences between them make that manual awful helpful.

Hot Link: Solid State Logic (http://www.solidstatelogic.com/)

The consoles made by SSL are completely outside the price range of the desktop musician, but they're good to know about (see Figure 17.3). These fabulously high-end units are the Rolls Royces of the mixing desk world.

Figure 17.3

If you want to up your coolness quotient, make an occasional reference to SSL.

Equalization: What a Beautiful Bottom End You Have

Equalization, or EQ, is the art of turning up or down various frequencies, from the lows to the highs, to make your various tracks sound better. Understanding EQ is pretty easy; using it to its full advantage is one of audio's most upper-level challenges.

All sorts of devices have basic EQ controls, from boom boxes to your car's CD player. Turn up the bass fader and that male voice gets fuller sounding; push up the treble and the song gets brighter. These simple controls are great for mass market electronics, but you want to go way beyond this in tone shaping your song's sounds. To get the best sound, you have to make subtle and precise adjustments across the complete frequency spectrum, from the deep dark around 20Hz to the airy stratosphere around 20kHz.

You might have several goals in mind when you start to adjust EQ. Perhaps you want to add a quality to an instrument that it doesn't have, like more fullness to a vocal. You might be (oh no!) trying to correct a problem in the recording itself, like having a not-so-good mic, or a poorly positioned mic. You might want to adjust highs or lows to make your tracks blend better with each other. Or, you may have some completely off the wall creative idea in mind—that last one is quite common.

When it comes EQ, you're working by ear—if it sounds good, it's right—but you don't want to work by ear alone. You'll need to know the layout of the human hearing spectrum to really work the magic of EQ:

- **Lows (20–200Hz).** This bottom end is often felt as much as it's heard. This basement range tends to be the rapper's favorite; a powerful bass line is important for this genre. Take care when turning up this powerful lower range—just a little bit can add punch.

- **Low Middle (200–1000Hz).** All sounds are made up of a fundamental frequency and a series of related higher frequencies called harmonics; both the fundamental and the related harmonics play a critical role in determining that sound's qualities. Since the fundamentals of many sounds are in the 200–1000 range, turning up or down frequencies in this area can affect the entire frequency spectrum.

- **High Middle (1000–5000Hz).** Turning up this mid range has a pronounced effect on an instrument's brightness and "presence." Turn this range up on an instrument that you want to be more dominant in the mix—but be careful, because this range can quickly sound tinny.

- **Highs (5,000–20,000Hz).** Add brilliance and shimmer to a sound by turning up the highs; up in this range is your instrument's higher harmonic frequencies. This range tends to be very exciting for the ear; the human ear has a fondness for brightness—it's kind of like sugar for the tongue. Again, though, a little bit goes a long way.

techtv
tip

Can You EQ Out the Noise?

Occasionally, you might hear an unwanted sound in your track—more than occasionally, probably. If it's an isolated sound, you can simply select it and delete it. But it's often mixed in with the original recording. In this case, you might be able to reduce that noise by finding its frequency and turning it down. However, because it's part of the audio you want, you need to find a balance between reducing the unwanted sound and maintaining the sound quality of the original track.

Sounds are rarely made up of a specific frequency. Most sounds are complex combinations of a broad range of frequencies. So it's difficult to simply find the unwanted sound's frequency and turn it down, because it's blended in with the audio you want. Attempting to reduce an unwanted sound with EQ is a kind of balancing act: How much damage to the sound you want can you tolerate in your effort to reduce the sound you don't want?

The Many Flavors of EQ

When you're ready to adjust your tracks' EQ you need to boot up your equalizer, which might be a graphic EQ, a parametric EQ, a shelf EQ, or some combination of these. Each has its use, but if the typical audio engineer were stranded on a desert isle with just one, I'm guessing that most would prefer a parametric.

Before we look at the various EQ units, it's important to understand the term *bandwidth*. Within EQ this refers to how wide a frequency spectrum you're boosting or cutting. You may, for example, decide to boost 3kHz to give your vocal track more bite. But do you want to boost *exactly* that frequency, or do you also want to boost frequencies on either side? Do you want to boost everything from 3kHz to 5kHz, or everything from 2kHz to 3.5kHz—how wide a bandwidth do you want to boost? Your decision about bandwidth is key part of the EQ process.

The various EQ units handle bandwidth in different ways:

- **Graphic EQ.** The graphic EQ is often the one that new users grab because it simplifies the EQ process. It offers faders set at predetermined frequencies with a predetermined bandwidth. Some graphic EQ units offer as many as 30 choices of frequencies to affect; others are more simplified. A typical graphic EQ unit lets the user cut or boost, for example, 130Hz, 250Hz, 500Hz, 1kHz, 2kHz, 4kHz, 8.3kHz and 16.5kHz. If you want to boost exactly 3kHz you're out of luck—it's not one of the choices. However, if the tone shaping you're doing isn't that detailed, the graphic EQ is fine.

- **Parametric EQ.** When it comes to equalizing, the parametric is where it's at (see Figure 17.4). It enables the user to determine which frequencies to adjust, how much to adjust them, and by how wide a bandwidth. The bandwidth is determined by the Q setting: the larger the Q number, the narrower the bandwidth.

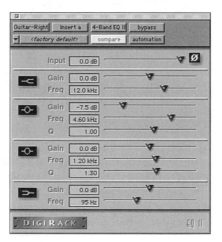

Figure 17.4

This is a parametric EQ set to cut 7.5dB at 4.6kHz, with a Q of 1.

Because a parametric offers more variables than the graphic, it requires more experimentation (and knowledge) to get good results. But it allows highly detailed sound shaping, so you can produce some really impressive results. All of the modern music you hear on the radio, in any genre, has been mixed with extensive use of the parametric.

A parametric can provide a vocal track with, for example, a 3dB boost at 500Hz, with a bandwidth, or Q, of one octave. The center frequency is 500Hz, so the one octave bandwidth is distributed on either side of the center frequency.

You can adjust the Q to be very wide, more than an octave, or down to a tiny notch, as small as one individual frequency. To set the Q, remember the formula $Q=Fc/B$. To put that in English, Q equals the center frequency divided by the bandwidth. Say your center frequency is 1000Hz. If your Q setting is 2, then the bandwidth must be 500Hz, because $2=1000/500$.

Using the parametric is often a case of adjusting its variables and then listening. Try a wider or narrower Q. Try shifting the center frequency up or down. If you're boosting the track by 3dB, try just 1.5dB. If your software allows it, it's ideal to be shifting variables as you're playing back the track, so you can hear a number of different settings back to back. Remember as you work: The math is big help, but your ears are the final judge. Usually a broader Q, and a gentle boost or cut, is the most pleasing to the ear, and is safer.

Filter, and Then Filter Some More

Beyond the parametric and graphic EQ, you may choose to use an array of other EQ filters on your mix. Some of the following filters can be created with a graphic or parametric; some are created using standalone EQ units.

- **Shelving Filter.** The name *shelving filter* is a good description for this equalizer (see Figure 17.5). You use it to adjust all the frequencies above or below a user-determined frequency. In effect you create a shelf—either a higher or lower shelf—to which all the tones above or below a selected frequency range adjust in level. You might, for example, want to eliminate the highest frequencies from a synth track because it sounds overly bright. So you could run the track through a shelf EQ that turns down—attenuates—all the frequencies above 8kHz.

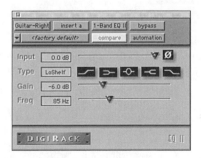

Figure 17.5

This shelf EQ is set to attenuate frequencies beneath 85Hz by 6dB.

- **Bandpass Filter.** A bandpass filter lets the middle band pass, but attenuates the highs and lows. It enables you to set the high and low frequency cut off points beyond which all the higher and lower tones are cut. A bandpass filter can create a very mid-rangey sound; it's sometimes used to create a deliberately telephone-like effect on a lead vocal. However, a bandpass could be any frequency and bandwidth—for example, a half octave centered around 80Hz.

- **Highpass Filter/Lowpass Filter.** A highpass filter lets the highs pass and cuts the lows. A lowpass filter lets the lows pass and cuts the highs. A typical use of a high-pass filter would be to reduce the low end amplifier hum or other unwanted low frequency noise from a track. Most all equalizers provide you with a highpass/low-pass filter. For example, the Filterbank EQ plug-in has a good one (see Figure 17.6) .

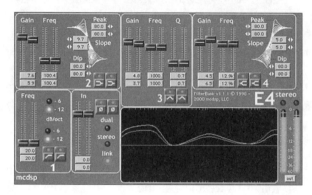

Figure 17.6

The Filterbank EQ plug-in uses software to emulate both tube and solid state equalizers, and lets you mix and match among the sounds of a variety of compressor units.

PRACTICAL APPLICATIONS

Okay, so you're ready to EQ. Where do you start? Here are some suggestions for frequencies to begin the process of experimentation. Realize that these suggestions are just starting points—your instruments may or may not need the same EQ as anyone else's. In each case, you want to adjust more than the stated frequencies; you want to use your parametric or other EQ unit to adjust a bandwidth around these center frequencies:

- **Kick drum.** Adjust the low end depth around 60–80Hz. Adjust percussive attack around 4kHz.

- **Snare drum.** Add or subtract fullness by adjusting around 240Hz. Adjust level of presence and cut-through by tweaking 5kHz.

- **Cymbals.** Adjust depth around 250-750Hz, add or subtract brilliance somewhere between 8kHz to 12kHz.

- **Tom Toms.** Beef up the toms by boosting 80 to 240Hz. Adjust attack around 5kHz.

- **Bass guitar.** Add or subtract bottom around 60–100Hz. Give the bass a more pronounced attack by boosting 700–1000Hz.

- **Acoustic guitar.** Give it more fullness by boosting 240 to 500Hz. Adjust clarity and attack at 2kHz to 6kHz.

- **Synth Pad.** Your EQ really depends on the synth itself, but generally, tweak the bottom from 100 to 250Hz, adjust dominance in the mix at 1 to 3kHz, and give it more high-end sheen from 6kHz to 12kHz.

- **String section.** Increase the fullness at 240 to 400Hz. If you're lucky enough to have real strings, you can emphasize the string/bow friction sound around 6.5 to 10kHz—but too much of a boost can result in harshness.

- **Horns.** Add fullness around 240Hz. Cut the sometimes piercing brightness around 4.5kHz to 8kHz.

- **Vocals.** Wow, dealing with vocal EQ is a vast subject, and depends greatly on the individual vocal and the genre. Generally, add fullness at 120Hz, presence from 1.5 to 3.5kHz, and clarity around 6.5 to 12kHz.

A note to remember about EQ. Boosting frequencies can cause distortion if your track's level is already close to the maximum output level. If you've normalized a sound file to maximize it, an additional 6dB boost (or less) at any frequency can possibly cause digital distortion, which is a pretty ugly sounding thing.

Instead of boosting, you might try cutting various frequency ranges. Cutting frequencies that don't sound good is often more effective than boosting frequencies that do sound good.

By the way, even in this software-driven age, not all EQ is software-based. Most well-equipped studios have an array of hardware EQ units, such as the Yamaha EQ in Figure 17.7.

Figure 17.7

Although you'll probably use software EQ units, hardware units like this Yamaha also come in handy. Each one of the faders allows you to boost or cut a given frequency.

Photo courtesy of Yamaha.

Which brings us to the bottom line of EQ use: First, do no harm. It's better to use EQ sparingly, only as far as it is enhancing the sound; if you're in doubt as to whether you've gone too far, back off your setting. The EQ process is sort of like adding spices to food: Just the right amount of spice is great, and too few spices creates a bland taste. But if you put too much on, you can completely ruin a dish.

COMPRESSION: MY TRACK IS LOUDER THAN YOURS

Have you ever wondered why the commercials on TV are louder than the program? There are a number of reasons, some having to do with EQ, but a key reason is compression. Highly compressed audio is punchier, more "in your face," more likely to grab the listener's attention.

Compression reduces the difference between the quietest and loudest parts of a song or other audio program. It does this by turning down the loudest passage; the compressor has a threshold, and any material that exceeds this threshold is automatically attenuated.

A song's dynamic range, that is, the variations between the soft and loud passages, can be quite dramatic. However, every medium has a ceiling above which a program can be no louder. Whether that medium is CD, playback off of a hard drive, or radio broadcast, that ceiling can not be exceeded. A song's loudest passages will reach this ceiling; if its soft passages are too quiet in comparison to its loud passages, they will get lost in the noisy modern world we live in.

Anything designed for commercial broadcast on radio or TV (in other words, all the commercially produced music by all major artists) must be compressed so that it sounds as loud as the other professionally produced material.

Without compression, a sound wave's dynamic range might look like Figure 17.8.

Figure 17.8

A sound wave before compression.

After substantial compression, that same sound wave will look something like Figure 17.9.

Figure 17.9

The same sound file as in Figure 17.8, after compression.

Notice that the dynamic variations are smaller in the compressed sound wave. A greater percentage of this compressed sound file is close to the ceiling. It will be perceived as louder, and will behave better in a mix. That is, if you set its volume level to 3db under the lead guitar, it will stay consistently at 3dB under the lead guitar, instead of having constantly changing volume levels.

Attenuate

Remember, always use the word *attenuate* instead of "turn down." They mean the same thing, but using "attenuate" will impress your friends.

Compression can easily be overdone. Something that's over-compressed sounds like it's had all the life squeezed out of it. Yes, it will be loud and sonically assertive, but it won't be very musical. The trick with compression, like EQ, is to control the dynamic level only as much as you have to. After you've compressed a track, listen to it. Is it still pleasing to your ears?

Okay, so you've got a track and you want to compress it. What do you do? You must set the following parameters in your compressor:

- **Threshold.** This is the level at which the compressor begins to attenuate your audio. The sound above the threshold is compressed; the sound beneath the threshold will not be affected at all. How high or low you set the threshold levels determines how much of the dynamic range you'll affect. If you just want to turn down the loudest sections, set a higher threshold—this is a more natural sound. If want a highly compressed signal, set a low threshold—this will squeeze the entire amplitude range.

- **Compression ratio.** This determines the relationship between input and output. For example, if you set your ratio at 6:1, for every 6dB of input above the threshold you'll only get 1dB of output—a fairly steep compressor setting. You can achieve a lot with a threshold setting between 3:1 and 6:1. If the compressor's ratio gets steep enough, it functions as a *limiter*. A limiter, in effect, says to the sound wave: You're not going much higher. Limiters have ratios like 10:1 or 20:1, or even infinity:1 (you'll see the little infinity symbol on the controls). At its most extreme setting the limiter is said to be a brick wall. This setting is useful when you want to set your output to your system's absolute maximum; it prevents the signal from going the additional .5dB or so that would cause distortion (now you know why those TV commercials are so loud. They are severely limited). Since you're using your PC for audio production, you'll probably be using a software compressor. To explore a popular hardware unit, take a look at Figure 17.10.

Figure 17.10

As a desktop musician, you'll probably rely upon your software's built in compressors, or perhaps a compressor plug-in. But if you're looking for a hardware compressor, the DBX 160 is unit used by many studios.

Photo courtesy of DBX.

Ratio and Threshold Work Together

A compressor's threshold setting and compression ratio are interlocking variables. You can set a low threshold but use a gentle ratio, like 3:1. This will affect the entire track from its softest to its loudest passages, but only lightly. Or, you can set a very high threshold with a severely limiting ratio like 40:1. This will only affect the signal's highest peaks, but it will reduce them greatly.

- **Attack time/ Release time.** A compressor's attack time setting affects how quickly it responds to incoming signal. You might think it's advantageous to have a fast attack time (and often it is), but too fast an attack can lessen the difference between a sound's peaks and its compressed section. The peaks are exciting. You don't want to squash them all together. Try an attack time of 10 to 30 milliseconds for voice; try a bit longer for lower frequency sounds. The release time setting determines how long the compressor stays engaged after all signal has fallen beneath its threshold. If it's set too fast, it can cause a "pumping sound" as it attempts to change dynamics too quickly. Like the attack time setting (and all of a compressor's settings) the final judge is your ear.

The De-Esser

You'll want to consider using a de-esser on many of your vocal tracks. It's used to reduce the harsh vocal sibilant sounds like "sss," and "tch." A de-esser is a frequency dependent compressor, reducing frequencies within a user determined frequency spectrum in the 2–10kHz range, which is where the voice's unpleasant "s" sounds occur.

The Expander

Think of an expander as the opposite of a compressor. You can use it to *increase* your music's volume variations instead of squeezing them smaller. An expander uses ratio and threshold settings to both attenuate the softer passages and boost the louder passages. For example, a musical passage with a 40dB dynamic range can be run through an expander to give it a 55dB range. Additionally, since the soft passages are attenuated, expanders are quite often used to reduce unwanted low volume noise on a track. At its more extreme setting, this attenuation of a passage's low volume acts as a noise gate. But what exactly is a noise gate?

Noise Gates

A well-named device indeed, the *noise gate* acts as a gate that can be used to keep out noise. Signal that exceeds a noise gate's threshold is allowed to pass without any effect. However, sounds *underneath* a noise gate's threshold—here's where they come in handy—are eliminated, or at least reduced in volume. So say you recorded a singer in your bedroom. The house was quiet, except for low volume TV rumble coming from down the hall.

You could put a noise gate on the singer's track. Set it so the singer's voice is above the threshold but the TV rumble is underneath the threshold. When the singer sings, the gate opens up. His volume is so loud in contrast to the TV rumble that it masks this unwanted noise. But when the singer stops singing, the gate closes completely, eliminating the distracting TV sound. (This assumes you don't want Regis Philbin in your song.)

THE EFFECTS: AN EVER-EXPANDING PALETTE

When you talk about the effects that you can use to color your mix, the list seems to get a little longer every year. There are the classics that go back further than guitarists with big hair, old stand-bys like reverb, chorus, delay and flange. But with the profusion of plug-ins and the constantly morphing state of audio software (see Figure 17.11), there is a crowd of new ones. Some of them are combinations of the old ones, like a chorus-flange-pitch shift effect. Some of them take advantage of digital technology's ability to mimic other sounds, like the Amp Farm plug-in that re-creates classic guitar amps. Then there are little apps that enable you to trigger a MIDI module with an audio file—not exactly an effect, but a way to add new sound to old. Then there are the just plain "out there" ones, that do some kind of phase reversal-sample analysis-whatjamacallit to the sound. If you think you know all the effects, wait for next year—there will be new ones.

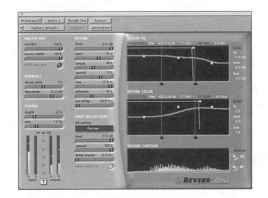

Figure 17.11

Made by Digidesign, the ReverbOne is an all-in-one processor plug-in, giving you a wide array of reverb and delay capabilities.

The more obscure ones might not get used that much, but there are a few basic effects that are used to mix every kind of music, from country to disco to techno. If you're going to mix your own music, these are the effects you need to know about…

Delay

At the root of many effects is one central idea. A device, either software or hardware, takes an input signal and holds it—delays it—for a user-determined amount of time. It then outputs this delayed signal, allowing you to combine it with the original. You might mix this delayed signal at an equivalent level with the original, at a much lower level, or at an overpowering level, depending on what you're trying to achieve. The amount of time between the original and the delayed signal may stay constant or may vary, and is typically measured in thousandths of seconds, or milliseconds (ms).

A super short delay, in the 1–8 ms range, is called *phasing*. As is the case with many delay-based effects, the delay time is often varied as you use it. As the delay varies from 3ms to 9ms to 5ms, it causes a "swirly" sound, a kind of psychedelic effect. In fact, phasing and its close neighbor, *flanging* (when the delay is 10–15 ms) was often used in '70s guitar music. For that reason it was very out of style in the '80s, but has since returned to coolness—unless you use it too much, in which case it's quite corny.

Increase the delay time still further (say 18 to 30 ms, and be aware that many of these times are approximations) and you get into *chorusing*. It's an accurate description because this delay creates the illusion that there is a chorus of instruments playing the part, not just one. Chorus is good way to add a fuller, rounder quality to a sound.

At around the 30–40 ms range, the ear begins to perceive delay as a distinct echo. From around 80–120 ms, it's such a rapid echo that it's called slapback, or "slap." This has been used as an effect on lead vocals in many genres.

Above the 120ms range, a delay is clearly perceived as a distinct echo, echo, echo. It's this range that people are usually referring to when they say, "let's add some delay." These echoes, especially if mixed at a soft enough level to be complementary without overpowering, can add a really pleasing effect to a sound. Delay is used on many instruments across many genres.

One of the primary mixing tricks is to set a delay time that coincides with the music's beats. So each echo coincides with the song's 16th notes, 8th notes, or quarter notes. In fact, if your echoes are out of time with the music, it fights the song's tempo and really works against the music.

Reverb

Ah reverb, sweet reverb, every voice sounds better with it. It's the first effect that almost every mixer goes for.

Reverb is created by sending some of the delayed signal back into itself, mimicking the rich array of echoes we hear in real life, as in a concert hall. Take a look at the TCMegaVerb in Figure 17.12 to see a program that offers many reverb options.

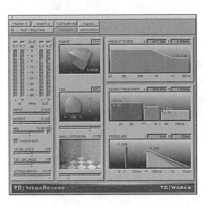

Figure 17.12

This software effects unit by TC Works allows you to give your tracks detailed spatial dimensions.

You might hear people say, "let's add some reverb and delay." What they mean is, they want to add an overall echo-ey quality (reverb) along with individual echoes (delay).

But of course adding reverb isn't just a question of booting up the reverb program and clicking "echo." There are all sorts of parameters—without obscure technical settings, what fun is audio?

- **Dry/Wet balance.** This determines if the original track will be drowning in echo (that's wet), or has just a slight ringing quality (that's on the dry side). While reverb seems to improve most everything, be careful about adding too much. It really adds a pleasant quality, but a sure sign of a novice mixer is that "submerged in reverb" sound.

- **Decay Time and Room Setting.** In nature, these two setting are interrelated. If a room is really big, it will naturally have a longer decay time to its echo (unless it's all carpeted, but how many concert halls are completely carpeted?). In a reverb device, however, you can have a room as small as a closet that rings for three seconds. Or, you can have a room that's as large as a cave, but that only echoes for .5 seconds. Adjust to taste.

- **Pre-Delay.** In a live environment, we hear some sounds directly, with no reflections from that environment's surrounding hard surfaces. Within a second, however, we begin to hear the many reflections that make up the room's natural reverb. Reverb devices, to re-create the time gap between the original and the reflections, give you a parameter called *pre-delay*. You can use this to help you create a sense of closeness or distance to an instrument. If you want an instrument to sound close, use a longer pre-delay time; since a close object's original sound would reach you more quickly, the later reflections would take longer to arrive, hence the longer pre-delay time. Conversely, use a shorter pre-delay time on an instrument to make it sound further away.

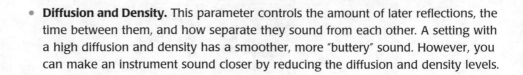

- **Diffusion and Density.** This parameter controls the amount of later reflections, the time between them, and how separate they sound from each other. A setting with a high diffusion and density has a smoother, more "buttery" sound. However, you can make an instrument sound closer by reducing the diffusion and density levels.

CHAPTER **18**

MIXING, PART 2

In This Chapter

- Go step by step through an actual music mix
- Learn an efficient process for mixing your music
- Find out some typical settings to use in your mixes
- Discover many helpful tips to maximize your music's sound
- An interview with a musician/engineer who has worked with some of the biggest names in music

LET'S SIT IN ON A MIX

Rather than talking about mixing, let's do one. Mixing is a hands-on art form. Yes, there's plenty of theory, but ultimately you have to get in there and do it yourself. So this chapter goes step-by-step through an actual mix process.

Although the mix we're about to watch is a fictional one, the techniques used are the same ones used by professionals in top studios. What's important is not the particulars of this mix, but overall concepts you can use in polishing *your* music tracks.

But remember, mixing is highly subjective—many people have many opinions, and there's plenty of disagreement. Is there a precisely right way to mix? Definitely not. But this chapter will provide you with a series of techniques to get you started. At a later date you might look back and view them as totally wrong. That's fine. But for today, let's make some music.

Time to Get Going

It's a Saturday afternoon and Rachel, our desktop musician, is about to mix her band's latest song.

Her setup is pretty straightforward. She's got a fast PC with audio software that handles recording and editing as well as MIDI sequencing. Her MIDI module is one of her more expensive purchases: It's full of great sounds and has 128-voice, 16-patch multitimbral capability. She has a 20GB external hard drive dedicated to audio. After searching the Web, she found a handful of plug-ins to jazz up her main software; she also found a cheap software sampler. Her audio card contains a high-quality A/D converter with four microphone inputs. As for mics, she borrowed four for the recording session she's about to mix. She has a pair of near field monitors that are known for flat frequency response (not like the commercial stereo speakers that are designed to enhance music). She also has a third speaker, a junky little thing that gives her a "real world" listening test—this speaker is about as good as many low-end car radio speakers. When she's done mixing she'll use her CD burner to create a master disc.

Rachel's band, Twisted Little Thing, is hard to describe. It's kind of rock band, so it has all the rock instruments: bass, drums, guitar (both electric and acoustic), keyboard, lead vocal, and vocal harmonies. But there are all sorts of unusual little additions: world beat, kind of a driving techno feel, and a lot of the songs contain a rap section.

What that means for her mix is that she'll be combining a lot of elements. Real instruments with MIDI, traditional musical genres with some weird stuff she's making up as she goes along. And like all good desktop musicians, she makes the mix a creative process. Sure, the tracks are all recorded, just waiting to be blended, but the mix will have as much to do with how the music sounds as how it was composed or performed.

Hot Link: Music Producers Guild (`http://www.mpg.org.uk/`)
This group is a professional organization that facilitates creative networking between musicians, composers, and producers. (See Figure 18.1.)

Figure 18.1

Find other music professionals to share techniques with at the Music Producers Guild site.

Her ultimate goal is to take all the tracks and combine them into a finished song. At the moment, within her computer are about 20 or so separate tracks. Each is completely independent of the others. So in this afternoon's mix she will assign a relative volume to each—the drums this loud, the guitar this loud, the vocals the loudest of all. She will also give a unique sonic color to each instrument as she places it in the mix. When she's done, she will have blended all the elements—mixed them—into a stereo master.

She takes a gulp of Jolt Cola and looks at her track list. Here are the various tracks she will mix down to a finished master:

- **Kick drum.** Recorded live in her living room.
- **Snare drum.** Ditto.
- **Overheads.** A stereo recording of the entire drum kit, using two mics placed a few feet above the drums.
- **Percussion.** A stereo MIDI part that plays along with the drums. Her drummer e-mailed her a variety of Brazilian percussion samples, which she loaded into her software sampler.

- **Bass.** A live bass player recorded with an electric bass guitar into a DI box (To find out about Direct Insertion boxes, see Chapter 12, "How to Record and Edit.")
- **Rhythm guitar 1.** A live guitar player, strumming an acoustic guitar.
- **Rhythm guitar 2.** A MIDI electric guitar track.
- **Keyboard.** A stereo MIDI synth part.
- **Lead guitar.** A live guitar player recorded with a DI box.
- **Sample track 1.** A broad array of city street sounds. The playback of these samples will be triggered by MIDI.
- **Sample track 2.** A wide variety of animal growls. Rachel has placed these samples at various points throughout the song.
- **Vocal harmonies.** Two tracks of band members singing a chordal music part.
- **Lead vocal 1.** Rachel sings on this track.
- **Lead vocal 2.** She raps on this track.

Building from the Bottom Up: The Kick Drum

It's a lot to combine, isn't it? But here's the trick, the technique that's used in most all good mixes.

Work on one track at a time, making sure it sounds good before adding the next track.

First, build the foundation: the song's rhythm tracks. The foundation of the rhythm is the drums; the foundation of the drums is the kick drum. The kick drum is kind of an unsung hero, giving the song its drive and energy without getting much glamour. Notice that practically every genre, from Big Band to disco to punk, uses a kick drum. It a critical part of a song's energy: If the kick ain't working, the song ain't working.

So Rachel turns on *just* the kick drum track and listens to it. It has a kind of "boxiness" to it, a kind of dull, unfocused quality. She uses her software's EQ to make adjustments. She turns down the frequencies around 300Hz quite a bit—as much as 12dB—to clean out the muddiness. To add presence and attack, she does some experimenting: She boosts a variety of frequencies between 1kHz and 7kHz until she finds a sweet spot around 2–3kHz. Boosting that range gives the kick drum a pronounced attack.

Hot Link: Musicians Junction (http://www.musiciansjunction.com/)
When you're done with your mix, this site lists places to sell your tracks, as well as any other musical services you offer (see Figure 18.2).

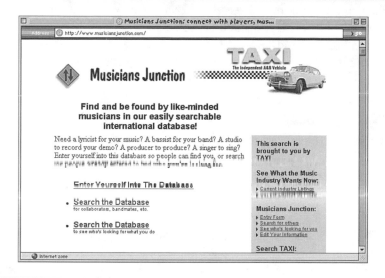

Figure 18.2

The Musician's Junction site offers a marketplace for musical services.

The drummer played the kick drum at varying volumes throughout the song, which Rachel wants to even out. So she runs the kick through a limiter, using a very quick attack time. (However, if it's too quick an attack she'll lose the "snap" of the drum attack). This reduces the variation between the soft kick parts and loud kick parts by about 8dB. It now has a rock solid feel. She adds just a touch of reverb; a tiny room tone that's just enough to keep the kick from being too dry.

The Language of Mixing

Talking about music requires using words to describe sounds, which is an inexact science at best. What exactly is a *muddy* sound? What does it mean for the guitar to sound *honky*? But when you mix with someone (or when you write about mixing), you have to use words. So realize that when you say to your mixing partner that you want to *brighten* the lead vocal, that person may interpret it differently than you do.

The Snare Drum

Rachel turns off the kick track and turns on the snare track, listening to it by itself. It sounds kind of hollow and anemic, so she subtly boosts the frequencies around 250Hz to give some fullness. She knows that she can give the snare some bite—a pronounced percussive attack—by turning up the upper mid range. But she's not sure exactly what mid range frequencies to boost. So she boosts the snare EQ setting by 6dB, and then sweeps the frequency setting across the mid range...1kHz—no, doesn't help; 3kHz—much better; 4.5kHz—yeah, that's it. Now the snare sounds sharp. She gives it more punch by compressing it, using a 4:1 ratio, adjusting the controls until she sees about 2–4dB in gain reduction.

But there's some noise on the snare track. The snare rings whenever the kick drum is played, muddying up the track. Rachel decides to use a noise gate to clean it up. She sets the gate so that it only opens when the snare plays—the ringing sound is eliminated, because its volume is beneath the gate's threshold.

However, when she listens closely she hears the noise gate opening and closing. She knows she could adjust the settings, but she wants this track to be perfect. This is *her* music. She decides against the noise gate. Instead, she finds the track in her editing software and goes through, measure by measure, cutting all the noise between snare attacks. It takes about a half hour for one track, but why not? There's no studio time clock adding charges to her bill. She can take the time to be obsessive.

After cleaning up the snare track, she adds some reverb. It's a medium-sized room setting, with a 1.8 second decay time. That's a fairly wet snare sound, but the song calls for it.

Hot Link: Yahoo's Music Producers (`http://dir.yahoo.com/Entertainment/Music/Producers/`)

One of the Internet's most interesting resources, the list of producers from various genres is a true education. Find out about the background and aesthetic approach of producers who have created some of pop music's best mixes.

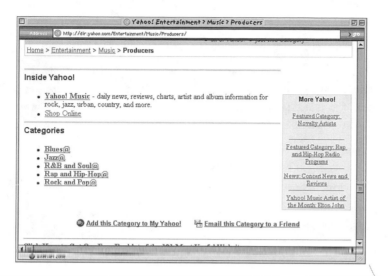

Figure 18.3

No matter what your style, you'll find a producer who works in that genre at the Yahoo Music Producers site.

Listening Volumes

It's best to listen at a medium to low volume as you mix. First, a loud volume quickly exhausts your ears—and your ears may need to work for several hours straight. Also, loud volume enhances music's perceived low and high frequencies, so it's less accurate to use in decision making. A mix that sounds good at a low volume tends to sound good in a diversity of listening environments.

Now Rachel turns the kick drum track back on, and listens to it in combination with the snare. She wants to find a relative volume for the two tracks. Hmmm...she gets it close, but she's not sure, so she puts in one of her favorite CDs by a major band. She listens to it as a reference. In comparison, her snare is softer, so she pushes up its volume. (Of course she doesn't want to push the overall volume too much—she needs to leave headroom for the other elements in the mix.)

The Overhead Drum Mics

Rachel now has a sweet little kick 'n' snare thing going, but she turns off those tracks to listen to the overhead tracks. These two mics captured the entire drum kit: kick and snare, tom toms, hi-hats, and miscellaneous percussion.

The overhead mics create a stereo image—two tracks—so she pans one all way left and the other all the way right. (The kick and snare are both panned up the center.) The overhead tracks have a muddy-sounding lower mid range, so she clears that out by turning down frequencies in the 500–800Hz range. And there's something really unpleasant sounding in the almost sub hearing range—so low we feel it as much as hear it—so she uses a shelf EQ to clear it out. She sets a shelf at 70Hz that turns down the basement range by 6dB. The overheads have a lot of room tone to them already, so she adds no reverb.

She turns the kick and snare back on and listens to them in combination with the overheads. She sets a relative volume level, letting the kick and snare find a roughly equivalent volume with the overheads, so that the combined tracks sound like a real drum kit.

> **Hot Link: Original and Remix Producers** (`http://www.slangmusicgroup.com/`)
>
> This is an example of a boutique shop of independent producers. (See Figure 18.4.)

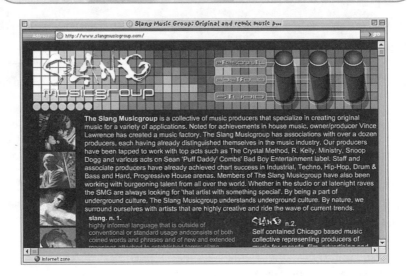

Figure 18.4

Based in Chicago, the group produces mixes for techno, hip hop, rave, and other new music styles.

MIDI Percussion

Rachel turns off the real drum tracks and turns on the MIDI drums. Her bongo-conga-timbale samples sound pristine and perfect in contrast to the real drum sounds; in fact they almost sound too perfect. She adds some reverb to help them blend, a small room setting with a 1 second decay time. Then she boots up a plug-in designed to add a lo-fi sound; this plug-in makes things sound grainy. It's unusual to use it on drums; it's more typically added to guitar or perhaps voice. She just adds enough of the plug-in grunge to make the MIDI drums blend with the real drums.

She gets the MIDI drums sounding more or less like real drums, then listens to them with the real drums. It's kind of strange: Both are going at exactly the same tempo, but the MIDI drums sound like a machine. They are, unlike a human drummer, precisely on the beat. So she selects the MIDI drum track and uses the Humanize function. She shifts the MIDI drum attacks away from the beat by milliseconds so it no longer sounds too perfect.

The drums are now done. As she keeps building her mix, Rachel continues the same process: She listens to a track in solo mode, makes sure it's perfect by itself, then turns on the other tracks to blend in the new track. She wants each additional track to blend in both volume level and sonic color.

Before she goes on, Rachel provides herself with a "safety net." She does a Save As. She saves this version of the mix with a descriptive title (maybe the date and a version number) so she can always get back to it. She does this periodically throughout the mix process, so that she can instantly go back to an earlier version if she needs to.

What Does a Producer Do?

Music producers wear many hats, but one of their key roles is directing the mix. They typically work in conjunction with an audio engineer and one or more band members. They make decisions about reverb settings, EQ, relative volume, and so forth. Top producers have ears that enable them to create mixes that compete with the most highly polished radio mixes. Additionally, they play referee; maybe the guitarist wants the guitar at a higher volume, or the vocalist wants his voice mixed hotter in relation to the music. The producer is an objective critic, hopefully providing guidance that overrides individual band members' egos. Of course, many desktop musicians are their own producers—so while you're exploring hardware and software options, you might also pick up a book on diplomacy.

The Bass Guitar

Now it's on to the bass. The bass, like most of the rhythm section, must have a rock solid volume level. The band's bass player is pretty good, but the track needs more punch. So Rachel runs it though a limiter, really squashing the heck out of it, until it has dramatically less variation in volume. It begins to lose a little of its "humanness," but it has a lot more power—and the rhythm section must drive the train. She gives the bass a more pronounced attack by boosting the 700–900Hz range. The very bottom is too dark, so she uses a shelf EQ to cut most everything under 70Hz. She adds just a touch of reverb, a small room size with a less than one second decay time.

When she turns the drum tracks back on to hear them with the bass, she switches to her junky speaker. It's a little sobering. Everything sounded so good through the bigger speakers, the near fields. Through the little speaker the snare cuts though a bit too much, so she pulls it down just a tad. Rachel goes back and forth between the good speakers and the junky little speaker, adjusting the bass and drum mix until it sounds clear in both listening environments.

Hot Link: Producers and Engineers (http://www.recordproduction.com/producers_and_engineers.htm)

Take a look at this site's interviews with some top producers, talking about how they worked on big budget mixes in studios like Abbey Road. (See Figure 18.5.)

Figure 18.5

Get the scoop on what it's like to work on major mixes at the Record Production site.

The Acoustic Guitar

The first of two rhythm guitar tracks is a strummed acoustic guitar. It's got a good bright sound to it, but Rachel improves it by cutting some of the "boxy" sound around 800Hz to 1.5kHz. She also subtly cuts the 240Hz region to enhance the instrument's clarity. To give the guitar some added brilliance, she adds a shelf filter to the guitar track, boosting everything above 12.5kHz.

In this song, the guitar needs a special dose of compression. In the song's chorus section, many of the other instruments drop out and the guitar strum must keep the energy going.

To make sure the guitar has the punch to keep the song going, she limits it by a 10:1 ratio, squashing it until the controls show 6dB of gain reduction. Rachel uses a slow attack time, so the guitar's initial attack is allowed to keep its spunk.

To give the guitar a thicker, rounder tone, she adds a chorus affect. This gives each strum a short echo, which is slightly pitch modulated from the original track. She uses a special chorus plug-in to add chorus, balancing the original guitar track with its chorused version. The 100 percent chorused version sounds cool, but in a moment of tasteful restraint, Rachel adds just 15 percent or so of the chorus effect to the original. She pans the acoustic guitar to the right side.

The MIDI Guitar

Rachel's challenge with the MIDI rhythm guitar is to bring it to life. It will be a complementary part with the acoustic guitar—the MIDI guitar panned left, the acoustic panned right. This MIDI electric guitar doesn't need to be compressed; she's able to use her software to keep the MIDI note volumes within a narrow range. But it needs an effect to add some sonic interest. She doesn't want to call too much attention to this part—it's essentially a supporting track. So Rachel adds a subtle delay, a short echo that she can set the relative volume of. She spiffs it up by making it a two-part delay: One echo is a soft one set to echo in time with the song's 8th notes; the second echo is a still softer one that echoes in time with the song's quarter notes.

The Magic of Pan

Each track can be panned to the right, left, or up the middle. The lead instruments are often placed right up the middle, but every position in the stereo image should be filled. Don't just pan things up the middle, all the way left or all the way right. You can create a more interesting stereo image by panning some items just halfway left of right, or to even more subtle pan positions. Be aware, though, that not all playback systems can reproduce the halfway pan. If you make some subtle halfway pan decisions, don't be surprised if they play back hard left or hard right when you hear them in different listening environments.

Hot Link: House Music Producers (http://www.housemuzak.com/housemuziq/)

You'll find a big crowd of house music producers linked here, from both Europe and the U.S.(see Figure 18.6). Take a look at their bios and discographies, or post your own.

Figure 18.6

If you're into house music, this site is a must visit.

Keyboard

The song's MIDI keyboard part is the mix's no-brainer. It's a "pad" part, a soft chordal accompaniment intended as background filler. It's a bit dull coming out of the keyboard, so Rachel dials in a parametric EQ setting to perk it up: an octave-wide bandwidth starting at 8kHz that's boosted about 3.5dB.

The tricky thing about this pad part comes in when she combines it with the other instruments. Listening on her tiny speaker, the pad part is barely audible. She starts to push it up, at which point this mushy pad part turns the whole mix into soupy mess.

It's at this point that Rachel remembers one of the great truths of mixing: Not everything can be dominant. Some parts need to be soft, some very low, some even subliminal. A few of the elements of a mix will be heard only by careful listeners. If you try to make everything loud, you end up boosting levels inch by inch across all the tracks until the mix is distorted. With that in mind, she pulls the keyboard synth pad down to a subliminal level.

The Lead Guitar

Ah, the lead guitar; that's the cool part. It's a wailing track, part grunge, part funk, and Rachel wants to do something weird with it. First she gives it a basic sonic treatment: She adds brightness around 5–7kHz, which gives it an aggressive edge, and then she fills in a bit of bottom end around 250Hz. She compresses it, around 6dB gain reduction with a 6:1 ratio. She looks at the part in her software, and decides…to reverse it. She selects the various riffs, section by section, and uses her software program's Reverse option. She adjusts the start time of the clips to make sure the part still works rhythmically. Strange.

But not strange enough. She adds an auto pan effect to the lead guitar, so that the guitar sounds like it shifts from left to right and back again as the song plays. Still not satisfied, Rachel gives it a variable flange effect, automating the effect so that it's very light during the verse, but quite heavy during the chorus. Okay, it's definitely strange enough now.

The Sample Tracks

Two tracks of Rachel's mix are coming from her software sampler. She decides to use them as a complementary stereo pair: The track full of samples of city sounds will be panned left; the track full of samples of animal growls will be panned right.

For the track of city samples, she routes the output of her sampler to a plug-in that adds the sound of a vintage guitar amplifier. Rachel chooses the sound of a 1959 Fender amp. But instead of just adding this grungy sound to the track, combining the sample track with a retro version of itself, she uses only the output of the plug-in. So her samples of city sounds—cars, buses, city bustle—sound as if they were played by an electric guitar. Weird but cool.

For the track full of animal growls, she uses a time compression plug-in. She pitch-shifts them down an octave, down low enough so that they still sound like growls, but it's hard to say what kind. For good measure she adds a bit of reverb; since these animal growls occur only occasionally, she adds a long decay to them, about 3.5 seconds, but uses a small room setting so the sound doesn't get too spacious.

Hot Link: Reggae Producers (http://www.reggaefusion.com/ Production/Producers.html)

From Jimmy Cliff to Winston "Merritone" Blake, here are all the cool Jamaican mixers and producers. (See Figure 18.7.)

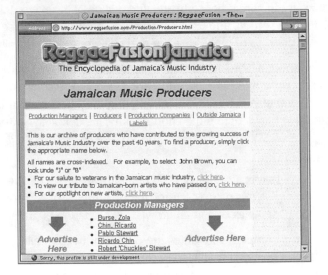

Figure 18.7

The producers at the Reggae Fusion site are adept at creating that laid-back Island sound.

Filling Out the Frequency Spectrum—Without Conflict

The ideal mix has elements across the entire frequency spectrum, from deep lows to pleasant mids to nice shimmering highs. Some musicians listen to their mix specifically with this in mind. They listen and ask, not what musical composition element should be added, but what frequency should be added? Is there something filling the 6–8kHz range? Is my low end filled up? Conversely, you don't want conflict in a given range. For example, the bass can sometimes conflict with the kick drum because they exist in a similar tonal range. One solution to the problem of competing frequencies is to carve out the competing frequencies from one of the instruments. For example, cut some of the instruments' 3kHz range to prevent them from overriding the lead vocals.

The Vocals

Finally, Rachel is ready to add her lead vocal track. (The vocal harmonies are the one thing she'll mix after the lead vocal; they rely completely on the main voice track for placement.) If every other track received loving care, this track gets the super-deluxe-obsessive treatment. For most listeners, this is what they respond to the most directly.

First, Rachel goes through and cleans the track, using her editing software. She removes any extra noise until the track is squeaky clean. If there's a breath she doesn't want, she cuts it. Some of the breaths add naturalness, some are just gasps for air—the difference is a matter of opinion.

Her lead vocal track contains a rap section and a traditional singing section. She splits the lead vocal into two tracks so she can treat them separately.

The Rap Section

Rachel wants this rapidly spoken track to be right up front, to jump out of the mix and assault the listener. She runs it through a limiter, using 20:1 ratio, getting about 8dB of gain reduction. She decides to give it a telephone effect, so she runs it though a bandpass filter, cutting all the frequencies beneath 800Hz and above 2.5kHz. What's left is just a narrow mid range, which makes the rapping voice sound like it's over the telephone. Then she adds delay, which creates an echo (which she mixes in pretty loud) that coincides with the song's 8th note rhythm. Then she adds a tight reverb, a .7 decay time with a small room setting. This is a nasty rap.

Traditional Sing

In contrast to the rap section, Rachel wants her singing to have a full, rich sound. She goes through the track phrase by phrase, boosting or cutting her voice's volume; her goal is to get consistent volume levels with as little compression as possible. When she's done with this painstaking process, she wants still more punch, so she compresses the vocal with a 4:1 ratio, setting it so that there's only 3–4dB of gain reduction. But, after listening to the voice with the fill mix, it still needs more punch—much more. So she routes the vocal through a limiter at a 10:1 ratio. She sets the limiter so that only the vocal peaks are affected.

Rachel runs the voice through a de-esser to minimize the vocal sibilance, the harsh "s" sounds. To add fullness, she finds a nice range right around 600Hz, defines a bandwidth that ranges from about 450Hz to 750Hz, and boosts it by 3.5dB. To make the vocal stand out, she nudges up the track's mid range, in the 3kHz range, by about 4.5dB. Then she gives the track dramatic brilliance by using a shelf EQ at 14kHz, boosting everything above this by 8dB.

The vocal reverb is the most spacious of any element in the mix: a 3-second decay time with a big hall setting. Rachel adds delay sparingly, a light echo that coincides with the song's 8th notes. She sets the delay so that the echoes ping pong back and forth between the left and right side.

Hot Link: Music Producer's Journal (`http://www.livejournal.com/community/music_producers/`)

This site is an ongoing discussion forum where mixers and producers ask advice and share comments about music projects in progress. (See Figure 18.8.)

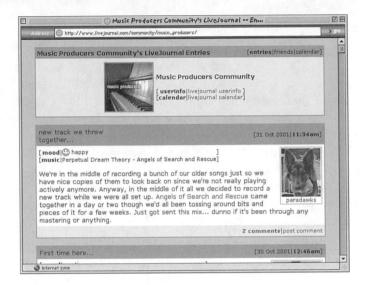

Figure 18.8

Nobody learns to mix all by themselves. This site is a good place to get the feedback necessary to keep improving your mixing skills.

Vocal Harmonies

For the stereo vocal harmony tracks, she pans one side left and the other side right. She compresses each track lightly, using the same setting on both sides so that they match. She gives the harmonies an EQ that puts them in back of the lead vocal. She turns down the mid range so they won't compete with the lead, and she adds only a touch of brightness to the top: a 1.5dB boost around 10kHz. Rachel adds a medium reverb setting and sets the volume so that the harmony tracks blend with the lead vocal without overpowering it.

Voice and Music Levels

What exactly is the right voice-music ratio? How hot should the music be in relation to the lead vocal? That's a question with a dozen answers, depending on your personal taste and what style of music you're making. Compare bands from recent music history and you'll hear a blizzard of different approaches. Groups like Pearl Jam and the Red Hot Chili Peppers, for example, mix their music hot in relation to the voice, at times even obscuring the lyrics. Madonna, on the other hand, always makes sure her voice is highly prominent. Country music is mixed very conservatively, with the voice much louder than the supporting tracks. Punk buries the lead vocal in a turbulent sea of noise. If you're looking for guidelines, listen to a well-produced CD of a band in your genre.

Finishing Touches

At this point Rachel has shaped and placed all of the tracks, listening to the overall mix as she's added each part. She takes some time to listen carefully to the mix in both the near fields and her little junk speaker, listening at both medium and low volumes. If all the elements are still clear at a variety of volumes, in both monitoring configurations, the mix will stand up to any listening environment.

After listening back and forth, Rachel decides to sub-mix. This is a popular technique that's often used to control a mix. For example, in a drum sub-mix, all the drum tracks are sent to a single stereo pair of channels. This way all six or so of the drums tracks can be easily controlled with a couple of faders.

Rachel creates a sub-mix that contains all the instruments except the voice. From the drums to the keyboard to the sample tracks—even the vocal harmonies—everything gets combined into one stereo pair.

This "all tracks but the voice" sub-mix allows Rachel to better control the most crucial element of the mix: the relative volume between voice and music. It's important to pull the voice back into the music—they must be fully merged. But Rachel spent hours writing the lyrics. She doesn't want the voice to be buried in the music. Finding the proper relationship between voice volume and music volume requires real finesse.

To better control the music sub-mix, Rachel compresses it. Even though each track has been compressed individually, by compressing the sub-mix she will further blend all the music. After compressing the sub-mix by an additional 3dB at a 3:1 ratio (a gentle squashing), the combined music tracks sound like one wall of sound. Additionally, the music is less likely to have a surprise surge that drowns the voice track.

Hot Link: Top Music Producers (http://www.record-producers.com/)

From the Cure to Depeche Mode, Ziggy Marley to the Talking Heads, these are the people who have created sounds that have sold a lot of records (see Figure 18.9).

Figure 18.9

Arguably the most impressive collection of big name music mixers and remixers profiled at one site.

It's time for the final listen. Whew, it's been a lot of work—is everything absolutely perfect? This would be a good time to take a break—since her studio is in her home she has the luxury of resting whenever she wants. Maybe even let it sit a day. Come back to it with fresh ears. Does the music-voice level still sound good when you listen the next day? How about the reverb setting on the snare? Should you make it a little less wet? It's a good idea to listen to your mix in as many listening environments as possible before pronouncing it finished.

When you're ready to master, you may have to find a way to route the entire mix back into your computer. The particulars of how to do this depend on your setup. Typically it's a matter of creating two new tracks in your record software, routing all your tracks to this stereo pair, and then going into record. If you can keep the music in the digital domain, that's vastly preferable. In other words, avoid sending the music out a D/A converter, because it will have to be re-digitized when you're ready to create a CD. Most programs offer a "bounce to disc" mode, in which your complete mix is saved as a file on your hard drive without needing to be routed in and out the digital converter (although you do have to find a way to record your MIDI tracks as audio). If your program has this option. It's the best way to go.

Bear in mind, too, that to burn a CD your audio files must be 44.1kHz, 16-bit audio. If you've been working in, say, 96kHz, 24-bit, you'll need to find a way to convert down, which is why some people choose to work in the format required by a CD.

INTERVIEW WITH A WORKING PROFESSIONAL

Richard Hilton has been a professional musician and recording engineer for the past 22 years, and has worked with a dazzling array of artists, from Bob Dylan to the B-52s. He is currently the chief keyboardist, programmer, and engineer with producer Nile Rodgers. We talked with him about his approach to audio production work.

What's your favorite studio tool, the piece of gear you most enjoy using?

My current favorite tool is probably the computer running Pro Tools. I find this to be an extremely enjoyable and productive environment in which to create. I don't miss tape one bit. I don't miss console automation, either. I've basically always wanted to work this way; I just had to wait a few decades for it to come along.

What do you listen for before you decide a mix is done?

I listen, in no particular order, to musical excitement and authenticity; the story being told (assuming it's song form). Some kind of sense of intimacy with the singer/story-teller. Groove integrity and pitch integrity. Sonic integrity; frequency balance, broad spatial presentation, textural variety, vocal clarity, and track punch. A smile on the producer's face. A smile on the artist's face. A smile on the A&R guy's face.

What was one of your favorite music projects, and why?

There have been so many positive musical experiences for me in the past two decades that to pick just one would seem to disrespect the others. David Bowie was a joy. Stevie Ray and Jimmie Lee Vaughan were too. Bob Dylan, Eric Clapton, The B-52s, David Lee Roth—they were all a blast to do. The Strangefolk record we did in 1999 was a big production opportunity for me, and I really loved working with those guys. The recent *We Are Family* tribute CD for disaster relief was definitely a highlight, as I got to record about 200 talented people, including some of the most well-respected vocalists in the history of pop music. The Tina Arena record we did this year was also a great opportunity and great fun. Diana Ross, Charlie Sexton, Lionel Ritchie, Steve Winwood, Freddie Mercury, Chic... I love music, and I am so grateful to have gotten to work with so many of my favorite musicians and become friendly with them.

Where do you see the future of music technology going?

Unfortunately, I see a smaller base of talented players of music in general, partially brought about by the easy availability of more versatile tools to the masses. Hopefully, this will even itself out and the real players out there will once again have the ability to rise to the top and be heard.

As for technology itself, I see, as with most things, the gear getting smaller and cheaper. I see very few commercial recording studios succeeding in this environment. I see budgets getting smaller and smaller, and more records being done mostly or entirely in home studio environments. I see record company corporate bullies and A&R guys who "always wished they'd kept up those guitar lessons" getting much more musical input than their specific musical talents would suggest they deserve, much to the detriment of the music and the creative process in general. Unfortunately, it is no longer an artist-driven business.

Any advice for desktop musicians that are just starting out?

Don't forget to learn how to play and understand music. Stay current. Broaden your tastes to the greatest extent possible. Be familiar with a wide range of styles and try to understand them. Listen to advice, even from those who might seem to be less qualified, because sometimes there's a diamond in the rough and a missed opportunity is a great waste.

CHAPTER **19**

DVD AUDIO AND SURROUND SOUND MIXING

In This Chapter:

- Learn about the various DVD recordable formats
- Discover the DVD application formats, such as DVD-Video and DVD-Audio
- Explore the music mixing technique that uses these formats: 5.1 surround sound
- Learn about the equipment and techniques of surround sound mixing

COMING TO A (HOME) THEATER NEAR YOU

The best word to describe the relationship between desktop musicians and DVD is…evolving. The DVD industry is in flux—major flux—and mixing for this new medium is just beginning to be possible for the average user. However, DVD will have a major impact on audio, and forward-looking musicians are feeling a healthy techno-lust in anticipation of its creative possibilities.

DVD offers distinct advantages over CD. First, it can hold substantially higher-quality audio. In contrast to CD's 44.1kHz, 16-bit audio, DVD can hold 192kHz, 24-bit audio—an impressive leap. In contrast to CD's two-channel stereo format, DVD can deliver discrete multi-channel audio, the 5.1 surround sound format (not to mention high-quality video). You can create an immersive mix with the surround sound format, placing the listener in the middle of your sound design. To top it off, DVD has the capacity to hold much more music than CD.

But unless you're a Hollywood movie studio, DVD is not yet the ideal medium for your product. One of its drawbacks is that only about 30 percent of U.S. households can play a DVD (maybe 40 percent by the time you read this). And those with a player probably have it in their living room or on their PC. But what about the listeners who want to enjoy it in their car or in their portable player? Give them a shiny DVD and they'll say…do you have a CD?

But still, you have an itch to mix your tunes in surround sound. That's a cool idea—but not yet for your major album. The task of mixing in the 5.1 format is daunting even to seasoned professionals. Heck, mixing in good old fashioned stereo is tough (that is, to do it well). Surround sound mixing not only adds an additional 3.1 channels, it adds an exponential leap in mix complexity. You might want to start to learn it, but in terms of putting out your album in 5.1, it will take you three times as long to record and mix it, and you'll still wonder if it's right. Fun, yes. Practical, not yet.

Hot Link: DVD Demystified (http://www.dvddemystified.com/)

Wondering about DVD bit rates, player compatibility, and the ever-changing DVD industry? DVD Demystified has most of the answers to most of the questions about DVD (see Figure 19.1).

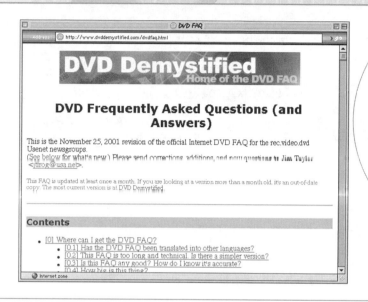

Figure 19.1

The FAQ section of DVD Demystified is the best online source of information about this rapidly evolving format.

Compatibility issues are also slowing things down. Not all DVD players will play home-pressed DVD discs, and there are a confusing handful of recordable formats, some of which are incompatible with each other. There are—surprise—manufacturers who are not working in a cooperative fashion with other manufacturers.

And of course, cost is still a factor. By the time you set up 5.1 mix and DVD premastering capability, you could have bought that extra bank of MIDI modules you've been looking at. (Some cost-conscious musicians have commandeered the home theater system for their surround music mixes. But these musicians do not tend to have happy home lives.)

The one exception to this "not yet" attitude is DVD-RAM. It's a good storage medium, and it's gaining popularity among musicians who need an easy way to archive audio. You can buy a DVD-RAM unit suitable for backup for less than $500, and archive your audio in considerably larger chunks than with a CD-R (although the blank media is more expensive, and for really big projects you might need to use multiple discs).

Also, now we have DVD+RW (from Phillips) and DVD-R (Pioneer, others). Those are becoming more widespread. It's an alphabet soup of confusion out there.

JARGON

DVD stands for both Digital Video Disc and Digital Versatile Disc, depending on who you talk to and what time period you're referring to. Funny, isn't it: one acronym, two meanings. But actually, the DVD Forum (the medium's governing body) has stated that it's just a mark with no defined meaning.

But don't be too discouraged by all this nay-saying. Looking to the future, DVD looks like it will leapfrog over CD-R as the desktop musician's medium of choice. Although penny-pinching creative types might sit it out for a while, it's a good trend to be aware of as it evolves. And if you're on the bleeding edge of technological progress, you're ready right now. So let's take a look at this medium in progress.

DVD: FORMAT VERSUS MEDIA

The DVD medium itself is fairly straightforward—in essence, a DVD is just an improved CD. It uses technology similar to that of a CD (which is covered in Chapter 20, "CD Burning, The Basics"). Like a CD player, a DVD player uses a laser to read digital data from a disc, interpreting an ocean of ones and zeros as it scans a disc's surface. A DVD, however, is able to hold (in some cases) more than 25 times the data of a CD. It can do this because the information stored on the surface of a DVD disc is in a much more compact form, and a mass-produced DVD can have more than one layer of information. A DVD laser, therefore, must be able to focus its beam of light on these various layers. This is one of the reasons a DVD player can play CDs but a CD player cannot play DVDs.

By the way, the newer blue-laser DVDs can hold 25 gigabytes of information on a single side.

Multiple Layers of Information

Whereas a mass-produced DVD can contain more than one layer of information, DVD-Rs contain just one layer.

Hot Link: DVD Made Easy (http://www.dvdmadeeasy.com)
DVD Made Easy, shown in Figure 19.2, is geared for the DVD content creators. You must register to peruse this site's articles, but it's free.

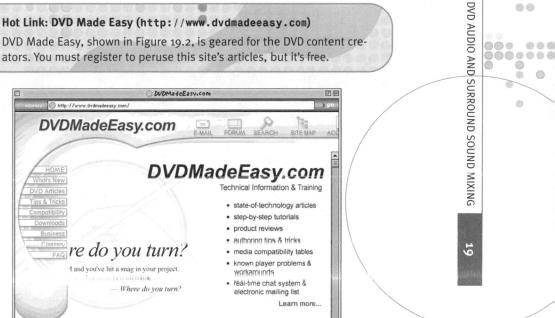

Figure 19.2

If you have questions about creating your own DVDs, browse the library of articles at DVD Made Easy.

So that's the physical media of a DVD—nothing too earth shaking. But the world of DVD starts to lose its simplicity after that. As if its sole aim is to confuse and befuddle the consumer, DVD has a small crowd of recording formats, not all of which are compatible. Let's take a deep breath and dive in.

DVD-R

DVD-R is the most common type of recordable DVD, and it has been on the market the longest. However, this format is itself divided into two subdivisions: DVD-R General and DVD-R Authoring. DVD-R Authoring is considerably more expensive, but it enables you to create a replication master that can be used for disc manufacturing (in the Cutting Master Format, CMF). DVD-R General is geared for non-professional users, is considerably cheaper than DVD-R Authoring, and will most likely be the format used by desktop musicians. However, there are restrictions on what kind of replication master you can make with DVD-R General, and the format includes all manner of copy restrictions. (You weren't thinking of renting a Hollywood release and copying it to your home DVD-R, were you?) Both forms of DVD-R may be unplayable on some consumer DVD players, although this tends to be more of a problem with older players.

Hot Link: DVD-R Compatibility (http://www.apple.com/dvd/compatibility/)

Apple maintains a page that lists whether or not a given consumer DVD player can handle discs created with its SuperDrive DVD-R burner (see Figure 19.3) that burns both DVD-R and CD-R media. By the way, the SuperDrive, which is actually the Pioneer DVR-103 DVD-R, has become a widely used burner on both Windows and Mac setups.

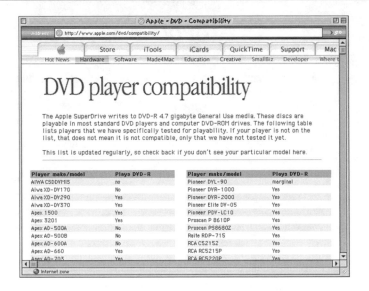

Figure 19.3

Find out which DVD players can handle discs created in the SuperDrive DVD-R unit at this site maintained by Apple.

DVD-RW

In contrast to DVD-R, which uses a dye that changes color as its writing medium, DVD-RW uses a metal alloy. This alloy's durability means that DVD-RW discs are good for 1,000 or more write/rewrites. If you have a DVD-R drive, it most likely handles DVD-RW as well. But the DVD-RW blanks are quite a bit more expensive; depending on what you're doing, it may be cheaper to simply burn DVD-Rs. In terms of distributing your material on DVD, DVD-RW shares the same compatibility issues as DVD-R. In fact, some consumer players will play DVD-Rs but not DVD-RW.

DVD+RW

This format is being promoted by a group of companies called the DVD+RW Alliance, which is made up of plenty of industry heavyweights, including Philips, Dell, Yamaha, Hewlett-Packard, and Sony. The Alliance promotes its format as "the compatible, rewritable format." The claim is that its recordable discs are compatible with consumer players. However, it's not compatible with DVD-R or DVD-RW. This means the DVD recordable industry has not yet settled into a fixed, one-size-fits-all standard. It's hard to say which standard will prevail. DVD+RW got to market later, but with as many companies as are promoting it, it's not safe to bet against it.

DVD+R

Promised for a long time, this format is finally making it to market. It's a write-once DVD format, much like DVD-R, but one that works with DVD+RW recorders. Blanks should run about a third the price of DVD+RW media

Hot Link: The DVD+RW Alliance (http://www.dvdrw.com)
This is the group of manufacturers who are promoting a standard that competes with DVD-R (see Figure 19.4). Will one standard prevail over another? Stay tuned.

Figure 19.4

Learn all about the DVD+RW format at the official DVD+RW Alliance Web site.

DVD-RAM

You mean...there's *another* recordable DVD format? Cool! The DVD recordable industry is about as organized as a general admission rock concert—everyone's just grabbing seats in a mad rush to beat everyone else. But of all the formats, DVD-RAM is the most useful for desktop musicians. Even though it has virtually no compatibility with consumer DVD players, it's a reasonable alternative for audio archiving. For this reason it's thought of as a "bit bucket"—you can dump your files to a DVD-RAM disc in 4.7GB increments. There are already plenty of musicians using DVD-RAM, and as the drives and blank media fall in price it will gain popularity.

USES FOR MUSICIANS: DVD-VIDEO, DVD-AUDIO, AND SACD

We've seen that there are a number of different DVD *physical formats*, such as DVD-RW, DVD+RW, and DVD-RAM. But there are also a number of *application formats* for DVD. The term "application format" refers to how information and content is presented on a DVD disc. Possibilities include DVD-Video, DVD-Audio, and SACD (Super Audio CD).

At this point, you might be frightened and confused: even more subcategories? You may be tempted to go back to your CD-R burner and wait until the DVD industry settles into a predictable pattern. That's a reasonable response. Since you might be a little bewildered by this medium in progress, now would not be a good time to tell you it gets worse: Not all DVD-Video players will play DVD-Audio discs, and DVD-Audio and SACD are competing to see which will dominate (or perhaps both will survive, who knows?)

Let's take a look at the various application formats.

DVD-Video

This is the format used on the movies at the neighborhood movie rental store; this is the format the general public calls "DVD." Since DVD-Video has reached the consumer mass market, you can find consumer-level authoring programs for under $100 (of course you'll also need to buy a DVD-R drive). The audio on a DVD-Video can be in a number of formats, including the impressive 24-bit, 96kHz, stereo. However, the multichannel surround sound audio on a DVD-Video must be compressed in the Dolby or DTS formats (more on them in a moment). Since DVD-Video was not intended as a music-only delivery medium, to press your own you'll need some video, although some authoring programs enable you to use stills. DVD-Video might become the medium of choice for musicians, yet there are two other formats specifically geared for audiophiles.

Interactive Links

Many DVD authoring programs contain a feature called Web linking, which enables you to embed hyperlinks into your DVD.

Hot Link: DVD Software (`http://www.roxio.com`)

Roxio's Video Pack for Windows can be used to make DVD-Video (see Figure 19.5).

Figure 19.5

Roxio is a leading name in disc creation software. Exploring the company's site is a good way to learn about DVD software.

DVD-Audio

If you're a musician or sound designer, this format is a deluxe option. It will hold PCM stereo audio (that's uncompressed audio, and therefore higher quality) at a dazzling 24-bit, 192kHz resolution. And it will even play surround sound audio at 24-bit, 96kHz. However, DVD-Audio has come to the market slowly. Part of the delay was due to copyright protection concerns, especially those created by DeCSS, a DVD descrambler code that allows copying of DVD discs. Additionally, the first generation DVD players couldn't handle DVD-Audio discs (they required their own players). This however has changed, and as DVD becomes the consumer standard, DVD-Audio looks like it will rise with the tide.

Because DVD-Audio is still in the process of gaining mass consumer acceptance, the authoring tools are still few and far between—and expensive. As of this writing, a DVD-Audio authoring package costs $5,000–$10,000, with a full-featured package costing considerably more. However, there are reasonably priced DVD-Audio programs on the horizon, including one by Minnetonka Audio that should be out in 2002.

SACD

The Super Audio CD standard was developed by Sony and Philips. Its super high resolution audio is a product of what's called Direct Stream Digital (DSD), a proprietary encoding technology. These discs contain both a multichannel surround version, which requires a SACD player (these players also play CDs), and a two-channel version, which will play in a CD player. (To add confusion, some SACD discs have either stereo or surround, but not both.) There are relatively few SACD titles available; about 500 SACD titles (and only about 180 DVD-Audio titles) existed in fall 2001. In terms of creating SACD, the hardware and software required is geared for the professional market, with no consumer-level authoring packages in sight.

How will these formats shake out? It's entirely possible that they will live side by side for an extended period. There are now some consumer players that handle all of the formats. The average consumer's eyes must glaze over as they read all the formats that some of today's players handle: DVD-Video, DVD-Audio, SACD, CD. Huh?

For the home musician, however, the format to watch looks to be some form of DVD-Audio. As the players continue to populate living rooms, and reasonably priced authoring software becomes available, more musicians will be experimenting. This format looks ready to begin to overtake the CD—but not overnight. On the other hand, it's far from certain. The DVD-Video format provides sound that's good enough for all but the most demanding audiophiles, the authoring software is cheaper, and there are a lot more players. Keep your eyes open.

Hot Link: DVD-Audio News Source
(http://www.digitalaudioguide.com/)

This site tracks the emerging DVD-Audio standard with an emphasis on available albums and player compatibility issues (see Figure 19.6).

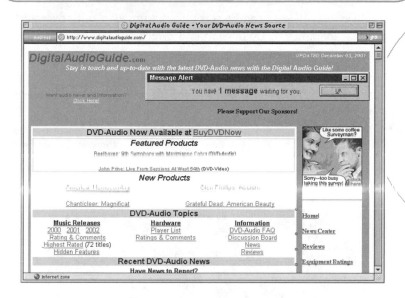

Figure 19.6

This site helps you keep up with audio developments in the constantly changing DVD industry.

THE MAGIC OF SURROUND SOUND

We've examined the physical format that holds surround sound: DVD and its many permutations. What about surround sound itself? First, we'll look at where it came from, which will help you understand the compression schemes you'll need, and then we'll look at how it works on the desktop.

It was from the movies that the original immersive sound experience was born. Seeking to pull us deeper into its world of make believe, Hollywood wanted a way to surround audiences with music and audio. The spaceship must not only fly toward us onscreen, we must *hear* it flying toward us—and hear it disappear somewhere in the murky depths of space behind us.

Early surround sound allowed moviegoers to hear a film's audio from four different points: left front, center, right front, and rear. This rear channel contained limited bandwidth, just the low end, and was used to enhance special effects (the evil spaceship is hovering…). Many theaters split this rear mono channel into two speakers to more fully surround the audience.

But the problem was how to compress all this information onto two channels of 35mm film stock. That solution was Dolby Surround, which has provided movie fans with years of explosions, terrified crowds, and triumphant music.

> **Hot Link: The Epicenter of Movie Sound (`http://www.skysound.com/site.html`)**
> Skywalker Sound, the audio studio for LucasFilms, could be considered nirvana for movie sound buffs (see Figure 19.7). Even the Web site has cool sound effects.

Figure 19.7

Take a virtual tour of one of the most advanced film sound facilities at the Skywalker Sound site.

With the advent of the digital age, the 5.1 format was developed (pronounced "5 dot 1" or "5 point 1"). A 5.1 surround sound system contains six discrete channels. (A discrete channel is completely separate from its accompanying channels. So a stereo signal, in contrast to a 5.1 signal, contains two discrete channels.) Five of the channels are full bandwidth, 20Hz to 20kHz, and the sixth channel—the ".1"—is for the basement lows, from 5 to 125Hz (although the idea of a speaker's subwoofer reproducing down to 5Hz is pretty theoretical). The 5.1 channels are referred to as left, right, center, left surround, right surround, and LFE (low frequency effect).

Dolby Laboratories, again on the forefront of sound technology, developed a codec to squeeze these six digital channels of information into less bandwidth than two channels of stereo PCM audio (remember, PCM stands for pulse code modulation, and refers to uncompressed digital audio). This codec is called Dolby AC-3 (or just AC-3), and is used on many commercial DVD titles. Its more common commercial name (you'll see this on the box in the store) is Dolby Digital.

> The term *codec*, short for "coder, decoder," refers to a device (or piece of software) that can compress and decompress digital information. A codec is used to squeeze data into a smaller space, or to decompress it to watch or listen to it.

But of course, few industry standards exist without competition. With the release of *Jurassic Park*, the public first heard DTS, a 5.1 surround sound codec developed by Digital Theater Systems. The DTS codec compresses the audio data less, and thus requires more data storage capacity than AC-3. For some listeners, DTS sounds more faithful to the original uncompressed audio than Dolby.

DTS has also made a foray into the music market, using one of its codecs to fit surround sound on a CD. However, to play these 5.1 music CDs, you need a DVD or CD player that can read DTS data, along with a DTS decoder and six channels of amplification. As you might expect, these specialized equipment requirements have so far kept DTS CDs from gaining a huge audience.

> You've probably seen the logo *THX* in movie theaters. THX was developed by LucasFilm in the early 1980s. George Lucas (the *Star Wars* director) wanted his movies to look and sound good no matter where they were played, so the company developed the THX set of theater standards to ensure optimum movie playback. According to legend, the term is named after both *THX 1138* (a Lucas film) and Tomlinson Holman, then LucasFilm's technical director.

YOUR STUDIO'S SURROUND SETUP

Although surround sound started in the movies, it's now gaining a presence on the desktop. Now many of the SoundBlaster sound cards—perhaps the most common piece of gear in the audio desktop universe—support 5.1 surround sound playback.

(Interestingly, one of these popular cards is called "SoundBlaster Live MP3 +5.1." So the unit handles everything from MP3s—an audio form we love, but let's face it, pretty low grade—to 5.1, a full bandwidth format intended to immerse the listener in sound. That's the state of modern audio—all manner of standards exist side by side.)

Surround Sound Mixing Setup

While the SoundBlaster supports surround playback, actually creating surround sound takes some special gear and a 5.1 speaker configuration (see Figure 19.8).

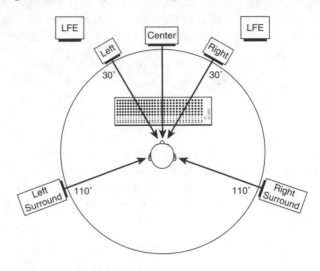

Figure 19.8

This configuration is the Audio Engineering Society configuration for 5.1 mixing. Note that the left and right front speakers are 30 degrees from center, and the surround speakers are 110 degrees from center.

At this point the home setup that has the resources to mix in the 5.1 format is rare. To create surround sound in your studio, you'll need the following:

- **Surround sound software.** The software designed for surround mixing is similar to regular multitrack audio software, with a key difference: It's set up to output to six channels, and so allows you to pan to six discrete spatial points. Examples of desktop surround packages are Nuendo, Digital Performer, Pro Tools, and Minnetonka Audio's Mx51.

 If you're wondering whether you can use the multitrack software you already have, you can, but it's awkward. Most audio software is set up to output to two channels for a stereo master. To create a six-channel surround master, you have to use your software's aux sends or sub groups to create a multichannel output. This ties up your sends that you would use to add reverb to your mix, so it's a limited solution.

- **Multitrack audio recorder—or maybe not.** Finishing a surround mix means finding a way to store six discrete tracks (see Figure 19.9). This can be done with hardware or software. For the hardware option, a multitrack digital deck is often used; the Tascam DA-88 is a popular choice. This multitrack master can then be sent off to DTS (among other places) to create a surround master. For the software option (probably more feasible for the average user), the finished surround master is a group of six discrete audio files stored on your hard drive. Once you have your six files, pressing a DVD-Audio disc is a matter of using your authoring package to assign which file is assigned to which 5.1 surround channel, and clicking "burn."

Figure 19.9

This is Minnetonka's Mx51 surround sound software. Notice the six output channels on the right side.

- **Five speakers and a subwoofer.** The key here is to get matched speakers. You want at least the three front speakers to be the same make and model, otherwise differences in the speakers themselves will lead you to make inaccurate mix decisions. So it's far from ideal to simply assemble speakers from your available stereo pairs. If you're experimenting with surround on a budget, you might look at the $150-for-a-set surround cheapies that are cropping up in local electronics stores. Some studios are getting five of their favorite powered nearfield speakers (for example, five Genelecs) plus the matching subwoofer. This way, all the speakers match, are equal in size, and have their own amplification.

- **Amplification.** To prevent yourself from spending the family fortune on power amps, a home setup is best served with a consumer home theater receiver. This will give you five discrete channels of power. It will also enable you to control volume on all speakers simultaneously, a requirement of a good surround setup. Ideally, the receiver will provide you with Dolby Digital and DTS decoding, as well as a way to bypass the decoders; you'll want to listen to your mix without decoding (because the material has not yet been encoded; that comes later). To compare your mix with those of Hollywood, you can pop in a commercial DVD and listen through the system's decoders.

Balancing Speaker Volumes

When you have your speakers hooked up to your receiver, you need to be sure all your speakers have the same relative volume. Attempting to mix the outputs of six discrete channels with speakers whose levels have not been balanced leads you quickly into an audio quagmire. Balancing your speakers' volumes entails playing back test audio through your system while using an SPL (sound pressure level) meter to guide you in setting equivalent amplifier gain for each speaker; the LFE speaker is set to a higher output. The particulars of this procedure vary according to your setup; you may need to check the dreaded manual.

- **Encoding software—or maybe not.** Your encoding needs depend on what your final medium will be. To encode for the DTS format, you can use, for example, Surcode DTS by Minnetonka Audio ($499). This enables you to encode six discrete surround tracks, which you can use to create a DTS CD with any standard CD burning program. (Listening to this CD will require a CD or DVD player with a DTS decoder.) To encode Dolby Digital files, examples of programs include Sonic Foundry's SoftEncode 5.1 ($995) or Winnetonka Audio's SurCode Dolby Digital ($995). Both programs enable you to create a 44.1kHz version of an AC-3 file, which you can burn to a CD-R disc. (Again, though, you can't simply play this in your CD player—you'll need a Dolby Digital decoder.)

The most desirable option is no encoding at all. If, as it looks at this point, the DVD-Audio format becomes the medium of choice, unencoded surround sound audio (with a stereo option on each disc) will become the standard mixdown format. That would be good. Encoding is a process that most musicians would gladly leave behind. It colors audio profoundly and, for many listeners, in undesirable ways.

Meridian Lossless Packing (MLP) is an audio compression technology that enables you to fit about double the amount of audio on a disc. Unlike Dolby or DTS, it does not discard any information as it squeezes the audio.

The Surround Panner

Figure 19.10 is a close-up of the surround panner like from Minnetonka's Mx51 software. This enables you to not only place sound anywhere in the 360 degree environment, but to automate your position changes; you can constantly shift the spatial location of each channel over the course of a song.

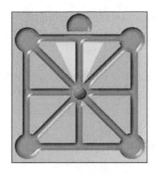

Figure 19.10

Surround sound software is equipped with a panner like this one that enables you to place each sound anywhere in the 5.1 environment.

SURROUND MIXING: THE QUANTUM LEAP

So, you're ready to do a 5.1 music mix. You're not sure whether to feel excited or overwhelmed. There you are, surrounded—by choices. That ".1" subwoofer means you have a wider frequency range; you not only have audio all the way up to 20kHz, now you have additional choices in the sub-150Hz spectrum. And you have exponentially more choices for spatial placement: With six discrete outputs, the difficulties of stereo mixing look like Easy Mix 101. What to do with this daunting array of options?

First, realize that, more than ever, it's up to you. Music surround sound mixing is a new art form—there are few, if any, firm rules. If you're doing it anytime in the early 21st century, you're part of the group that's making up the rules as they go. For movie sound, there's an established orthodoxy: Generally, the characters' voices are panned to the front, and the support sound effects move around them to the side and back.

But for music? The movie mixing rules no longer need be gospel. Of course, you probably don't want to assign the lead vocal to the .1 subwoofer—although undoubtedly some major group will try it for at least part of a song, and it will be seen as an incredibly cool effect.

The key concept here is that it's an aural playground. Experiment. Try it and listen—you don't have to print it to disc, but you want to hear it. It's reasonable to assume that, as music surround gets established, it will use the following approach as its overarching guideline: The lead vocals positioned in the front and the supporting instruments panned around them. In other words, a fuller, more interesting version of stereo.

But the really imaginative surround mixers will find a way to make a surround mix a really surprising departure from traditional stereo mixing. As you begin your experiments, consider these ideas:

- **Positioning reverb returns.** It's a standard technique in two-channel mixing to position the voice up the middle and pan that voice's reverb returns to the left and right. But 5.1 opens up possibilities like placing a stereo recording of the voice in the front left and front right, and panning the reverb to the surround left and right speakers (see Figure 19.11 for an example of a surround plug-in to aid panning). Or, placing the voice in the right surround (as if the singer is right next to the listener facing the front of a home theater), and panning the reverb returns to the front speakers. Be careful about placing your singer in only the center front speaker. Your mix might get played back in one of the many home systems that use the television speaker as the front center speaker. Listeners might ask why your vocalist lacks fullness.

Figure 19.11

Designed for Pro Tools, SmartPan Pro is one of a growing number of plug-ins to facilitate desktop 5.1 mixing.

- **Dueling stereo pairs.** You can use the left and center speaker as one stereo pair, and the right and center speakers as a second stereo pair. This works well with any kind of a call and response situation, like when a horn phrase answers a guitar riff. Or, you can alternate placing the same instrument between the left and right stereo pair, changing how this track is affected each time they appear; first the background singers have no reverb, next they're drenched in echoey reverb and delay.

- **Omniplacement.** This technique entails placing one aspect of a song's multi-part instrumental section in each of the speakers. It works well for the drums or an extended percussion setup, which has many parts. You would, for example, assign the kick and snare up front, with the tom toms and other support drums spread across the surround left and right speakers. This can be really aurally exciting as the percussion immerses the listener in the song's rhythmic elements.

- **EQ sweep.** An equalizer sweep is when all the elements of a mix are equalized as one, and simultaneously altered for dramatic effect. (The term *equalization*, you'll remember, refers to the process of boosting or cutting the high, low, or mid frequencies of sound.) An EQ sweep is used, for example, to simultaneously turn down all the high-end frequencies, and then restore them—sweeping the EQ setting up the frequency range, dramatically restoring the mix to life. With a 5.1 setup, you can move this EQ sweep spatially, attenuating and restoring the high frequencies in each segment of the 360 degree environment.

- **Movement.** Surround sound almost begs to hear a guitar or a vocal travel around in a circle—this might become the first 5.1 music cliché. However, it would be intriguing to hear, say, a single plucked bass, and then hear the reverb travel around in a circle before dying away. There are interesting possibilities here, but be careful of gratuitous use.

- **Use the recording itself.** In stereo mixing, mix decisions are based partially on how the recording was made, and this plays an even bigger role with surround. Using surround to its fullest requires recordings made with five microphones placed in a complete surround pattern (although three mics can accomplish a lot also). Alternately, you can position a track recorded with one omnidirectional mic in the center of your mix. But you don't have to have these elaborate recordings to create a large presence in your 5.1 mix. As long as the various recordings are discrete, you can place them around the environment to take advantage of the space. In the years ahead there will probably be a host of new mic techniques (and maybe mics) developed to make the most of 5.1.

- **The LFE (care and feeding of the subwoofer).** Most surround sound home theaters use a technology called *bass management*. This technology directs all the really low end energy to your subwoofer, which is best equipped to reproduce it (see Figure 19.12 for an example of a subwoofer). What this means for your mix is that you don't need to assign low-end tracks to this output; the system itself will do it for you. If there's a really special low-end instrument or other effect you want to assign to it, go for it, but it's not a good idea to assign all sorts of things to it just because it's there. Realize also that some home systems do a great job of reproducing low end. If your mix environment isn't equipped to reproduce these powerful lows you might be unpleasantly surprised when you play your music in a nice surround system. There you were, cranking up the bass to get your studio subwoofer pumping, only to realize that on a nice system it's almost volcanic. (This is a particular danger if you're mixing with a $150 set of surround speakers, or if you're sort of cheating by using just a regular speaker in place of the subwoofer.)

Figure 19.12

The Tannoy PS110B is an active subwoofer that you can pick up for about $400.

Photo courtesy of Tannoy.

AND DON'T FORGET: STEREO IS STILL THE DEFAULT

Downmixing is what happens when the home theater owner decides to push the "stereo" button on their receiver. Suddenly your meticulously created surround mix is collapsed into two outputs. You want to make sure your 5.1 mix can be downmixed and still sound good. If you don't mix with this in mind, listening and checking occasionally, when all your surround tracks are combined there may be some very non-musical conflicts. Phase cancellation is a major concern here. A well-equipped surround sound setup has a single button that collapses your mix-in-progress into stereo.

Additionally, it's a good idea to do a good old-fashioned stereo mix of your song while you're doing the 5.1 mix. The DVD-Audio format enables you to place both a surround and stereo version on one disc. In fact, while you're at it, you might as well do a 44.1kHz, 16-bit mix for a regular CD. In the time period we're living in, a small crowd of formats live side by side.

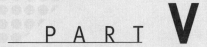

PART V

THOSE DISCS WERE MADE FOR BURNING: DESKTOP CD BURNING

CHAPTER **20**

CD BURNING, THE BASICS

In This Chapter:

- Find out about the technology of compact discs
- Learn about audio CDs, data CDs, and mixed CDs
- Discover the write modes necessary for recording CDs
- Learn about CD burning drives

THE INNER WORKINGS OF A COMPACT DISC

Let's pretend for a moment that we are little microscopic creatures, so small we can fit inside a CD player and see how it works. We'll go inside a disc player, down to the surface of a CD, and take a look at what's going on. What we're trying to figure out is this: How do you get raging guitars, power drums, and impassioned male vocals all from a little plastic disc?

We know that when audio is stored digitally, it's stored as ones and zeros, millions and zillions of ones and zeros. Down on the surface of the CD, at the microscopic level, we see how these ones and zeros are represented: millions of small raised and lowered areas. These areas are known as *lands* and *pits*. The lands represent ones and the pits represent zeros. But how does a CD player read them?

That's the Pits

A standard compact disc holds about 2 billion pits.

As we're looking at the surface of the CD, someone presses play on the disc player. The disc starts to spin, rapidly. As it spins rapidly, we see an intense beam of light—the CD's laser—reflecting its light off of each of these lands and pits, one after the other. A photodetector interprets these millions of lands and pits as the millions of ones and zeros that make up a digital file.

These pits and lands are what we'd see on the surface of a store-bought CD, which is made in a replication plant designed to turn out large quantities of compact discs. If this were a disc that someone created with a home CD burner, which uses a CD-R (CD-Recordable) disc, the surface would look different.

In this case, the disc's raised and lowered areas would instead be marks in a layer of organic dye. These marks are created by the heat of the CD's laser (hence the term "burn a CD"), which focuses on the organic dye and pulses in response to the stream of ones and zeros it's receiving from a digital file. The marks created by the pulsing laser on the layer of organic dye have the same reflective properties as pits and lands.

Down here on the surface of the CD-R, we can see how densely the data is packed. There's a spiral track that guides the laser, which makes a mind-boggling 22,188 revolutions around the surface of a CD. The length of this spiral track, from where it begins in the center of the CD to where it ends on the CD's edge, is close to 3.5 miles long.

Hot Link: Andy McFadden's CD-Recordable FAQ (http://www.fadden.com)

Almost any question about compact discs can be answered at this CD-Recordable FAQ site (see Figure 20.1) .

Figure 20.1

Andy McFadden can be called the guru of CD-R. His site is arguably the best online source of information about creating CDs.

LET'S GET STARTED: FIRST, CD-R OR CD-RW?

You have all the basics you need to start creating your own CDs, and you're eager to get started. So you have, or are about to buy, a PC with a CD recorder (often called a "burner"), software that reads and writes CD information, and some files—probably music files—you want to put on a CD.

But before you plunge into creating your own CDs, you've got a question. You've heard there are two types of recordable CDs, CD-R and CD-RW. Which one is better? Because CD-RW (CD-Rewritable) can be written to and erased repeatedly, it must be better, right?

Well, not exactly. Both CD-R and CD-RW have their own burners and their own blank media. Burners that burn only CD-R discs are becoming rare birds. Visit your local electronics store and all the shiny burners for sale are CD-RW burners. However, a CD-RW burner will burn a CD-R disc.

So, CD-RW burners are becoming standard operating equipment for today's desktop PC, if they're not already. But most people are using these CD-RW recorders to burn CD-Rs. Why?

Compatibility with CD players is a major reason. Some CD players (especially older ones) will not play CD-RW discs. You'll hand people your new music mixes on a CD-RW disc and they hear nothing in their player. But an even bigger determinant is price. CD-RW blanks are approximately double the cost of CD-R blanks, and used to be considerably more (although price depends on retailers and quantity, and the cost difference between CD-R and CD-RW media seems to be lessening all the time).

Of course, CD-RW media has its advantages. If you want to update a disc's existing material, CD-RW will allow this. If you're working on an album in progress, perhaps doing a number of mixes until all the band members are happy, you might want to reuse a CD-RW disc (although it's probably true that most musicians simply burn a fresh CD-R).

To add a bit of confusion, there is a way to write to a CD-R disc and write to it again later. You can't erase old material, but you can add to existing material. As we'll see when we look at the write modes, CD-R media has some of the flexibility of CD-RW.

Hey, Let's Use All Those AOL Discs

What about all those AOL sign-up discs that blanket America? Can we use them in our CD burner? After all, there are so many of them it appears that there are 3.1 for every U.S. citizen. Unfortunately, these discs, like store-bought CDs, are released on discs that cannot be recorded on again.

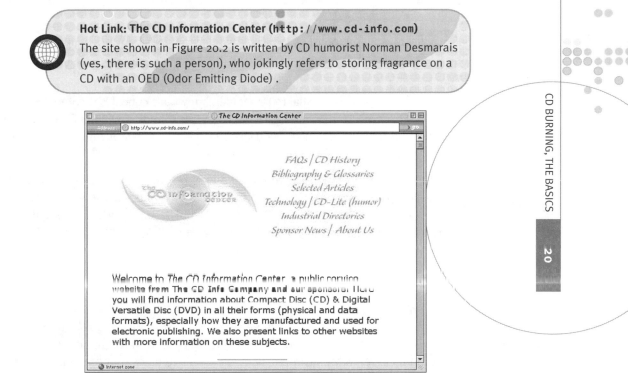

Hot Link: The CD Information Center (http://www.cd-info.com)

The site shown in Figure 20.2 is written by CD humorist Norman Desmarais (yes, there is such a person), who jokingly refers to storing fragrance on a CD with an OED (Odor Emitting Diode) .

Figure 20.2

Another good source of burning information, this site actually has a humor section about creating discs.

Preparing to Burn: What Kind of CD Are You Making?

So, what kind of CD do you want to make? Is it an audio CD, like a disc with all your favorite tunes or your recent music mixes? Or is it a data CD, which you'll use to store your files for later use? Or perhaps it's a mixed CD, which combines music and data on one CD? A mixed CD is often used as a promotional device for a band; a group distributes photos and interviews along with their songs.

The type of CD you're burning determines what format your files must be in. And if you're burning a mixed CD, it also determines what writing mode you need to use. Let's look at the three types of CDs, and then we'll look at the writing modes.

The Audio CD

You've got a handful of songs, saved as digital files on your hard drive, and you want to make a CD to listen to in the car. But first, you must be sure your files are in the Red Book format.

The format's name is not essential to remember, but what's critical is the Red Book specs: 44.1 kHz, 16-bit, stereo. If your music files aren't in this format, you can't burn them to an audio disc. If you're using Windows, you'll need WAVs, or on a Mac you'll need AIFFs, but either way, they have to be 44.1 kHz, 16-bit, stereo.

But what about all those MP3s on your hard drive? Yes, you can create a music CD from them, but first you must convert them to the Red Book standard. The good news is that some of today's CD-burning software does this for you. Load a bunch of MP3s into one of the programs that can handle them, and the software itself will say "hey, wrong format, I'll change it to Red Book." It's one of those rare instances where computers make our lives simpler.

On the other hand, you also can burn a data CD (see the section "The Data CD," later in this chapter) with your MP3s without converting them to Red Book standard. Some of today's portable CD players, along with newer car stereos, as well as your CD-ROM player, can play a CD with MP3 files without needing them to be 44.1 kHz, 16-bit. Why put native MP3 files on a CD? With MP3 compression you can fit 10 times or more music on a single CD. That's 10 hours or more. Your portable CD player's batteries will die before you listen to all the music on that CD.

In comparison, the maximum number of Red Book audio tracks you can put on audio CD is 99. The typical amount of playing time is 74 minutes, although 80 minute CDs are becoming more and more common, and almost as cheap as the 74-minute version. Be careful, though—some consumer CD players, particularly older car stereos, will choke on those discs.

Converting Software

If your CD creation software doesn't convert files, you'll need to convert them before loading them into the program. In many cases you can use your audio recording/editing software to do this. Simply import your files into a program such as Cool Edit, and save them as 44.1 kHz, 16-bit files. To find additional conversion software, look at Chapter 7, "Software: The Extras."

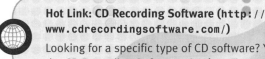

Hot Link: CD Recording Software (`http://www.cdrecordingsoftware.com/`)

Looking for a specific type of CD software? You'll find most every type at the CD Recording Software site (see Figure 20.3) .

Figure 20.3

This site has an exhaustive selection of CD-related gear from all the major manufacturers and software developers.

The Data CD

If you want to create a data CD, otherwise known as a CD-ROM, you've got a lot more flexibility in terms of file format. You can use a data disc to store MP3s without converting them to Red Book standard. A data disc can store audio files at any resolution, from those low-bandwidth 22kHz files that you'll post on the Web, all the way to those beauties at 192kHz, 24-bit. Data discs are often used by musicians to archive audio. Once a project is done, they simply burn all the source audio to a data CD, and then erase it off of their hard drive.

Like an audio CD, a CD-ROM holds 650MB (although, again, you may find blank media that holds more). Unlike an audio CD, a CD-ROM will not play in a regular CD player.

The recording protocol for a data disc is ISO9660 or HSFS (High Sierra File System). (You may see these terms in your burning software. In some programs, you must select the ISO9660 option to burn a data disc.) This protocol dictates things like character filenames; the most basic form of HSFS allows only file names with 8 letters and a three-letter extension. Because of these limitations, extensions were developed to add functionality. At this point, today's leading CD creation software allows you to vary from the "8.3" naming convention.

Mixed CD

A wonderful thing, the mixed CD contains both music and data files. Sometimes called Enhanced CDs, they turn your PC into a little multimedia show: You can listen to the disc's music, watch QuickTime movies of concert footage, and peruse carefully airbrushed photos of the band. While this is a technique used by major-label artists, you can create your own mixed CD. Distributing them at gigs is a wonderful self-promotion tool.

You can play the music on a mixed CD in a regular CD player, but you'll need a CD-ROM drive to enjoy the accompanying data files. To create a mixed CD, you'll need to burn it as a multisession CD, which is one of the writing modes we're about to look at.

 Hot Link: Nero CD Creation Software (http://www.ahead.de/)
Nero CD software has a loyal following. Find out about this popular program at the Ahead site (see Figure 20.4) .

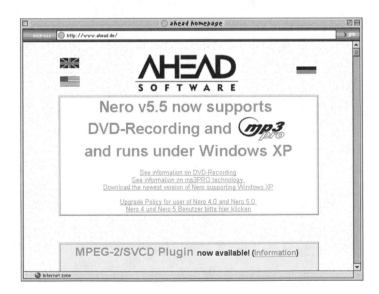

Figure 20.4

Made by Ahead Software, Nero CD software is one of the leading CD burning programs.

The Writing Modes

So, you've got all your files (in the right format) loaded into your CD creation software, you've got a blank CD-R (or CD-RW) disc in the burner, and you're about to click Record. But you need to give your burner some instructions about how to lay that information onto the CD—you need to choose a writing mode. There are four modes: Disc at Once (DAO), Track at Once, Multisession, and Packet. You'll find these choices in your CD software, although various software programs may refer to the modes differently (and some programs can't do all of them).

By choosing a writing mode, you're telling the CD recorder's laser how to operate. You are, like a superhero, taking control of a powerful beam of light. (Well, it's actually no more than 8 milliwatts, but still, it is a laser. By the way, a CD's laser uses one setting to write, 4–8 milliwatts, and a lower setting to read, .5 milliwatt.)

Disc-at-Once

This is the most straightforward way to burn a CD, and the most likely choice to burn a music CD. Choose which Red Book audio files to load in your burning software, make sure it's in DAO mode, click Record, and shortly thereafter you're done. Pop the finished CD in a regular CD player or a CD-ROM drive and it plays your music (that is, if it's an audio CD—if it's a data CD you'll need a CD-ROM drive to access it) .

In DAO mode, a CD burner's laser writes all the selected files from your hard drive to the disc in one uninterrupted session. This includes the Lead In (which contains the disc's Table of Contents, or TOC), the Program Area (the files themselves) and the Lead Out (1.5 minutes of null data that lets the player know the disc is finished).

If you want to create a master for mass duplication, this is the mode to use. You can send a DOA disc off to a mass replicator to run thousands of copies of your album. DOA has another great benefit—it eliminates the need for two-second gaps between each track.

Why would you want to do this? Well, let's say your band just went on an epic tear, 73 minutes of non-stop music, covering eight songs from five different artists. You want to make a live CD, but you don't want to have to break that long jam into eight songs with a two-second gap between each track. With DAO, you can drop those seven track changes directly into the song, and have it play seamlessly without breaks.

Track-at-Once

This mode turns off the laser between each track. Track-at-Once allows you to keep adding new material to a disc over the course of several days or weeks. Say you have only six of the ten song files that you want to include on an album, but you want to burn a CD. You can burn those first six to disc, adding songs as you finish them. But here's the limitation: Until you close that disc, you won't be able to play it in a regular CD; you'll need a CD-ROM drive to listen to it. Because of this limitation, many musicians simply burn a DAO disc with the first handful of files, and burn yet another when they have all their files. A TAO disc is not suitable to send to a duplicator.

Multisession

As the name suggests, multisession mode enables you to burn more than one discrete program to a disc, so you can combine music, movies, photos, and more on one CD. It's similar to Track-at-Once, but each session has its own Lead In (with TOC), Program Area, and Lead Out.

The trick to creating an enhanced CD is to burn the music session first—this makes the music playable by regular CD players, which can only read a disc's first session. CD-ROM players, which offer users more control, can play any of the sessions; the user simply has to click on the file to access it. Again, though, your limit is 650MB—and the null space between sessions eats up 23 MB—so you need to be aware of how large your files are.

Of all the modes, multisession is the trickiest in terms of choosing the option in your software; it varies considerably from program to program. Typically, you have to turn off the Disc-at-Once mode, because that burns the CD in one fell swoop. In many cases you want to choose your software's Track-at-Once mode and close your audio session before writing your accompanying files to disc.

Hot Link: Roxio (http://www.roxio.com/)

Roxio is the big dog when it comes to CD software. Visit the company's site to learn all about its many programs (see Figure 20.5).

Figure 20.5

Visit the Roxio site to find out about two very popular CD burning programs: Easy CD Creator (Windows) or Toast (Mac).

Packet Writing

Packet writing isn't suitable for creating a music CD, but it's a good way to back up files. With packet writing, your CD recorder becomes like a removable storage drive. You can write to a CD-R or CD-RW as if it were a big floppy—just drag and drop. Packet writing enables you to delete information from a CD-R (and of course also from a CD-RW). The files aren't actually removed, but the disc's directory is updated so that they're inaccessible.

Discs created with packet writing use the universal disc format (UDF) format, which is not universal—not all operating systems can accept it. Traditionally, it's been a Windows-only format (DirectCD is the leading software choice), although Mac OS 8.6 and later support it.

Copying a CD

Forget all the write modes—what if you just want to make a CD copy of a CD? No problem (usually). To do this, it helps to have both a drive to play CDs and a CD-R drive connected to your PC. Choose your software's Copy option (but realize that different programs handle this differently), and write directly from disc to disc, otherwise known as copying on-the-fly. But if you only have a CD burner, you can still copy a CD—most software lets you use a two-step process to copy a CD. First, copy the CD files to your hard drive, and then burn those files onto a blank. It takes longer, but the results are the same. This is also a great way to ensure you don't make a coaster (ruined CD) on slower systems, which happens when the CD burner waits too long for data from the original CD drive.

Hot Link: CDR-Info (`http://www.cdrinfo.com/`)

A site that lives up to its name, CDR-Info provides tips and techniques for burning digital information to disc (see Figure 20.6) .

Figure 20.6

CDR-Info is packed full of CD as well as DVD information.

BURNING: IT'S EASY, EXCEPT WHEN IT'S NOT

Although there are a few things to know about burning CDs, such as file formats and write modes, the actual burning process tends to be a no-brainer. The programs that you use to create CDs are some of the most intuitive of any audio-related programs. With a program like Easy CD Creator, Toast, or Nero, the software itself practically guides you. Choose which type of disc you want to burn, select the files you want to record to CD, make sure everything's turned on and there's a blank in the burner, and you're in business. If only all audio could be so easy.

But, that's not to say you won't run into problems. While the typical burn is easy as can be, most everyone who's ever burned CDs has turned a few blank discs into unusable "coasters." (They're also good for propping up a table that wobbles to one side, but not much else).

So, if you're running into problems, be aware of a phenomenon that causes quite a few CD burning snafus: buffer underrun.

When you burn a CD, information must flow from your hard drive to the CD recorder in an unbroken stream. Within the CD-R driver is a buffer that temporarily holds the information that's about to be recorded to CD. You'll encounter problems with buffer underrun when information is not fed to this buffer fast enough. This causes your attempted burn to fail—there's no way for the CD-R drive to restart that disc burn when the data flow is broken.

Not all CD-R drives are created equal in terms of buffer size. Some have larger buffers, which should theoretically result in fewer problems with buffer underruns. However, apart from buffer size, there are some things you can do to guard against buffer underrun:

- **Record at a slower speed.** If you choose to burn your disc at 4x rather than 8x, you're reducing by half the amount of data that must flow in an uninterrupted manner; this lower data requirement is easier for your system to handle. (In fact, some users choose to burn their all-important archive discs at a maximum of 4x to make it a "safer" burn—less prone to run into problems. Other users feel this is unnecessary.) You might also check to see if your CD creation software has a Test mode. In Easy CD Creator, for example, you can choose either the Test Only or Test and Create CD option. In the Test mode, the software will verify that it can write the disc without actually doing so; in Test and Create CD it will verify, and then actually burn the CD. In Toast, you can use the Check Speed option to verify that the writing speed is sufficient to record your source file to disc. (On the other hand, at $.50 a disc, you might throw caution to the wind and simply hit Record, unless you've been having problems.)

- **Quit other applications.** It's sometimes necessary to quit all other programs you have running prior to burning a CD, although many have broken this rule and gotten away with it. Again, the idea is to avoid creating extra burdens on your computer's CPU which might cause an interruption in data flow. If your computer can handle running other programs and burning a disc at the same time, go for it. But if you're turning blanks into coasters, this is one of the first things to try.

- **Defragment your hard drive.** To keep data flowing continuously from your hard drive to your burner, your computer's operating system must be able to quickly find the data on your hard drive. But your hard drive, after a long period of use, may become fragmented. This condition forces your computer to store large files in noncontiguous segments, which means it takes longer for your system to find the files. If your hard drive is too fragmented, it will take so long it may cause a buffer underrun, especially if you're trying to write at faster speeds. To defragment a Windows system, you can use the defragmenter tool that's built into the OS; with Mac, you'll need a special piece of software like Norton Utilities.

JARGON

Subcodes are the event pointers embedded in a disc during writing, otherwise known as indexes, that tell a CD player how many tracks are on a CD, and how long each track is. The CD format could use a total of 8 subcodes, but currently only the P and Q subcodes are used. (But don't be confused—each of these two subcodes can be used multiple times on a CD, so you can place many more than 8 tracks on your discs.)

Hot Link: Shopping for a Burner (http://www.mysimon.com/)

Rather than surf from one site to the next looking for the best price on a CD burner, visit the MySimon site (see Figure 20.7) to get multiple price quotes in one place.

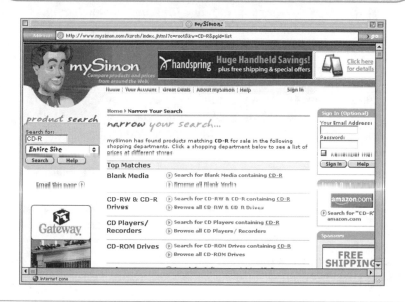

Figure 20.7

One of the easiest way to find the best deal on a CD burner is to use MySimon, a site that compares products and prices from a wide array of retailers.

HARDWARE: HOW CHEAP CAN IT GET?

You won't be able to burn a CD with your CD-ROM drive; you'll need a drive specifically designed to record to CD. Buying a CD recorder for home use will cost you about $30,000— oh, wait, wrong year. That was the 1991 price, when Sony introduced one of the first desktop units. As other manufacturers entered the market in the early '90s, the price soon fell to the $10–12,000 range, for units that burned at 1x rate (so a 74-minute CD took 76 minutes to create; the extra minutes were needed to write the TOC and close the disc). Yamaha stepped up and bested everyone in 1994 by offering a 4x-speed recorder, and at $5,000 you could hardly resist it. Hewlett-Packard offered the first burner for under $1,000 in 1995, and the prices have since tumbled to the under $200 level. You can now get one of the Sony models for $75.

So, with units for less than a \$100 and the media at less than a dollar, the CD-R drive is today's cassette machine—but with a lot more recording options and offering vastly better sound quality.

If you're thinking about buying a CD burner, there are a few factors to be aware of:

- **DVD-R/CD-RW.** You've gone to buy a CD-R burner, and then realize: For a bit more money (actually considerably more in some cases) you could also get a drive that burns DVDs. That's enticing. But realize a couple of things. In terms of price, the DVD-R/CD-RW recorders are where the CD-RW drives were a few years ago. It's likely they'll fall to comparable levels, or at least head that way; if you can wait you'll save a few bucks. Also, there are lingering format wars. Do you want a DVD burner that creates DVD-Rs or DVD+RWs? For a discussion of these format conflicts, see Chapter 19, "DVD and Surround Sound Mixing."

- **Internal or External.** The decision as to whether to get an internal or external CD-R drive is pretty easy if you don't have the necessary extra internal slot in your PC. If not, that's okay; the external drives have their advantages: There are fewer technical hurdles involved with installation, and they're portable (although of course whatever machine you connect it with will need burning software, too). The internal drives also have their selling points: You'll have more room on your desktop, less cable spaghetti to keep track of, and one less power outlet to provide—an internal unit gets its juice from your PC. The internals also tend to be cheaper than the external drives. You'll need to be aware of what interface the unit requires: Typically the internals will require IDE or SCSI, and the externals will require USB, SCSI, or FireWire.

- **Read/Write Speeds.** Shopping for a CD-RW drive entails deciphering odd-looking numbers like this: 8x/4x/16x. In this instance, this drive will record CD-R media at 8x (full CD takes about 9 minutes), record CD-RW media at 4x (full CD takes about 18 minutes), and read CD-ROMs at 16 times real-time. Audio CDs are always read at 1x—any faster and the singers would sound like they just inhaled helium. The number that many users care about the most is the first one: Since this measures CD-R write speed (which many users use for audio CDs), this determines how long you have to wait for your CD to be done. The faster, the better. Plextor now makes a 40x burner.

CHAPTER **21**

CD CREATION, PART 2: BEFORE AND AFTER THE BURN

In This Chapter:

- Learn how to transfer your cassettes and albums to CD
- Find out about mastering and restoration
- Discover software programs that aid mastering and restoration
- Learn how to make your CD packaging look good

THE LEAP FROM ANALOG TO DIGITAL

In the privacy of our own homes we can admit it: We're not totally digital yet. We know that everything's headed for digital, but still, analog is part of our lives. In particular, we have music we enjoy on (it's okay) cassette tapes, some of us even have vinyl albums. But CD players are everywhere, and you'd like to transfer your music collection to this more convenient format.

So you might ask what is perhaps the most universal question in the world of desktop audio: How do I make a CD from my cassettes or record albums?

Whether your source material is cassette or vinyl or some combination thereof, the process is essentially the same. You'll need to make a digital sound file from those songs on tape or vinyl. To do that, you'll of course need a cassette deck or turntable for playback. (And the turntable must have its own phono pre-amp, which almost all of them have. If not, you can buy a standalone unit at Radio Shack for about $25.) Additionally, you'll need

- **A cable to connect your cassette deck or turntable to your computer.** You will most likely need a cable with two RCA on one end (you plug this into your cassette deck or turntable outputs) to an 1/8 inch stereo miniplug (this goes into your computer's sound card). This is sometimes referred to as a "Y cord." Finding such a cable will probably require a trip to the local electronics store.

- **Audio Recording Software.** This doesn't have to be anything heavy duty; if you're doing any work with audio recording you probably have a sufficient program. But it must be able to not only record but also edit; you'll need to be able to trim up the front and back of your audio files. To learn about software that does this, take a look at Chapter 6, "Software: The Basics."

For cassette transfer, now is the time to clean the playback heads on your tape deck—few tape deck playback heads have been cleaned this century. This is a matter of buying some cotton swabs and some head cleaner (again, at the local electronics store), opening up the little door to the cassette compartment, and gently scrubbing the heads that come in contact with the tape. Or, to make your life simpler, pick up a cassette head cleaning kit—you can get one for just a few bucks. Either way, your tapes will sound brighter and clearer.

For records, you'll also need to do some cleaning. You can buy special vinyl cleaner, and will need to apply just a bit and carefully wipe it clean with a cloth. Some vinyl aficionados claim that it reduces a record's pops and clicks to leave a very thin film of record cleaner on the record as you play it.

Hot Link: Pristine Sound (http://www.alienconnections.com/products.htm)

Alien Connections' Pristine Sounds is specifically designed to clean up old records and tapes (see Figure 21.1).

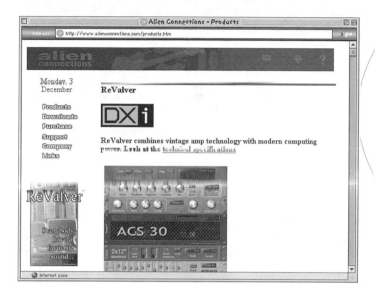

Figure 21.1

For an example of software specially designed to clean up records and tapes, take a look at Pristine Sound.

A few setup tips: In your audio software, you might need to select Line In (as opposed to Mic In). You'll also need to put your recording software in Input mode, so you can check levels before you record. Remember, you want your recording level to be as hot as possible without causing distortion. It's worth a moment to check input by finding and playing the loudest part of the song; set this section to the maximum input level and the rest of the song will be fine.

To make it easy to burn a CD, record your audio at the Red Book standard: 44.1kHz, 16-bit, stereo. That way, when you're done with recording and trimming up your files, you're that much closer to being ready to burn.

It's time to record audio. Cue up your cassette or turntable to right before the song, click record on your software, and start your analog playback unit. Congratulations. You are now creating a digital file from analog media. This process is called *digitizing*.

To speed up the process, you may want to record several songs at once, and then go back and edit them into separate sound files. Remember though, 25 minutes of music at CD quality eats up a whopping 250MB of your hard drive space.

When you're finished recording, your audio files will look something like Figure 21.2. Trim up the front and back of each song file so it will start promptly when it's on CD. To do this, simply select the undesirable noise between cuts and press Delete. Save each song with a title you can remember, and you're ready to load them into your burning software and create a CD.

Figure 21.2

To convert your tapes and records to CD, you need to turn them into a digital file.

 Gaps Between Songs

Although many CD creation programs default to a 2–3 second gap between songs, you can change this. You can use the program's preferences to select a new time increment between songs, or, depending on whether the program you're using supports this, even cross fade between songs.

(IMPROVING) THE SOUND OF MUSIC: RESTORATION AND MASTERING

But there's a downside to transferring music from cassette or vinyl onto a CD. The audio doesn't automatically turn into high-quality sound when recorded onto a CD. In fact, recording audio onto a digital medium can be a wonderful way to draw attention to its flaws. You've got a CD with…hiss, or, if you transferred from vinyl, you've got a CD…with record pops. What can you do to make those analog-to-digital transfers sound better?

Cleaning up and improving the sound of your analog masters involves the processes of *restoration* and *mastering*. While these two activities are different, they are closely related. As we take a look at restoration and mastering, here's the key point to bear in mind.

You can use many of the techniques involved in either restoration and mastering for two purposes:

- To clean up your tapes and records prior to transferring to a CD
- To optimize the sound of your music mixes prior to creating your CD master for duplication

Let's look at restoration and mastering in more detail.

Restoration is the process of improving the sonic quality of deteriorated recordings, attempting to make their flaws less noticeable. These techniques are more applicable to your old vinyls and cassettes. Restoration often involves balancing the remedy with the defect. That is, many of the fixes involved with restoration also act to limit the vitality of the music. Eliminating the hiss can also eliminate the brighter frequencies; filtering out all the records pops can also filter out some of the desirable musical transients like elements of the drum set. If you go too far with restoration work, you can end up with music that's pristine but lifeless.

Mastering is the process of optimizing an audio master for duplication. Even though a highly experienced audio production team has tweaked the mix down to the last quarter of a dB, still the mastering engineer gives a final polish. A master for a large budget album might be sent to, for example, well-respected mastering engineer Bernie Grundman, who gives the audio the final gloss necessary to make it sonically comparable to major label radio hits. As in restoration, though, it's critical to balance the improvements with the music itself. A mastering engineer may desire a tad more brightness, but if he adds too much brightness the music sounds tinny. More compression can add punch, but too much compression makes music sound dull.

Hot Link: Cool Edit Pro's Click and Pop Eliminator (`http://www.syntrillium.com/cep/proinfo.htm`)

Cool Edit Pro comes with a click and pop elimination utility that aids the process of tape and vinyl clean up (see Figure 21.3).

Figure 21.3

If you have the popular Cool Edit Pro program, you already have an audio cleanup utility.

In both restoration and mastering you're working to improve a finished master. Unlike in the mix process, you don't have access to an individual instrument. You're working on the complete mix, so when you turn down 7.5kHz, you're turning down everything at 7.5kHz—voice, rhythm guitar, drums, and anything else. Like the mix process, the technology you're using has to serve the music. The idea is to make small changes and listen, letting certain "problems" remain if doing so allows the music to sound its best.

While some tasks within restoration and mastering are completely different—you probably don't want to run your final mix through a filter designed to eliminate record pops—some of the problems you'll encounter in both desktop restoration and mastering will be similar. For example, if your mixes were done in different home setups at different times, you'll probably need to work on getting volumes and overall EQ to sound similar prior to burning. Similarly, if you're combining music from several tapes or vinyl albums, you'll probably need to tweak levels and EQ to make them sound similar.

The Master/Restoration Philosophy: Less Is More

Before plunging into specific techniques and software, remember an axiom that may help your restoration and mastering efforts: When in doubt, do less. As you're tweaking, realize that the average person, the majority of your listeners, are listening to the music itself. There aren't very many people who say, "Wow, I really liked that Weezer tune, but I wish there was more 12kHz in the drums," or "that old jazz song was great, but that record pop just ruined it for me." So don't get so hung up on fixing a perceived problem that you somehow lessen the music's overall impact.

On the other hand, audio production standards have increased dramatically over the years. If a major label were to put out a CD that had the low-fi sonic quality of some of those '50s and '60s recordings, even the general public would say "It just doesn't sound very good"—even if the music was great. So it is worth painstakingly optimizing your music for CD, but realize that, at the end of the day, it's probably the music itself that will sell it or not.

Hot Link: Sound Forge (http://www.sonicfoundry.com)
Sound Forge 5.0 comes with what its developers call Wave Hammer Mastering Tools, a compressor and volume maximizer that will enhance your CD-burning process. (See Figure 21.4.)

Figure 21.4

Sound Forge 5.0 comes equipped with a suite of mastering tools.

The Basics: Volume Levels and EQ

If nothing else, you want your volume levels and relative brightness/low end to match from song to song. It's really distracting if they don't.

Normalize Volume

Select each of your audio files and normalize them individually (you'll find the normalize option in your audio software's edit functions list). Normalizing audio lifts the volume of the entire sound file by the same amount; it's often used to push the music to its maximum volume without distortion. It's important that you normalize each file individually—if you don't, you're merely maintaining the volume differences in your various audio files. However, since making equivalent volume levels is your goal, you may not want to lift each file to 100 percent of its maximum (many audio programs give you the ability to normalize by a certain percentage, say 80 percent). Due to factors like compression and EQ, two audio files at 100 percent volume may be perceived as having very different volume levels. That tune you mixed at your house sounds a lot louder than the tune you mixed at your band member's house because one is much more compressed, and has more high end. This is also true of music from cassettes from different years, and it's always true when making a compilation tape that combines vinyl albums and cassettes.

Realize that your system's VU meters (volume unit meters, which display your program's output level) may read as if the music is equal volume, but it may not sound that way to the ear. Always use your ears as the final judge, not the meters. As you deal with volume levels and other issues, make sure you're making your ears happy. When you're not sure, ask yourself a simple question: Which way sounds better?

Volume Levels Versus Perception

To see how inaccurate your VU meters can be in terms of human perception, put an extremely bright piece of audio right next to one with a more balanced EQ. Adjust the volume levels so that the meters are even. Note that the brighter piece of audio sounds significantly louder, even though its meter reading is equivalent.

> **Hot Link: Dartech's Dart Pro 98 (http://www.dartech.com/New.asp)**
>
> The Dart Pro 98 program is an advanced audio restoration program. (See Figure 21.5.)

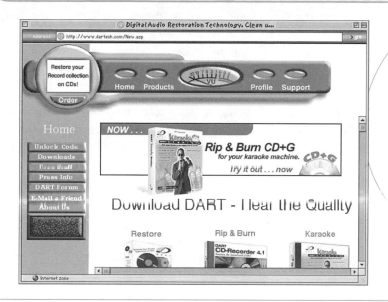

Figure 21.5

Dartech's restoration application offers the user sophisticated control over all aspects of an audio cleanup job.

Equalization

It would be great if there were an EQ preset that you could simply boot up and use for all your files prior to laying them on CD. Unfortunately, for both the obvious problems of old tapes and the more subtle work of optimizing your lovingly mixed audio masters, there is no one-size-fits-all solution.

For audio cassettes, you'll be dealing with a lot of hiss. You can eliminate this by attenuating frequencies in the 5–10kHz range, but this is also the range that gives you brilliance and presence. Turning it down is like putting a blanket over the music—it sounds muffled. But you can find a balance: Turn it down a bit, but also be prepared to live with some remaining hiss.

For mastering your mixes, now is good time to use a commercial CD as a reference. You may have used this in your original mix, but listen yet again, this time for subtleties. Are your highs as bright? Or do they need to be slightly pulled down? Could it use just a dash more bottom end? Listen to the mix on as many speakers as possible to see if any EQ adjustments make sense. Equalizing the master is a perilous process and here, more than ever, less is more. Any kind of major EQ is best done back in the mix process, when significant EQ changes could be balanced track by track. Now that you're affecting the entire mix, you probably want to think in terms of 1–5dB boosts or cuts at most.

Software Programs

Arboretum Systems makes some highly useful restoration and mastering software for both Mac and Windows. In particular, Ray Gun (http://www.arboretum.com) comes in handy for eliminating distracting pops from vinyl albums. Note that in Figure 21.6, the Pop elimination setting is adjustable. Simply setting it to the maximum will overdo it and eliminate portions of the audio you want to keep. Again, listen and carefully adjust until you've reached a balance between getting rid of pops and maintaining the audio's musicality. Ray Gun offers other cleanup functions like a noise reduction utility and a low end filter to cut rumble.

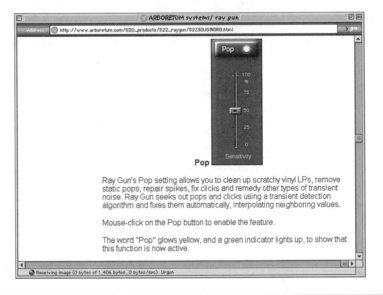

Figure 21.6

The Ray Gun restoration software allows you to vary your pop elimination setting.

Other tools to look at for restoration include Alien Connections' Pristine Sounds, Cool Edit Pro's Click/Pop/Crackle Eliminator, Sonic Foundry's Noise Reduction (included with Sound Forge), the Waves Restoration Bundle, and Dartech's Dart Pro 98. Remember, though, that there are many good ones on the market, and there are often new ones introduced.

When shopping for a restoration/mastering program, it's good to find users who have used a given program on your type of project—various programs are better suited to different types of restoration jobs.

One particularly deep audio restoration program is Diamond Cut's Millennium program (`http://www.diamondcut.com/Catalog/mainofmill.htm`). Not only does it have many tools for handling both tape and vinyl problems, as shown in Figure 21.7, it has a section called CD-Prep, specifically designed to prepare your files for digital discs.

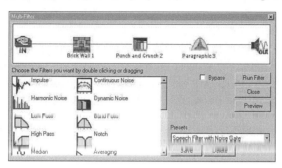

Figure 21.7

Diamond Cut's Millennium program gives you many tools to work with thorny restoration jobs.

You'll notice by looking at Figure 21.7 that the Millennium program provides a number of ways of attacking restoration problems. You can view an audio file's waveform, zooming in to problem areas to work on them individually, or you can use any of a number of tools to filter the file as a whole. The Impulse filter, for example, cuts record pops by eliminating transients (extremely brief but powerful increases in volume); the Band Pass filter allows you to cut a narrow frequency range, perhaps a particularly nasty area of hiss in the 7kHz range.

techtv tip

Don't be discouraged if a pop filter doesn't remove all your record's pop on the first filtering. Sometimes you may need to run an old record through more than once, making gradual adjustments to the pop elimination setting.

A Mastering Engineer's Master Tools

One of the most effective tools for mastering (and also useful for restoration) is the multiband compressor limiter. Available in many software programs, a multiband compressor limiter enables you to divide the frequency range of an audio file into discrete regions for the purpose of assigning a different compression ratio to each. You may, for example, want to leave the mid range alone, because it already has enough punch, but instead compress the 7–9kHz range quite heavily. The multiband compressor limiter offers a daunting array of choices; the user must decide which frequencies to compress, by how wide a bandwidth, by what ratio, and with what attack and release time. Various multibands offer still other variables.

Using such a tool to its full advantage takes knowledge and experience, but it's one of the mainstays of the mastering engineer. One of the first things to try with a multiband is to cut some of the frequencies in the 150 to 500Hz range (try a gentle ratio like 4:1 first); too much energy in this frequency range can make a track sound muddy if it hasn't been tamed during the mix.

A limiter that's considerably easier to use but also quite useful for mastering is the *look ahead peak limiter*. This device allows you to get those extra few dBs of volume without causing distortion. It does this by looking ahead within an audio file to find all the peaks above a user-determined limit. By the time those peaks happen, the look ahead peak limiter has already attenuated them. This is its advantage over an analog limiter, which requires some fraction of a second before it responds to a peak. So the look ahead peak limiter allows you to set all of your audio file's levels closer to maximum volume, without worrying about distortion caused by an unforeseen peak.

And maximizing volume levels is an important part of the mastering process—you don't want your listeners to have to turn up the volume when your song plays immediately after another group's song.

A look ahead peak limiter program that's popular with both Mac and Windows users is the L1 Ultramaximizer, made by Waves (http://www.waves.com/). While the Ultramaximizer, shown in Figure 21.8, is useful for mastering your carefully mixed music, it's also useful for tweaking old cassettes and vinyls on their way to CD. Its ability to give you a louder signal helps you burn a CD from tapes and vinyls that's as loud as one made from digital files.

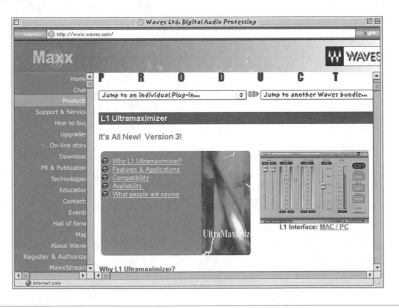

Figure 21.8

The L1 Ultramaximizer uses look ahead peak limiting to allow maximum volume without distortion.

A Little Secret

Before you pronounce your music done, ready to commit to final CD master, you might want to experiment with time compression. In other words, speeding it up just a bit. For many musicians, this is heresy—hey, they would say, if you wanted to change tempo, you should have done it back when you were laying down the track. That's a valid point, but still, sometimes quickening the tempo of a tune just a few percent is what gives it the energy to excite your listeners. Try perhaps 1–3 percent—it's almost subliminal, but it allows the music to deliver its message a tad faster.

Psychoacoustic Concerns

Once you've gotten your music sounding its best, there's a crucial decision you still have to make: song order. This is less important for making compilation CD from your favorite tapes, but vitally important for mastering your album.

It's an odd psychoacoustic phenomenon, but the order in which a listener hears a series of songs makes a significant difference in listener perception. There are no hard and fast rules, except: Don't put your best material last. With listener attention span sometimes measured in microseconds, they may hit Stop before they get there.

You want your listeners to fall in love with the music as early in the disc as possible, to ensure that—like any love relationship—they'll keep that disc playing even through material they're not sure about. So the process of ordering your songs forces you to take a hard look at your music and decide what's most compelling—which is where additional pairs of ears come in handy.

Because you are close to the material, you are probably the least qualified to judge which of your creations will appeal to the greatest number of listeners. So swallow your pride and get some uncensored opinions (which in itself may be hard to find). Distribute a test CD to as many listeners as you can corral before you create your final master disc. You can't necessarily count individual opinions, but if 6 of 8 people tell you they really like that one song, put it near the start of your CD.

DUPLICATION: DO IT YOURSELF—OR NOT

After you've tweaked and polished your master CD, you're ready to make multiple copies. If you have more time than money, you'll probably want to do this yourself instead of using a professional duplicator. You can run a few hundred at home and even make them look professional. We'll take a look at this.

If, however, you're going to run more than a few hundred, you may want to send your master off to a CD duplication facility. To get a good per unit price from such a facility you'll probably have to order a least a thousand, and the better price breaks come at even higher quantities. There are plenty of good CD duplicators; choosing one entails getting on the phone and getting prices from several, as well as a feel for the various companies' level of customer service.

One key point about working with duplication facilities: The reference disc is essential. Many duplicators insist that you get a reference disc, which is a test pressing, prior to running your full order. Always get a reference disc, and always listen closely to that disc. Duplication facilities send you a reference disc because they want you to take responsibility for the final product. They don't want to deliver 2500 CDs only to find out that—whoops—you really wanted that certain song to be first on the CD, and song 3 and song 4 are at different volumes. So listen to that reference, and realize it's a lot better to pay another $50 or so to have another master made, rather than run umpteen CDs that you're not happy with.

Hot Link: Discmakers (`http://www.discmakers.com`)

Discmakers is a well-known mass duplication facility that is geared toward working with musicians. (See Figure 21.9.)

Figure 21.9

Discmakers is one of many duplication facilities specializing in music.

In many cases there's no need to hire a duplicator. You can run enough discs for a lot of purposes using your home setup. If you need discs to sell at gigs, put in local record stores, or sell through your Web site, that home burner can do the job. Let's see, doing the math…if you can turn out one disc every six minutes, that's 10 an hour; it will take you 20 hours (perhaps spread over several evenings) to run a couple hundred. If more than one band member has a CD burner, you can have plenty of CDs within a few weeks, for much less than a duplicator would charge for a limited quantity run.

But just running the CDs isn't enough—you want them to be eye-catching. (In fact, this might contribute as much to a CD's success as the music itself, a fact you might not want to mention to your more idealistic band mates.) To make those shiny discs look sharp, you'll need a few basic tools. Depending on how polished you want your CDs to look, you have a couple of options. You can use

- **Stick On Labels.** This is the less expensive option, and can look quite good. Many CD creation programs have a label printing utility built in. In the case of Easy CD Creator, for example, the program is CD Label Creator. A program like this allows you to import graphics and select from a number of fonts to create a look that fits your style. All you need is a color printer and precut CD label paper from companies such as Neato or Avery. The labels have adhesive on them, so when you're done printing you can invite everyone over and have a labeling party (hint: don't get beer for the party). Putting them on can be a bit tricky, so you might want to buy a CD labeler specially made to help you get them on straight. These labeling helpers are made by Hewlett-Packard, Memorex, and CD Stomper, among others. But be aware that not all labeling devices work with all types of labels; check before you buy.

- **Printed on Disc.** For this option, you'll need a printer specially designed to print on discs. This is a slick look, and it also saves you the trouble of having to hand adhere your labels. If you or a friend know how to use Illustrator or a similar layout program, you can create some highly professional looking discs. (You can print directly from Illustrator onto your CD.) Prices vary considerably on CD printers. You can spend well over a thousand, or somewhere in the $300–500 range. The Signature Pro by Primera is a good unit (and also handles DVD-R printing), but as of this writing it's priced at around $1200. You might also consider the used market when shopping for a CD printer.

But the most important part of your CD packaging is of course the artwork on the jewel box. This is the first thing people see and it's what creates that all important first impression. If there was ever a time to make that extra effort, this is it—notice how much attention the major labels pay to album covers. It's an art form all its own.

Some musicians do their own CD duplication, but choose to hire a professional printer for the jewel box's artwork. Considering the importance of jewel box's appearance, this makes a lot of sense. It's a similar process to working with a CD duplicator in that you need to look at a test printing before you have your quantity run.

Hot Link: S&J Duplication Services (http://www.snjcd.com/)

S&J is set up to run both small and large quantity CD orders, and also does DVD duplication. (See Figure 21.10.)

Figure 21.10

If you have a smaller order (under 500) it may be worth shopping for a duplicator like S&J, which welcomes both small and large orders.

Again, though, you can print the jewel case artwork yourself with precut paper (or simply use standard photo paper and cut it yourself) from Avery, Neato, or other office supply companies. Better yet, you can hire a professional artist to create it but print it yourself. But realize that whether you work with a printer or do it yourself, the artwork as printed on paper will not look like it does on your computer screen. Many musicians have labored over cover art for countless hours, only to get it back from the printer (or print it themselves) to be surprised at how different it looks. Bottom line: Artwork looks different on your computer monitor than it does on paper. It's a good idea to print a test version on your home printer, so you can make adjustments as you work that actually look good when printed.

P A R T VI

THE INTERNET: THE DESKTOP RECORDIST'S BEST FRIEND

CHAPTER 22

PREPARING YOUR SOUNDS FOR UPLOADING

In This Chapter:

- Learn how to get the optimal sound for your Web files
- Find out about the popular Web formats
- Discover how to create streaming audio files
- Look at some examples of how major label musicians use the Web
- Learn how to copyright your music

GLOBAL SELF PROMOTION

It's pretty wild when you think about it: Post your music on the Web and, potentially, it could be listened to by about a quarter of a billion people (at last count).

Of course it's not that simple. It takes advertising and promotion—buzz—to get a crowd to visit. That's why record companies will survive. They have the publicity machines necessary to turn an artist into a massive commercial success.

But all musicians can create their own publicity, and having a Web site with your music on it is a central part of that. There's no easier and cheaper way to make your music quickly accessible to a mass audience. You can put a link to your music in any e-mails you send out, mention the site at performances, trade links with other sites to get traffic to yours—it's an essential promotional resource.

Although we won't look at mechanics of building a Web site or the HTML coding necessary in putting audio on the Web, we will look at making your audio sound its best before you put it out there. We'll also cover copyrighting your music, which is important to do before offering it for public distribution over the Web.

Part of preparing your audio for the Web is deciding whether you're prepping your files for download or for streaming. With the download option, the music you post becomes resident on the hard drive of those who download it, at which point they can listen to it. With streaming audio, your site's visitors can listen to an audio file as soon as they click on the song title or other Web link, without needing to download it; streaming files typically do not become resident on your listeners' hard drives. Streaming files have to be compressed more severely because they must be small enough to flow quickly across the Internet.

An audio *encoder* is a piece of software that converts a sound file into a given format, such as MP3, RealAudio, Windows Media Audio, or QuickTime.

Hot Link: Beastie Boys (http://www.beastieboys.com/)

The Beasties are just as happening on the Web as they are musically. Their site uses RealAudio to stream musical snippets (see Figure 22.1) .

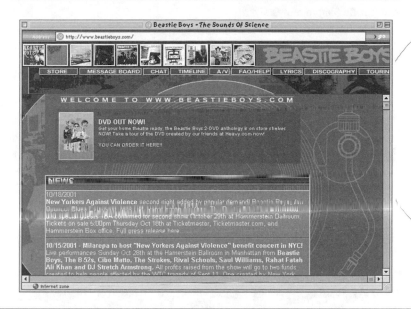

Figure 22.1

Visit the Beastie Boy site to see how it offers RealAudio clips of the group's music.

PREP WORK

When you prepare your audio for download, you might first have to make a mental adjustment. Because converting your music—those mixes you slaved over, that song that comes from the heart—means compromising audio quality for a shorter download time.

Sure, you want to upload CD-quality audio. But think about the file size: A four minute song at 44.1 kHz, 16-bit, stereo weighs in at about 40MB. And considering that most users have 56k modems, it's unlikely you'll get many listeners for that hefty a file.

So the mental adjustment comes in, realizing you have to lower resolution. This degrades the sound quality—sometimes quite a bit—which you're probably reluctant to do to your lovingly crafted music.

The trick is to make the audio compromises that take the least away from the music itself. You want to achieve the impossible: Hang on to high-resolution sonic quality while converting your audio files to a really small size. Musicians argue about which compromises are the best, but there are a few basics to keep in mind as you begin to degrade your music (sorry, that wasn't nice).

One thing to realize before we look at the audio preparation techniques: You'll probably need to experiment, trying several techniques in various combinations to come up with the best possible sound for your particular audio files.

Can't It Be Simple and Fast?

Be aware that you only need to do much audio prep work if you want the optimal sound for your music. If you want to make it simple, you can simply encode your audio in one of the formats covered in this chapter and post them. This works just fine for many musicians. The following steps are only for those few extra percentage points of sonic quality in the smallest file size feasible.

Hot Link: Radiohead (http://www.radiohead.com/)

No, the Radiohead site is not good way to hear the band, but it's an incredibly imaginative site. (See Figure 22.2.) It's a quantum leap past the "here are pictures of us" approach.

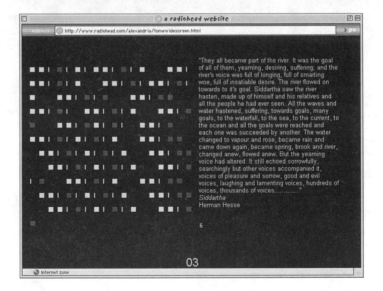

Figure 22.2

Radiohead's whimsical Web site is an effective promotional tool for the band in that it stresses the group's creative approach.

Help Yourself by Helping Your Encoder

You will probably want to encode your music into one of the popular Web formats: MP3, RealAudio, Windows Media Audio, or QuickTime. For each, you will need a piece of encoding software that will shrink your file for you. However—and here's the key point—you want to ask the encoder to do as little of the shrinking work for you as possible, because a given encoder will compress the file in its own way, which may or may not produce the optimal audio quality for your particular music.

So the more prep work you do to your files before you load them into the encoder, the more you're taking control of the process. This means shrinking them ahead of time as much as possible, and it also entails tweaking EQ and compression.

Mono-Stereo

When you convert a stereo file into a mono file, you instantly turn a 40MB file into a 20MB file—without degrading the sound quality of the audio itself. It's a no-brainer. Some musicians go so far as to mix a mono version if they know they're going to post that song on the Web.

But the stereo to mono conversion isn't an automatic choice. In fact it's one that makes some musicians groan in protest. If the audio you're encoding is short (which means it won't need much compression to make it small enough to download) or if the stereo aspect of your mix is critical to enjoying the song, keep the file as stereo. But converting it to mono will make the encoder's job much easier, by making the file size radically smaller.

EQ Tweaks

Many encoders cut the very high and very low frequencies from a file as part of their compression scheme. So you can do it for them and do a more careful job. An MP3 file, for example, doesn't have much above 15kHz. Before encoding, try cutting most of the frequencies above 12kHz and under 80Hz. If you need to get really serious about shrinking file size, like when you're preparing a streaming file, cut everything above the 6–8kHz range.

To help your file survive the encoding process with its punch intact, try gently boosting frequencies in the 2–4kHz range. To keep that bottom end full, give the 200–350Hz range a little boost as well. Your EQ decisions should reflect the music itself. If you're encoding hip hop, and really need that bass to stay strong, turn up the 150–300Hz range a bit more.

Hot Link: David Bowie (http://www.davidbowie.com/)

Bowie's site is an example of the maximum in self promotion, with a built-in all-Bowie radio station and a subscription plan (see Figure 22.3).

Figure 22.3

It's all Bowie all the time at DavidBowie.com.

Sample Rate Versus Bit Depth

Say you have your final mix in a file that's 44.1kHz, 16-bit, which is the format it needs to be in to burn a CD. You can cut that file's size in half by converting it to 22kHz, 16-bit. This is a much better choice than converting that file to 44.1kHz, 8-bit, which will also cut the file size in half. Reducing a file's sample rate chops off the audio's higher frequencies, but reducing a file's bit depth degrades its signal across all the frequencies. You may not decide to do either, but keep it in mind as a possibility. Remember, the smaller you can make your file before encoding, the less work the encoder will have to do—and it's often better for you to make the file reduction decisions yourself rather than leave it up to your encoder.

Remove DC Offset—Huh?

If you're poking around in your audio editing program's preferences, you might come across an option to remove DC Offset. *DC offset* is a shift in the audio waveform due to an electrical grounding problem. It's entirely possible your files have no problem with this, but if so, it's good to remove DC offset prior to encoding.

Squeezing Dynamics

If your music has a large dynamic range (meaning there's a big difference between the quietest and loudest passages), it helps to compress it before encoding it. If you don't, the encoder will, and again, you can take more care with it than an encoder, which tends to use a one-size-fits all scheme. Try a 3:1 compression ratio, setting your compressor so that it reduces gain by about -6 dB, though you may need to use a steeper ratio and a larger amount of gain reduction.

Just a Snippet

You might not want to post entire songs on your Web site. Instead, many musicians post teaser selections—just the hook, or just an interesting lead in. If you're going to do this, you'll want to edit your music prior to encoding it. Find a natural edit point to introduce the music, probably a downbeat that begins a measure or phrase. After letting the selection play, put a short fade out at the end so it doesn't cut off abruptly. Because these smaller clips don't require much file reduction to get them down to posting size, you won't have to use your encoder's most drastic file reduction scheme. So you'll be able to retain most of your music's sonic qualities. Additionally, with this "just a clip" method you're not giving away an entire song—it's just a teaser offer.

Normalize

After you've done all your other tweaking, normalize your files. This lifts its volume to the maximum without distortion. Be careful, though, because you may not want to normalize by 100 percent; this can sometimes cause distortion when you encode. Again, some experimentation is required.

> **Hot Link: Sarah McLachlan (http://www.sarahmclachlan.com)**
> The Canadian singer/songwriter's site, shown in Figure 22.4, is a good
> example of straightforward design, and includes plenty of music for fans to
> listen to.

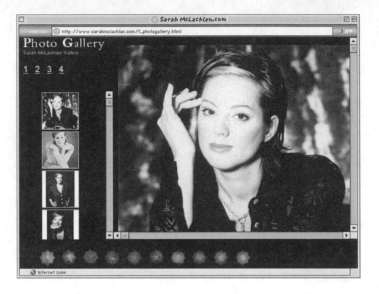

Figure 22.4

Sarah McLachlan's site veers away from flashy Web techniques, but does a good job of presenting the
artist.

The File Formats

All right, you want to make a million bucks? Here's how you do it. You create a Web music
player that plays and creates any kind of music file. It recognizes it and plays it (even converts it), with no further instruction. Unfortunately, we have no such application, but
instead a variety of file formats that require different players.

This is why many large sites offer files in more than one format. If you just want to use
one, MP3 is your best choice. For streaming files, RealAudio has the advantage of the
largest installed user base.

MP3

This is clearly the format that rules the Web. It's gotten so popular that virtually every audio editing program will let you save a file as an MP3.

As you encode your files as MP3s, you'll have a variety of choices. The format that seems to be the Web default is a stereo MP3 at 128kbps (kbps is short for kilobits per second, a measurement of data rate). This squeezes music to about 1/10th of its size. And it sounds amazingly good considering how drastic a compression scheme it is. If you have a particularly large file you're trying to get down to downloadable size, try 96kbps. Conversely, if you're just posting part of a song, you might try 160kbps. The file size is bigger, but 160kbps gets closer to fooling people into thinking it's CD quality audio.

You also might want to experiment with variable bit rate (VBR) encoding. When you choose the VBR option, your encoder adjusts the bit rate based on the audio itself; the passages that would lose quality from the standard compression rate are compressed less. This will improve the sound and, in some cases, make a larger file. However, not all MP3 players can handle VBR MP3s.

You can also set MP3s up for streaming, although MP3s are small enough that they download fast, and the extra technical steps required to set up streaming MP3s may seem unnecessary. Actually, it's pretty easy and it's free, but it does require basic Web building skills. In short, you need to create a text file that points the way to your MP3 file, and give this text file the .m3u extension. To take a look at the particulars of doing this, visit http://www.slackmaster2000.com/articles/streamingtutorial.htm.

Promote Yourself with Tags

And don't forget to tag your MP3s. This is a small information file that travels with the file wherever it goes. Put in your song's title, your Web URL, or any other relevant self-promotional material. This tag option is also available in the other formats covered in this chapter.

> **Hot Link: Prince (http://www.npgmusicclub.com/)**
>
> He's not at the top of the charts anymore, but the way Prince's site integrates graphics and music is really attractive. (See Figure 22.5.)

Figure 22.5

By the looks of his site, Prince spent some serious money on Web site development.

RealPlayer

Developed by RealNetworks, RealPlayer is able to stream video as well as audio. Streaming video over the Web is still of pretty sketchy quality due to bandwidth limitations, but streaming audio has come a long way since RealAudio introduced it in 1995. You'll need two things to maximize your site's RealPlayer offering:

- **Server.** The server that hosts your Web site should be set up to offer streaming RealAudio files. Most likely it is, but you usually have to pay a higher monthly fee to be able to offer RealAudio on your site, and you'll only be able to offer a set number of streams simultaneously. If you purchased the most basic hosting package, you may need to upgrade to be able to stream RealAudio. (If your server isn't set up to offer RealAudio, you can still stream RA files from it, but only one stream at a time and only at one data rate. The instructions for doing this are included with RealProducer.)

- **Software.** You can download a free encoder from the RealNetworks site, RealProducer Basic (there's also a deluxe version, RealSystem Producer Plus, for $199.95). Additionally, many of today's audio editing programs enable you to export RealAudio files.

Take a look at the RealProducer Basic software (`http://service.real.com/`) in Figure 22.6. Notice the option on the right side, Target Audience. This determines how severely your files will be compressed, based on connection speed: The slower the connection, the more severely the audio gets squeezed. You could choose 28K, which would allow virtually everyone with a Net connection to hear your streams. But the best choice here is 56K, which allows the majority of listeners to hear your streams, and keeps you from having to squeeze your music down to the frightening 28K level.

Because streaming encoding (by any developer, not just RealNetworks) is one of the most severe compression schemes, it's worth converting your files to mono prior to encoding. The smaller the file you feed that streaming encoder, the less detrimental effect that drastic compression will have on your audio.

Windows Media Player

Although Windows Media Player is as of this writing in the number two position behind RealPlayer in terms of users, it's probable that eventually it will take the number 1 position. It's a versatile program, with files that are both downloadable and streamable, and it's included with the Windows OS itself. This player's file format is called Windows Media Audio (WMA), and is supported by many audio editing programs.

To encode your songs for download, you can use the latest version of the Windows Media Player. (Including an encoder with the player is an important advantage this product has over RealPlayer.) Or, you can download the free Windows Media 8 Encoding Utility; this allows *batch encoding*, which is the process of encoding multiple files at one time.

To encode streaming files, download the free Windows Media Services program. The particularly impressive feature of this encoder is that you can get a decent-sounding file even at the low 96kbps rate, so your files are smaller and hence stream faster.

A Little Padding

When preparing files for streaming, some musicians add a moment of silence at the head of the file. This is certainly not necessary, but sometimes a streaming file suffers more drop outs (intermittent silence) as it begins to stream. The moment of silence at the head allows the stream to get established before your music plays. On the other hand, streaming technology keeps getting better, and there's less of a problem with this than there used to be.

Hot Link: Beatnik (http://www.beatnik.com/)

Beatnik, shown in Figure 22.6, is a tremendously cool form of Web audio, but it doesn't have the installed user base of the major formats.

Figure 22.6

Beatnik, founded by '80s pop star Thomas Dolby, offers some very creative Web audio options.

QuickTime

Although it's an also-ran in terms of user base, Apple's QuickTime is a solid application. It works well with both Mac and Windows machines. QuickTime is a good format for delivering video, but you can create audio-only files using the QuickTime .mov format as well. To convert your songs to QuickTime files, for downloading or streaming, you need QuickTime Pro, which will set you back $29.95. To use the encoder to convert files for streaming, simply chose Prepare for Internet Streaming, and Fast Start Compressed Header as you encode your music.

COPYRIGHTING YOUR MUSIC

Because putting your music on the Web means making it accessible to the entire planet, it's a good idea to copyright it first. A very good idea. Fortunately, it's pretty easy to do. Here's a step-by-step guide:

1. Record your song, with or without sophisticated technology. A home cassette deck will do. Even writing down the words and music on paper will do.

2. According to copyright law, this composition is now "fixed in a tangible medium of expression," and so is automatically copyrighted. You own all the rights to this music, unless you wrote it as a work for hire (which means someone else paid you to compose it, in which case they may have a claim on the rights).

3. Put a copyright notice on the tape or sheet music. It should look like this: © 2002 *Artist Name.*

4. To fully protect yourself, you need to register your copyright claim. To do this, download a copyright application form from the U.S. Copyright office forms site at `http://lcweb.loc.gov/copyright/forms/`.

5. Complete an application form for each work you want to copyright.

6. Create two copies of the work, either on tape or sheet music. These copies won't be returned to you; they'll be kept on file at the U.S. Copyright office.

7. Write a check or money order for $30 for each application.

8. Put the check, the forms, and the copies of the music into the same envelope and mail it to

Library of Congress
Copyright Office
101 Independence Avenue, S.E.
Washington, D.C. 20559-6000

When you've finished that, congratulations. You are now a fully copyrighted composer, and your music is stored on file with an incredible array of songwriters, from Irving Berlin to LL Cool J.

Attorney Michael P. McCready's site (`http://www.music-law.com/`) provides clear and easy-to-read information about music law.

CHAPTER **23**

FILE SWAPPING: INSIDE
THE REVOLUTION

In This Chapter:

- Find out what file sharing is
- Learn how this trend developed
- Discover how to use file sharing software
- Learn how file sharing may affect your desktop
  music

HERE TO STAY

File swapping is a controversial topic, with those on either side feeling passionately about their opinion. Ever since Napster (`http://www.napster.com`) was featured seemingly on every news magazine in America, the phenomenon of Internet file sharing has generated serious disagreement (see Figure 23.1). For some, it's the beginning of the end of music as we know it, completely immoral, really nothing more than stealing. To others, it's a much-needed shift in the way music is distributed, the best thing about the Internet, a global music fest to which everyone brings their favorite tunes.

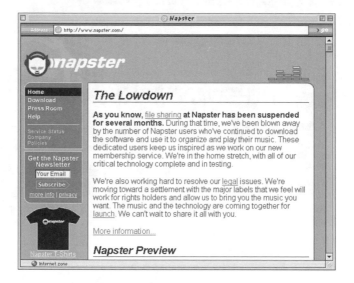

Figure 23.1

Is there anyone who hasn't heard of Napster? The site has received more press than any music-related Web site.

This chapter is not intended to persuade you that Internet file sharing is good or bad. (However, if this book were turned into an electronic file and swapped over the Internet, with no payment to the publisher, in that case our opinion is that file sharing is bad. Very bad. And no, we won't e-mail you the chapters in electronic form.) This chapter's intent is to give you an overview of the file swapping phenomenon. Because, whether file sharing is a scourge or a boon to music, there are a couple things that are very clear. First, it's here to stay, in one form or another. Second, it will play a significant role in desktop music making. If you're going to be using your PC to do sound design, you'll most likely encounter it. It's a good thing to understand.

The practice itself is fairly simple. Users download a piece of software from one of the many companies that have developed software for this purpose. The software is always free. Connect your PC to the Internet, and the software allows you to hook into a network of users who have downloaded that same program. Each of these users has designated a folder on their computer that's accessible to all the other users in the network. The software enables you to do a keyword search—enter your favorite band—and find a list of files to download. You can choose which file to download, and—presto—that file transfers from, say, a user's hard drive in New York to your hard drive in Florida. Since it links any number of computers as equal members of a network, it's also referred to as peer-to-peer, or P2P.

The choice of music available, at this point, seems to be growing to include the entire catalog of recorded music, although it favors the tastes of the younger, more technologically adept audience that uses P2P the most. You'll find more recordings by Weezer or Radiohead than by Woody Guthrie or Maria Callas, although you'd likely find recordings of any of those artists if you look long enough. And many of today's file swapping programs enable you to trade files other than music: graphics, movies, software, text files—if you can digitize it, you can swap it over the Internet. As file swapping grows ever more prevalent, it looks like it will affect everything from Hollywood to the record companies to software development, and all the industries that support these businesses.

Tracking P2P's Future

Visit the TechTV site (www.techtv.com) to find out about the constantly changing state of file swapping. Which program is the best? Which program has problems? TechTV covers it as it's happening.

WHERE DID P2P COME FROM?

The development of file sharing has been greatly facilitated by the MP3 file format. This compression scheme allows audio to be squeezed into about 1/12th the file size—and still sound good. Back before MP3s became popular, downloading a song was often a matter of clicking and waiting…and waiting.

But, as tens of millions of music fans know, creating, uploading, and downloading MP3s is fast and easy. The software for turning a track from a CD into an MP3—a process called *ripping*—is free and simple to use. And once you've converted a song to an MP3 file, its conveniently small file size makes it easy to quickly e-mail it to a dozen friends, who can each e-mail it to a dozen of their friends.

In 1997, an entrepreneur named Michael Robertson launched MP3.com (he had bought the domain name for a thousand dollars). Robertson built the site into a downloader's hotspot, mostly with unsigned bands, but offering plenty of free MP3 software and user forums. And MP3.com was far from alone. Other sites that facilitated music download kept popping up faster than you could keep track of them. IUMA.com, Garageband.com (which at one time offered a $250,000 signing bonus to unsigned bands), Ampcast.com, Farmclub.com, Audiofind (a search engine for MP3s)—suddenly, there was a whole lot of downloadin' going on. (The idea of the PC as music machine used by millions got a big boost during this time, hence the book you hold In your hands.)

MP3.com Goes Public

In 1999, MP3.com became a publicly traded company, selling shares on the NASDAQ stock exchange. On the first day its shares were available, they were priced at over $100 per share. As of this writing, the stock trades at about $5 per share.

But the problem was, it was still hard to find specific tracks. There was an ocean of MP3s being sent back and forth across the Internet, but it was tough to find exactly that Top 40 hit you wanted. You knew that someone, somewhere, had ripped it from a CD and posted it on the Web, but where?

Then came Shawn Fanning. His story has been told countless times, and he ended up on the cover of essentially every national magazine sometime in 2000. Still, his contribution to the Web was brilliant. And considering he created it at age 19, the creative vision that went into developing Napster was nothing short of jaw-dropping.

The core technology of file trading existed before Fanning. Networking together a group of computers so that each user could access the files of the others on the network was a common practice. Many companies network the computers of multiple employees using a LAN (local area network) or a WAN (wide area network). But Fanning saw the entire Web as one big wide area network.

Hot Link: Recording Industry Association of America (http://riaa.org/)

The RIAA is the industry trade group that represents the interests of the major record labels (see Figure 23.2). It led the legal battle against Napster. In the RIAA's view, Napster and the other companies that are involved with file sharing are helping listeners infringe on the copyrights of the artists whose works are downloaded. They point out that musicians and other creators spend years dedicated to their craft, and rightfully expect to be paid for their efforts.

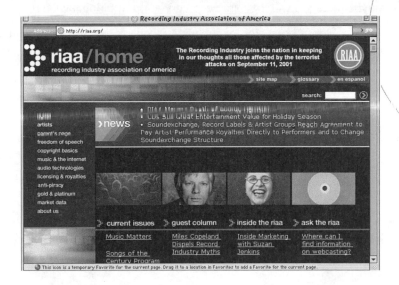

Figure 23.2

The RIAA went to court to shut down Napster, and continues to pursue legal remedies against other companies who are involved with file swapping.

He had encountered the same problem as a lot of MP3 downloaders. The file is out there, but where? So he created a piece of software, the Napster program, that allowed all the users who have it installed on their PCs to be a single connected network. These users designated a folder on their respective hard drives, full of MP3 files, as accessible to any of the other users. A Napster user could enter a keyword, like "Beastie Boys," and see a list of MP3 files available for download. The software did the searching for you, and delivered the file to your hard drive at no cost.

Suddenly, two very large things were united: an enormous body of music, the millions of MP3 files that had been ripped from CD, and an equally enormous audience, the millions of fans who wanted to find those MP3s. Napster, with no ad budget, registered 20 million users within one year.

But there was a problem. Some of the musicians whose music was being swapped on Napster—who had played in bar bands for years, finally gotten signed, sweated over creating a great album and toured relentlessly to promote it—got upset when they saw their music distributed for free. Of course it would have been no big deal if just the musicians were upset—musicians aren't good at hiring lawyers. But the major record labels were also upset, maybe more so, and they are very, very good at hiring lawyers.

Napster got in a lot of hot water for copyright violation, and as of this writing is in a kind of P2P backwater. It still exists, but you have to pay to download files.

> **Hot Link: Scour Exchange (http://www.scour.com/)**
>
> Scour Exchange, shown in Figure 23.3, was a favorite site of file swappers before it ran into some legal difficulties similar to those of Napster. In its new incarnation, Scour offers music and video titles as part of the "new, legal Scour."

Figure 23.3

Scour has changed the way it operates due to legal concerns.

But Napster, it turns out, was just a footnote in the history of file swapping, kind of like the Wright Brothers and aviation. Yes, they started things, but now it's a much bigger story.

Because today's big file swapping sites have found a way around Napster's legal troubles. Napster relied upon centralized servers to facilitate file trading. That means there's a central controlling organization, which means there's someone to sue.

But today's leading P2P programs don't use centralized servers. A given company develops and distributes its own file swapping software, but is not involved with what its users do with it. The software searches the users' network itself, without using centralized servers. This means there's no one for copyright holders to sue. You can't sue a pipe manufacturer because someone smokes an illicit substance with its pipe. And the record companies don't want to litigate against individual users—they are the labels' consumers. Besides, how do you sue 40 million people? So the big P2P sites operate unhindered. (However, in late 2001, the RIAA did file suit against MusicCity, KaZaA, and Grokster, some of today's most popular P2P developers. So, we'll see....)

How to Use P2P Software

Many file swapping programs have sprung up in the vacuum created by Napster's downfall. The biggies include KaZaA, Bearshare, and Audiogalaxy Satellite. But the program that appears to have earned the title "the new Napster" is Morpheus by MusicCity. This program has a number of strengths:

- **User base.** A file swapping program needs a critical mass of users to provide a huge selection to its user. Napster had tens of millions of users, which meant that someone, somewhere, was going to offer even the most obscure bootleg for download. As of this writing, Morpheus has been downloaded over a million times a week for months. It's reasonable to assume that its user base is close to what Napster's was.

- **Decentralized.** With Morpheus, the company that makes it (MusicCity), holds no copyrighted material; each user is a node on a network. This means (theoretically) that the system is not legally vulnerable as was Napster.

- **Multiple file types.** This is a big one. While Napster enabled the swapping of music files, Morpheus (and many of today's programs) let you swap anything that can be digitized: music, movies, text, graphics, software, and so on.

- **Ease of use.** One of the reasons Napster became so popular so quickly was that it required no special technical skills to use it. After a short learning curve, you had access to a vast treasure of recorded music. Morpheus's user interface is just about as easy.

As we look at how to use Morpheus (see Figure 23.4), realize that many of the programs work in a very similar manner. So if you know Morpheus, you can quickly get started with most of them. Let's take it step by step from the start:

1. **Get the Program:** Download the program from `http://www.musiccity.com`. It's free.

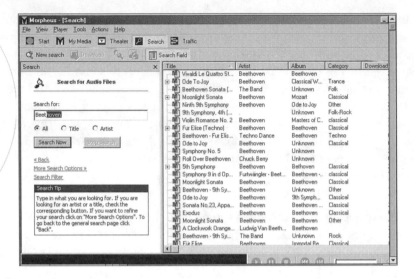

Figure 23.4

The Morpheus software, after a keyword search for "Beethoven." Notice the many possibilities for download on the right.

2. **Register:** After you install it (which the software does itself) and get it going, you'll need to register by entering a username, password, and your e-mail address. (Does anyone enter his or her real e-mail address?)

3. **Choose your download folder**: Go to Tools, Options and click the Download and Uploads tab. You can use the default folder that Morpheus chooses, or click the ellipsis (…) button to choose a new one. To better organize your searches, you can set up a main download folder, and put subfolders inside of it for video, music, and images, or for however you want to organize your downloads (maybe…rock, hip hop, and Cajun). It's better to keep things organized as you download rather than try to sort it out later.

4. **Search:** When you're ready to start downloading, make sure you're connected to the Internet, and click the Search button. In the left window, select the file type you're looking for: MP3, .WAV, .MOV, or whatever. Then enter any keywords in the search box and click Search Now.

5. **Download:** After the software hunts through the network, you'll see search results on the right side of the screen. If you see a file you want to download, double-click it. It will begin to download to the folder (or folders) on your hard drive you specified as your download folder. To see how your downloads are progressing, click the Traffic button. You can stop a download by right-clicking on Cancel Download.

6. **Listen:** If you want to play any of your files, click the My Media button. Browse the folders in the left window. Choosing a folder will reveal that folder's contents in the window on the right. Select anything you want to hear in the right window. Then click the Play button in the Player window in the bottom right.

Protecting Your Privacy

Any files you choose to share are potentially shared with the entire planet , so be careful about what you share. If you put your diary in your shared folder, 40 million people might read it.

Power User's Tips

Here are some techniques you can use to get the most use from your Morpheus software:

- **Creating a Playlist.** In the My Media section, select the files you want and drag them to the Playlist section—you'll see it in the bottom right corner. Or, you can select a file (or multiple files) and click the button Add To Playlist. You can save your playlist by clicking Save Playlist in the Player menu.

- **Sharing files.** Drop any files you want to share in the My Shared Files folder. (This is automatically created when you install Morpheus.) You'll see this folder in the My Documents folder and on your desktop. Or share entire folders by choosing Find Media to Share from the Tool menu, and then clicking on Folders.

- **Editing details of a file.** In the My Media section, right-click on the file you want to change and select Edit Details. This allows you to change the name and description of a file.

There are so many gazillions of files on the Internet that narrowing your search will save you time and hassle. You can limit your search to a media type—audio, video, and so on—by clicking on that corresponding media type right below the search field.

Click on More Search Options to further refine your search by criteria such as category, artist, or language. To get more search results, choose Options from the Tools menu and increase the search result from 50 (the default) to 100.

If you need immediate gratification—and who doesn't?—choose one of the files in your search results and click Download and Open. It may take 30 seconds (or so) to begin to play. If you want to stop it from playing but still download it, select Stop from the Player menu.

Morpheus classifies all users in terms of connection speed, from 1 (slowest) to 5 (fastest). You always want to choose the fastest possible users to download from.

Virus Alert!

It is possible to download a virus from a file swapping services. In particular, be careful about downloading executable files (they look like this: filename.exe), or Microsoft Word and Excel documents (.doc, .xls). It's a good idea to have some good anti-virus software handy, such as McAfee or Norton.

HOW FILE SWAPPING AFFECTS THE DESKTOP MUSICIAN

Using file swapping software is fairly easy. More difficult is answering the many questions it poses: What does it mean for the future of music? What does it mean for the many creative people who use their PCs as music studios?

Although there are some answers to those questions, the truth is that no one really knows. That anyone with a PC connected to the Internet, with a program like Morpheus, has fast and free access to the (almost) complete library of recorded music (and graphics, text, and so forth) is astounding. This amazing opportunity has not gone unnoticed. According to Internet research firm Webnoize, 1.81 billion digital media files were transferred using the top three file sharing applications during the month of October, 2001. And remember that Shawn Fanning didn't create Napster until 1999, so P2P has grown from non existent to 1.81 billion files traded monthly in about two years—an amazing growth rate.

So while it's unknown exactly what effect file sharing will have over time, the numbers demonstrate that it will be a profound one. Especially considering that many adult consumers, in addition to perhaps using file swapping programs, have grown up buying CDs. It's a kind of cultural habit, not to mention a good way of getting music. But what about that 10-year-old who grows up with file swapping? Will they still troop down to the record store and plunk down $15 bucks for whatever type of digital disc is currently fashionable? Those kids have CD burners and they know how to use them. So big changes are coming, although if you can figure out exactly what they'll be, you're way ahead of most of us.

As the chaos unfolds, there are couple ways that you, as a desktop musician, can stay take advantage of the phenomenon of file swapping.

Educate Yourself

Like nothing before it, file swapping is a great cross-pollinator. Every kind of music is available to everyone, with no more effort than a click of your mouse. Musicians of every stripe can know what other musicians are doing. So get out there and listen to what's going on.

Don't just download the stuff you know and like, but listen to a little bit of all of it. Listen to Zydeco and Ska and heavy metal and old jazz and those Posies songs that never made the radio (and when you find something you like, go out and buy the album). Make your ears really large by exposing yourself to everything you can. Creating interesting music—especially in the period we live in—is about creatively combining outside influences with your own sound. And just listening to commercial radio is sort of like trying to live on a fast food diet. It seems like you're filled up, but really your starving. Apart from spending thousands at the record store, adventurous use of your P2P software is the best way to be a well informed musician.

Promote Yourself

Whatever you think of Madonna's music, one thing is clear: She knows how to market herself. She was quoted as saying, "Napster could be a great way for people to hear your music who wouldn't have the chance to hear it on the radio." So take her tip and use file swapping software to get yourself heard. Giving away a sample as a way to get consumers interested in the product is a time honored business technique—it's like a "teaser," intended as an introduction to your style. So take one of your tracks, one of your songs with the most immediate crowd appeal, and make it available for all to download. You're not being stolen from, you're being listened to, and if you're not yet signed, that's the biggest obstacle. If you're lucky enough to have it downloaded—which is probably the toughest task—you're that much closer to having audience recognition.

But no matter how you use P2P, or even if you chose not to, it's worth keeping track of as a musician. Although file swapping is changing so quickly that it's a study in chaos—which musicians tend to be more comfortable with than many others—it's clear that it will profoundly affect music in the years ahead.

COLLABORATING ACROSS TOWN— OR THE GLOBE

In This Chapter:

- Learn about Rocket Network, an Internet-based method of music collaboration
- Find out about other technologies that enable musicians to work together regardless of location
- Look at the future of distance collaboration

THE BIGGEST STUDIO IN THE WORLD

This book began with a look at the past, all the way back to the early '60s, at what was one of that period's high-tech recording sessions: an early Elvis session. At that time, the facility that the King was using was the ultimate in recording technology.

In this last chapter, we'll look again at ultimate recording technology, but this time we'll look at one of the audio technologies of the future: the Internet itself.

The Internet is becoming an ever more central part of studio technology, a network that combines two of more studios into one facility. With the way that the Net enables studios across the country—or across continents—to become one facility, it's shaping audio production.

And, while Net-enabled distance collaboration is happening right now (it's as much present as future technology), it has only just begun to grow into what it will become.

Of course, many desktop musicians already use e-mail to send audio back and forth. Indeed, this has been a major advantage of the Net: Zip your files, e-mail them off, get some tracks added, keep on working. Or, lower tech but still useful, burn a CD and mail it off, which gets around the small file size limitation of e-mail.

How Small Is Your File?

The small file size of MIDI files makes them ideal for e-mail. From the earliest days of the Web, MIDI files were traveling back and forth between collaborating composers.

But the Net offers better methods. One of the best examples of the Internet as facilitator of distance collaboration is Rocket Network (`http://www.rocketnetwork.com`). Rocket is certainly not the only method of Net-based distance collaboration, but in its degree of organization and technical sophistication, it reveals the most about how the future may look.

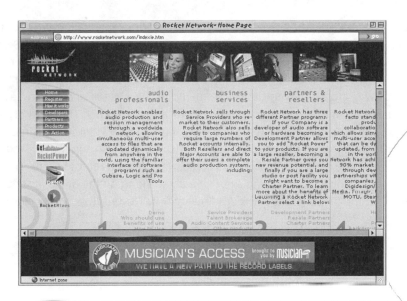

Figure 24.1

The Rocket Network is a leading Net-based collaboration system.

The company itself is based in San Francisco, although its actual physical location is not important to the many collaborations it assists. The company's technology has been used as part of high-budget projects in studios both inside and outside the U.S.

It works like this: When two musicians in remote locations want to work together, they can upload their project's audio to the Rocket server. One musician can make a series of edits, which he can upload to the server, which will update the master audio.

What, you might ask, is the advantage over simply e-mailing the files? What makes the Rocket system faster is that the audio itself does not need to be sent back and forth—just the edits to the audio. Audio has a hefty file size. A song with even a very basic mulititrack arrangement could eat up more than 100MB, and many arrangements eat up substantially more. But the information needed to make an edit is quite small. Say you want to draw in a cross fade on track 7. You could upload the data request necessary to make this edit using a very small computer file, which would therefore move back and forth much more quickly than the source audio.

Take a look at Figure 24.2. The two PCs on the left labeled Client 1 and Client 2 represent musicians working in different geographic locations. Let's say one is in Seattle and the other is in Chicago. The Rocket server in the middle is where the audio resides. It also resides on the local hard drives of both musicians. Notice that *objects* and *media* are flowing both ways for both musicians. The media in this case is audio, perhaps a multitrack music session with everything from drums to bass to vocals. The term *objects* is Rocket lingo for the edit data, which would be everything from a volume adjustment to any kind of fade to a change in plug-in parameters. MIDI data is also supported. (You'll notice that on the right side of Figure 24.2 there's something called a remote client. This could be an additional engineer or client who's not actually working on the audio, just downloading it. Notice that the media and objects are flowing only toward this remote client.)

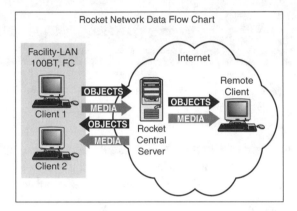

Figure 24.2

The Rocket Network uses a central server to enable musicians who are in different cities to work together quickly and easily.

It's vastly preferable to have a broadband connection to work with a system like this. Even though the musicians are usually just sending back and forth edit requests, not audio, to begin a multi-user session they have to upload the audio. Without at least a DSL line this might take one heck of a long time. To aid this, Rocket has its own compression technology. One of the compression schemes squeezes the audio by about 8:1, and there's an additional compression mode that uses a 15:1 ratio (for final mix, uncompressed audio is used).

As the musicians work back and forth from remote locations, they can also use the real-time chat utility built in to the Rocket system, although speaker phone has become popular as well. Within the system protocol is a method that prevents musicians from making the same edit (or conflicting edits) at the same time. There's a kind of "passing of the baton" built in to ensure that the collaborators always have only one version of the master audio.

Many of the leading audio programs are incorporating access to the Rocket Network, including Steinberg's Cubase, shown in Figure 24.3, Emagic's Logic, Digidesign's Pro Tools, and MOTU's Digital Performer. Although it may at some point be possible to work not just across the globe but also across applications—one musician has Cubase, the other has Logic—it's not currently feasible.

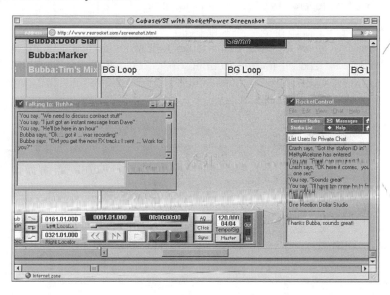

Figure 24.3

This figure shows what the CubaseVST user interface looks like while using the Rocket Network. Note the real-time chat utility on the left.

JARGON

What's a Mix Stem?

A *mix stem* is discrete track that's part of a multitrack mix. When sending a multitrack mix by CD (or DAT), musicians can lay each of the tracks on the CD as discrete tracks so that they can be mixed or edited however the recipient wants. Each of the mix stems has a *two pop* (a short beep sound, created with one frame of 1 kHz tone) to mark its beginning. To re-assemble the mix, you load all the mix stems into your PC and align all the two pops to the same moment.

An example of a Rocket collaboration was a last-minute mix for the movie *Bridget Jones's Diary*. Songwriter Jeff Trott was in Portland, mix engineer David Tickle was in Hawaii, and singer Sheryl Crow was in London. Yet they had to work together to meet a deadline that was just three days away. Songwriter Trott uploaded the tracks to the Rocket server, which enabled mixer Tickle to mix them in Hawaii. He uploaded his mixes so that Crow (in London) could approve them and Trott (in Portland) could make sure everything was okay. After some tweaks were made, the new mixes were uploaded so that production companies in London and New York could access the files and continue with that aspect of the film's production.

The Many Flavors of Distance Collaboration

The Internet is a major bridge for distance collaboration, but there are other technologies that facilitate this as well. Of the three following examples, only one uses the standard Internet. But each is proof that, somehow, some way, people will find a way to make music with each other, regardless of geographic location.

ICQ (http://groups.icq.com/Music/) is an Internet communication tool that lets you know who's online at any time, and enables you to interact with them. (See Figure 24.4.) If you have a PC and an Internet connection, you can download free ICQ software and hook into the network. You can find a friend online and simply chat in real-time, or, use the application for file transfer.

Figure 24.4

ICQ music groups let you share an interest in virtually any kind of music, from German speed metal to acoustic New Age. It's an effective tool for Net-based music collaboration.

In terms of music collaboration, communication over ICQ has helped with many projects. Indeed, complete albums have been conceived of and finished over ICQ—without the participants ever meeting each other in person.

The limitation, of course, is bandwidth—still the main slowdown in many Net-based collaborations. If the musical participants have only the data transfer capability of a 56k modem, sending audio files will either take a long time or require a conversion to lower resolution prior to transfer (say, to MP3 from CD quality). Because of bandwidth limitations, some ICQ collaborators limit their partnerships to MIDI files. And of course it's also feasible to send a CD through the mail to get the bulkiest audio files from place to place.

Although ICQ is not the highest tech solution to Net collaboration, it has its advantages. It's completely open—anyone can join for no cost. And by looking through the lists of interests at the ICQ music groups page, you can find collaborators in any part of the world with Net connections with virtually every musical approach. You're not limited to studio professionals, or musicians with a budget and a deadline, or even to people you know. It's an example of the Web facilitating both the social and technical connections necessary for creative collaboration.

And it's far from the only one of its kind. While you're exploring, take a look at the services offered by AIM (http://www.aim.com), Yahoo (http://messenger.yahoo.com/), and MSN (http://messenger.msn.com). Some musicians use Trillian (http://www.trillian.cc), which combines AIM, ICQ, Yahoo, MSN, and IRC.

THE TECHNOPHOBE AND THE MADMAN

Webcasting a music theater production over the Internet is itself a bit of a feat. But for the collaboration involved with staging *The Technophobe and the Madman*, shown in Figure 24.5, there was an additional challenge: Half the cast was in New York City, and half was in Troy, New York, 163 miles away. The show was Webcast over Internet2, a network that allows higher quality audio and video due to its greater bandwidth. Even with this higher bandwidth, a collaborative Net-based live performance posed the challenge of a split-second delay. The cast dealt with this by having the musicians in Troy start first, with the NY-based musicians following. The piece's composer, Robert Rowe, described the sound as a "free, temporal presentation of material that is not based on pulse." This kind of a project, which is just barely technically feasible, is an example of creative people using technology to push the boundaries of what's possible in terms of distance collaboration.

Figure 24.5

This project, `http://www.academy.rpi.edu/projects/technophobe/`, was a musical performed over Internet2, with cast members in two different cities.

ISDN: THE SPEED OF REAL TIME

EDnet is a high-speed data transfer network that uses ISDN (integrated services digital network) lines, which are digital phone lines. It's used by many recording studios all over the world. The technology has become so prevalent that it's practically a given that a professional audio studio of any size will have an EDnet connection. EDnet uses a private network that allows full resolution audio to be sent in real-time. The network is also used to transfer compressed video and multimedia files.

The EDnet connection is used, for example, when a film or TV producer based in Hollywood needs to record an actor who's traveling. In that case, the LA-based producer can send a video copy of a TV show though the mail to a studio in, for example, Chicago. The actor in Chicago can watch the video, and read his lines in response to the picture. The actor's voice is sent in real-time via the EDnet lines, allowing a full-resolution recording to be plugged into the master and shown on TV that evening. It's much faster than FedEx—in the world we live in, even 24 hours is too slow.

So far, the EDnet connection is used mainly by professional studios and home-based voiceover artists (they're the people who narrate commercials) with a substantial business. It's still pricey. Using EDnet requires you to buy a hardware codec, which is the unit that codes and decodes the signal as it is sent to and from its various geographic destinations. Additionally, there's a hefty fee for each connection made.

Talent Across the Country

Since EDnet became commonly used in the mid '90s, it has changed the way commercial voiceover talent work. A voice talent located in Connecticut, for example, may record commercials for studios all over the country from his or her home studio.

THE FUTURE...

It's almost funny when you look at some of the things futurists have predicted, and how far off they've been. By now, early in the twenty-first century, we were all supposed to have personal jet packs to transport us across town. Sadly, that's still in progress, but there are some more reasonable predictions that we can make about how technology will facilitate music collaboration (and you future people reading this, no snickering, please).

What if the technology that makes the Rocket Network possible was incorporated into music software on a one-to-one basis without the server in the middle? In other words, with a mouse click, you send just your edit changes to a colleague many miles away, a fellow musician who has the audio files resident on their hard drives. So even the most basic off-the-shelf software would enable real-time distance music collaboration of complex multitrack mixes. It seems like the developers will figure this one out one of these years.

And what if the technology behind EDnet—real-time, full-bandwidth audio transfer—becomes affordable and widely used for desktop musicians? That would require the hardware units to fall in price (but hardware always does) and it would require more usage of broadband lines (which they tell us are coming) and still better compression schemes (certainly a possibility). In that case, it would be commonplace for musicians in remote locations to be jamming, in real-time, with full-resolution audio. That would be a blast.

Put these two possibilities together, in the context of the affordable PC music studio. So remote musicians could record and edit, in real-time, with the same quality and immediacy they have if they're in the room together. Let's see, with a global Internet population growing from its current base of 230 million, imagining that anyone with access to a PC and low-cost hardware/software could collaborate, using high quality audio...hmmm...kind of makes you wonder what's possible....

APPENDIX A

TECHTV QUICK FACTS

Boasting the cable market's most interactive audience, TechTV is the only cable television channel covering technology information, news, and entertainment from a consumer, industry, and market perspective 24 hours a day. Offering everything from industry news to product reviews, updates on tech stocks to tech support, TechTV's original programming keeps the wired world informed and entertained. TechTV is one of the fastest growing cable networks, available around the country and worldwide.

Offering more than a cable television channel, TechTV delivers a fully integrated, interactive Web site. Techtv.com is a community destination that encourages viewer interaction through e-mail, live chat, and video mail.

TechTV, formerly ZDTV, is owned by Vulcan, Inc.

AUDIENCE

TechTV appeals to anyone with an active interest in following and understanding technology trends and how they impact their lives in today's world—from the tech investor and industry insider, to the Internet surfer, cell phone owner, and Palm Pilot organizer.

WEB SITE

Techtv.com allows viewers to participate in programming, provide feedback, interact with hosts, send video e-mails, and further explore the latest tech content featured on the television cable network. In addition, `techtv.com` has one of the Web's most extensive technology-specific video-on-demand features (VOD), offering users immediate access to more than 5,000 videos as well as expanded tech content of more than 2,000 in-depth articles.

INTERNATIONAL

TechTV is the world's largest producer and distributor of television programming about technology. In Asia, TechTV delivers a 24-hour international version via satellite. TechTV Canada is a "must-carry" digital channel that launched in September 2001. A Pan-European version of TechTV is planned for 2002.

TECH LIVE QUICK FACTS

Tech Live is TechTV's unique concept in live technology news programming. Tech Live provides extensive coverage, in-depth analysis, and original features on breaking technology developments as they relate to news, market trends, entertainment, and consumer products. Tech Live is presented from market, industry, and consumer perspectives.

Mission

Tech Live is the leading on-air resource and ultimate destination for consumers and industry insiders to find the most comprehensive coverage of technology and how it affects and relates to their lives, from market, industry, and consumer perspectives.

Format

Tech Live offers nine hours of live programming a day.

Tech Live is built around hourly blocks of news programming arranged into content zones: technology news, finance, product reviews, help, and consumer advice.

Tech Live news bureaus in New York City, Washington D.C., Silicon Valley, and Seattle are currently breaking technology-related news stories on the financial markets, the political arena, and major industry players.

The TechTV "Superticker" positioned along the side of the screen gives viewers up-to-the-minute status on the leading tech stocks, as well as additional data and interactive content.

Tech Live runs Monday through Friday, 9:00 a.m.–6:00 p.m. EST.

NETWORK PROGRAM GUIDE

The following is a list of the programs that currently air on TechTV. We are constantly striving to improve our on-air offerings, so please visit www.techtv.com for a constantly updated list, as well as specific air times.

AudioFile

In this weekly half-hour show, Liam Mayclem and Kris Kosach host the premiere music program of its kind that dares to explore music in the digital age. From interviews with artists and producers, to insight into the online tools to help create your own music, *AudioFile* discovers how the Internet is changing the music industry.

Big Thinkers

This weekly half-hour talk show takes viewers into the future of technological innovation through insightful and down-to-earth interviews with the industry's most influential thinkers and innovators of our time.

Call for Help

This daily, hour-long, fully interactive call-in show hosted by Becky Worley and Chris Pirillo takes the stress out of computing and the Internet for both beginners and pros. Each day, *Call for Help* tackles viewers' technical difficulties, offers tips and tricks, provides product advice, and offers viewers suggestions for getting the most out of their computers.

CyberCrime

This weekly half-hour news magazine provides a fast-paced inside look at the dangers facing technology users in the digital age. Hosts Alex Wellen and Jennifer London take a hard look at fraud, hacking, viruses, and invasions of privacy to keep Web surfers aware and secure on the Web.

Extended Play

In this weekly half-hour show, video game expert hosts Kate Botello and Adam Sessler provide comprehensive reviews of the hottest new games on the market, previews of games in development, and tips on how to score the biggest thrills and avoid the worst spills in gaming. This show is a must-see for game lovers, whether they're seasoned pros or gaming novices.

Fresh Gear

A gadget-lover's utopia, host Sumi Das supplies viewers with the scoop on the best and brightest technology available on the market. In this weekly half-hour show, detailed product reviews reveal what's new, what works, what's hot, and what's not and offers advice on which products to buy—and which to bypass.

Silicon Spin

Noted technology columnist John C. Dvorak anchors this live, daily, half-hour in-depth look at the stories behind today's tech headlines. CEOs, experts, and entrepreneurs cast a critical eye at industry hype and separate the facts from the spin.

The Screen Savers

Whether you are cracking code, are struggling with Windows, or just want to stay up to speed on what's happening in the world of computers, *The Screen Savers* is here to help. Leo Laporte and Patrick Norton unleash the power of technology with wit and flair in this live, daily, hour-long interactive show geared toward the tech enthusiast.

Titans of Tech

Titans of Tech is a weekly hour-long series of biographies profiling high tech's most important movers and shakers—the CEOs, entrepreneurs, and visionaries driving today's tech economy. Through insightful interviews and in-depth profiles, these specials offer viewers a rare look at where the new economy is headed.

INDEX

HYPERLINKS, EMBEDDING (DVDS)

INDEX

I/O (INPUT/OUTPUT)

INDEX

SOUND

X-Z

WHAT'S ON THE CD-ROM

On the CD for *TechTV's Desktop Recording: Producing Audio with your Home PC* you will find audio samples and a wealth of other applications and utilities.

SOFTWARE

- **ACID Xpress** by Sonic Foundry
- **Audiograbber** by Jackie Frank
- **CD-Maker 2000 Professional Trial Version** by NewTech Infosystems, Inc.
- **GoldWave** by Chris Craig
- **Nero** by Ahead Software
- **Noise Reduction 2.0 DirectX Audio Plug-In** by Sonic Foundry
- **SIREN Jukebox** by Sonic Foundry
- **SoundForge 5.0** by Sonic Foundry
- **SureThing CD Labeler** by MicroVision Development, Inc.
- **XFX** by Sounic Foundry

ABOUT THE SOFTWARE

Please read all documentation associated with a third-party product (usually contained with files named readme.txt or license.txt) and follow all guidelines.

INSTALLATION INSTRUCTIONS

Windows 95/NT 4:

1. Insert the CD-ROM into your CD-ROM drive (see NOTE at bottom of the page).
2. From the Windows desktop, double-click the My Computer icon.
3. Double-click the icon representing your CD-ROM drive.
4. Double-click the icon titled START.EXE to run the multimedia user interface.

NOTE: If Windows 95/NT 4.0 in installed on your computer and you have the AutoPlay feature enabled, the Start.exe program starts automatically whenever you insert the disc into your CD-ROM drive.

READ THIS BEFORE OPENING THE SOFTWARE

By opening this package, you are agreeing to be bound by the following agreement:

You may not copy or redistribute the entire CD-ROM as a whole. Copying and redistribution of individual software programs on the CD-ROM is governed by terms set by individual copyright holders.

The installer and code from the author(s) are copyrighted by the publisher and the author(s). Individual programs and other items on the CD-ROM are copyrighted or are under GNU license by their various authors or other copyright holders.

This software is sold as-is without warranty of any kind, either expressed or implied, including but not limited to the implied warranties of merchantability and fitness for a particular purpose. Neither the publisher nor its dealers or distributors assumes any liability for any alleged or actual damages arising from the use of this program. (Some states do not allow for the exclusion of implied warranties, so the exclusion might not apply to you.)

NOTE: This CD-ROM uses long and mixed-case filenames requiring the use of a protected-mode CD-ROM driver.